MAP OF EARLY PITTSBURGH

1. Peter Audrian—Smithfield & Cherry Streets.
2. James Ross—Smithfield & Cherry Streets.
3. Henderson's Ferry—"Hogg's Pond".
4. Morrow's Green Tree Tavern—Market & Wood Streets.
5. Adamson Tannehill—Market & Wood Streets.
6. Samuel Ewalt—Market & Water Streets.
7. John Ormsby—Chancery Lane & Ferry Streets.
8. Samuel Sample's Tavern—Ferry & Water Streets.
9. John Neville—Ferry & Water Streets.
10. Isaac Craig—Redoubt Alley & Water Street.
11. Redoubt.
12. Boat Yard—Short & First Streets.
13. Ab. Kirkpatrick—Short & Water Streets.
14. James O'Hara—Water & West Streets.
15. Old Fort Pitt—Winter 1758.
16. Fort Pitt—Summer 1759.
17. Fort Duquesne built 1754.
18. Redoubt.
19. Col. Wm. Butler's widow—Marbury & Penn Streets.
20. Gen. Richard Butler's widow—Marbury & Penn Streets
21. John Scull's—Market & First Streets.
22. Watson's Tavern—Market & First Streets.
23. Judge Brackenridge—Market Street.
24. Alexander Addison—Smithfield & Second Streets.
25. Jean Marie—Fourth & Grant Streets.
26. Gen. John Wilkins—Wood & Third Streets.
27. Chas. Richard—Ferry & Second Streets.
28. Maj. John Irwin—Liberty & Third Streets.
29. John Gibson—Ferry & Third Streets.
30. Benj. Richard—Chancery Lane.
31. John Wilkins Esq.—Fourth & Wood Streets.
32. Irwin's Hall—Market Street.
33. Black Bear Hotel—Market & Fifth Streets.
34. Wm. Cecil—Liberty & Pitt Streets.
35. Dr. Nath. Bedford—Liberty & Irvine Streets.
36. First Presbyterian Church—Wood & Sixth Streets.
37. Battle-ground—Grant Street.
38. Market-house—Market & Second Streets.
39. Jail—Market & Fourth Streets.
40. Fort Fayette—Hand & Liberty Streets & Allegheny River.
41. James Robinson—Franklin Road & Allegheny River
42. J. Lichtenberger—Smoky Island—On Ohio River.
43. General Wayne's stable—Stukes Run on Monongahela River
44. General Wayne's Headquarters—West & Second Streets.
45. First Post Office—Redoubt Alley & First Street.
46. John Johnston—Chancery Lane—First Street.

Redrawn from a map in the *Western Pennsylvania Historical Magazine*, XI, (1928)

PITTSBURGH'S COMMERCIAL DEVELOPMENT

1800-1850

By

CATHERINE ELIZABETH REISER

Pennsylvania
Historical and Museum Commission
HARRISBURG • 1951

ii

TABLE OF CONTENTS

ILLUSTRATIONS

PREFACE

PITTSBURGH in 1800 was little more than a frontier town with a most fortunate and strategic location. Already, as a French post, an English fort, a pioneer trading settlement, and from 1794 an incorporated borough, the region at the Point—now the Golden Triangle—had passed through the more elementary stages of pioneer economic activities. At the turn of the century a nascent industrialism existed. Pittsburgh was emerging from the domestic system of manufacture and growing impatient with her still almost primitive form of commerce, her lack of financial capital, her isolation, and her retarded transportation facilities. The necessity of the development of commerce and industry; the opportunities for economic progress; and the vigor and imagination of business leaders plunged the people of the region into a steady determined struggle for their material progress.

Pittsburgh's principal ambition at first was to secure an economic development which would relieve her binding dependence upon eastern manufactures. With this idea in mind, Pittsburgh built up manufacturing establishments to provide glass, cotton and woolen textiles, iron tools and agricultural implements. Manufacturing, therefore, was introduced of necessity and gradually arose to pretentious proportions only as commerce developed. Instead of striving for their own economic independence, Pittsburghers adopted a broad outlook and placed greater faith in commerce, based primarily upon their manufactures. Commerce and industry were thus so closely allied as to be inseparable—the prosperity of one meant corresponding success for the other, and consequently, any study of one must, of necessity, include the other.

The present study proposes to trace the development of Pittsburgh's economic activity during the first half of the 19th century, to show the influence of the growth of manufacturing and of the improvement of the channels of trade on Pittsburgh's commerce. No one factor can be credited with full responsibility for Pittsburgh's commercial growth. Consequently, this study reveals the effects of the interworking of natural advantages, mechanical improvements, a growing population, as well as the effect of favorable and unfavorable circumstances beyond Pittsburghers' control.

In the preparation of this manuscript, which was originally presented to the University of Pittsburgh as a doctoral dissertation, the writer is especially indebted to Professor Russell J. Ferguson of the Department of History of the University of Pittsburgh for his friendly criticism and numerous suggestions. As major advisor, Dr. Ferguson gave the writer the advantage of his deep knowledge and thorough understanding of Western Pennsylvania history.

The author is indebted to her sister, Caroline M. Reiser, for her aid in research and her editorial assistance. Special thanks must be extended to Miss Rose Demorest of the Carnegie Library, to Miss Esther C. Stewart of the Mellon Institute, and to Mrs. Lydia Landis Davis as well as to the many other persons who contributed in various ways to the final completion of this work. To all, the writer extends her gratitude and appreciation. The writer also wishes to express sincere thanks to the library staffs of the University of Pittsburgh, the Carnegie Library of Pittsburgh, the Western Pennsylvania Historical Society, the Historical Society of Pennsylvania, the Library of Congress, the State Library of Pennsylvania, the Cambria Library of Johnstown, and the Wheeling Public Library.

Grateful appreciation is also extended to the Pennsylvania Historical and Museum Commission which made this publication possible.

CATHERINE E. REISER

University of Pittsburgh
May 19, 1950

I

Pittsburgh, Gateway to the West

PITTSBURGH, the City of Three Rivers, is located at the forks of the Ohio River where the Allegheny and the Monongahela Rivers meet. The site was a natural depot for the products of the entire region of Western Pennsylvania, and the rivers flowing from the north and south were the principal arteries of travel and communication. The Allegheny River is a fine navigable stream 325 miles long, free from rock and uninterrupted by falls. It rises in Potter County in northern Pennsylvania, flows north into New York state and gradually turns southwest, re-enters Pennsylvania and then traverses the entire western area to Pittsburgh.[1] By means of the Allegheny River, Pittsburgh was thus able to tap the trade of the northwest area of the State. This river was the principal connecting link between northern and southern Pennsylvania prior to 1850. Two tributaries of the Allegheny River increased its importance; the Kiskiminetas and French Creek were navigable streams which flowed eastward and westward respectively and greatly enlarged Pittsburgh's trade area.

The Monongahela River, on the other hand, tapped the trade of northern Virginia and the extreme southern area of Pennsylvania in much the same way in which the Allegheny did in northern Pennsylvania. It rises in what is now Marion County, West Virginia, flows north to Brownsville, Pennsylvania, and then bears northwest to Pittsburgh. The Monongahela River was more dangerous to navigate than the Allegheny before 1844; and in length is only about one-third as long.[2] Together with its principal tributary, the Youghiogheny, the Monongahela River taps an area rich in mineral resources, and its importance as a trade way increased with the years. The Allegheny and the Monongahela unite at Pittsburgh to form the Ohio River, which in turn links Pennsylvania directly with the Mississippi River.

The town's location at this most strategic point at the headwaters of the Ohio gave a great impetus not only to the growth of the town's population, but also to the development of commerce and industry down to 1850. The strategic importance of Pittsburgh was particularly significant in the days when travel and transportation were limited to the packtrain, the wagon, and the river boat, or, until

---

[1] Cramer, Zadok, *The Navigator, Containing Directions for Navigating the Monongahela, Allegheny, Ohio and Mississippi Rivers*, 11th ed. (Pittsburgh, 1821), 17.

[2] Cramer, *The Navigator*, 14-16. In 1844 the Monongahela was slackwatered and navigation was decidedly improved.

the availability of the railroad. The settlement at the junction of these rivers was also one of the most accessible ports for westward migration. Transients on their way to the West, and settlers, for at least a half century, depended on the growing town for the necessities of life.

Pittsburgh's geographic importance was further emphasized because the Allegheny Mountains separated eastern and western Pennsylvania and seriously retarded transportation and communication between the two sections. Instead of relying upon the East as a market, people on the western side of the mountains looked to Pittsburgh for economic leadership. The region, consequently, had more in common with the Mississippi Valley than with the East, and all eyes turned westward. The Mississippi River system was the common bond which united Pittsburgh and Western Pennsylvania to the West, and this attachment persisted until internal improvements made possible cheap transportation eastward.

Pittsburgh was aided in her economic development because she was located in the heart of a rich agricultural area. The soil of Western Pennsylvania was fertile and the settlers were soon able to produce a surplus crop which they were extremely anxious to sell. The practical place for exchange or shipment was Pittsburgh, and for that reason, Pittsburgh was able to devote her energies to commerce and industry, thus becoming the middleman for the farmers of Western Pennsylvania.

Commerce will develop in some degree wherever men congregate in social life. It will not become established, however, until the population is secure in its position, and until a surplus of commodities can be produced. Settlers had begun to enter Western Pennsylvania even when the territory was still inhabited by the Indians; and despite repeated attempts on the part of the authorities to dislodge them, some settlers stayed, and their numbers were constantly increased by new arrivals.[3] These settlers laid the commercial foundations, hardly perceptible it is true, but still important because the ground work was established for future expansion. Until the beginning of the 19th century, commerce was more or less speculative, not the result of local enterprise, but rather due to the foresight of the old established commercial houses at Philadelphia that were interested in the fur trade carried on by the Indians. Such firms as the one of Baynton, Wharton, and Morgan, that of the Gratz Brothers, or that of Marmie, Turnbull and Company, had sufficient capital to speculate in the frontier trade; they could afford to wait for their profits without too much inconvenience because their main source of income was independent of the slow moving, but, at times, lucrative frontier trade. But by 1800

---

[3] Craig, Neville B., *The History of Pittsburgh with a Brief Notice of Its Qualities of Communication and Other Advantages for Commercial and Manufacturing purposes*, (Pittsburgh, 1851), 97-99.

Pittsburgh was an established town of about 2,400 inhabitants, having been in process of settlement for almost fifty years, and now ready for a commercial development in her own right.

The abundance of conveniently located natural resources furthered Pittsburgh's commercial and industrial development. The land was covered by timber which furnished cheap building material; once cleared, the land was fertile and usually produced a satisfying harvest, and eventually a surplus crop. As a result, an inexpensive, though meager, livelihood was guaranteed. Coal, found to be an excellent fuel, was also plentiful and cheap. Cramer observed that Pittsburgh:[4]

. . . from its geographical position alone . . . would be regarded as the great emporium of western commerce. But it has advantages which do not belong to any town in the interior of the United States, and are scarcely equalled to any part of the world.

Pittsburgh's "exhaustless beds of coal" were an advantage of incalculable importance. Industry of all kinds needs fuel, especially a fuel which is not too expensive. Coal, although discovered and in use in Pittsburgh for many years,[5] was not mined in large amounts until the industrial boom during the War of 1812. The iron and glass manufacturers found it a virtual necessity, and as these industries expanded, the coal trade also developed. Thurston, however, is of the opinion that: ". . . it was when the shipment of coal down the Ohio River commenced that the dawn of the Pittsburgh coal trade really began."[6] By 1817 coal was used to process five thousand tons of iron, which was no small amount at that time.

Iron ore too, was readily available to Pittsburgh. Although ore was not located in Pittsburgh proper, the source of supply was not too remote to be sent to Pittsburgh. The neighboring counties of Fayette, Westmoreland, and Somerset had abundant quantities of iron ore, and early developed furnaces from which the iron was sent to Pittsburgh to be made into nails, shovels, tongs, spades, scythes, sickles, hoes, axes, frying pans, cutting knives, vices, scale beams, augers, chisels, nail springs, locks, files, coffee mills, plane bits, door handles, and many

---

[4] Cramer, Zadok, *Pittsburgh Magazine Almanack*, 1817, 43-44.
[5] The Reverend Charles Beatty wrote in his *Journal*, September 8, 1766, that: "In the afternoon we crossed the *Monongahela* river, accompanied by two gentlemen, and went up the hill opposite the fort, by a very difficult ascent, in order to take a view of part of it more particularly from which the garrison is supplied with coals, which is not far from the top. A fire being made by the workmen not far from the place where they dug the coal, and left burning when they went away, by the small dust communicated itself to the body of the coals and set it on fire, and has now been burning almost twelve months entirely under ground, for the space of twenty yards or more along the face of the hill or rock, the way the vein of coal extends, the smoke ascending up through the chinks of the rocks. The earth in some places is so warm, that we could hardly bear to stand upon it; at one place where the smoke came up we opened a hole in the earth till it was so hot as to burn paper thrown into it; the steam that came out was so strong of sulphur that we could scarcely bear it." Craig, *History of Pittsburgh*, 95-96.
[6] Thurston, George H., *Allegheny County's Hundred Years*, (Pittsburgh, 1888), 123. Thurston sets the date at 1817; this was not the first shipment, however. In 1802 coal was sent as ballast to Philadelphia *via* the Ohio River on the ship *Louisiana*. There it sold at $.37½ per bushel or $10.50 per ton.

other articles too numerous to include.[7] Pittsburgh was fortunate to have access to the iron ore region, for the weight of the material was too great to allow its transportation from the East. Furthermore, the transient emigrants and the military expeditions created an urgent need for metal equipment. The manufacture of the much needed metal product was the beginning of Pittsburgh's industrial growth, and Pittsburgh grew in proportion as the demand for iron increased.

Pittsburgh's actual physical struggle against the frontier was over by 1800. The right to possess the land had been accepted; Indian troubles had been virtually non-existent in Western Pennsylvania since 1794; and the question of political relationship with the Federal government had been defined. But the Allegheny Mountains had not been leveled, and internal improvements, which might have made eastern connection possible, were too costly to be undertaken immediately on a large scale by either the State or Federal governments. Unfortunately, Pittsburgh, when she considered her situation, did not feel that she had the proper water connections to effect an easy commercial development. Three hundred miles of transportation overland · taxed the frontier's surplus too heavily to make an exchange with the East profitable.

As soon as Pittsburghers realized this fact, they began to make an adjustment. The agricultural surplus was shipped by way of the Ohio River to New Orleans, where it was sold for cash, and then the indispensable eastern goods were purchased at Philadelphia or Baltimore. Thus, commercial relations between the South and East were established, and Pittsburgh was the link that connected the chain. This arrangement was only a temporary measure; the increase in the population of the little commercial town, attended by a proportionate increase in surplus products and in the requirements of life, made irksome this long-distance, three-cornered system of trade. Pittsburghers began to feel oppressed by the weight of the chain; too much specie had gone over the mountains; and Pittsburghers began to build up a feeling of animosity towards the East. Pittsburgh felt that the Atlantic states held a financial advantage; and that she was only helping them to develop a fine economic system by absorbing the East's surplus manufactured goods, rather than developing her own economic possibilities. Naturally the eastern states found it to their advantage to have Pittsburgh develop her agriculture and to use eastern manufactured goods. The reason for Pittsburgh's increasing animosity to the seaboard was because of the fact that the consumers of her surplus products did not increase as fast as the producers of the crops. The supply was exceeding the demand, and sadly Pittsburgh became aware that "the people on the Western waters are already becoming rivals

---

[7] Cramer, *Pittsburgh Magazine Almanack*, 1817, 42.

to each other at New Orleans; and the Atlantic states are rivals to
us all."[8]

From that moment, Pittsburgh began to anticipate manufacturing
as a remedy for her commercial deficiency, and her efforts to encourage
local production were never relaxed. Manufacturing was not entirely
new to Pittsburgh, in fact, domestic manufacturing had existed from
the beginning. Self-sufficiency on the frontier had been necessary
because commercial intercourse was irregular; transportation was
difficult; and money was scarce. The food supply was almost entirely
furnished by each family unit; spinning and weaving were regular
household tasks; soap and candles were home-made; medicines were
obtained largely from herbs; in short, the home and the farm comprised
an economic unit which supplied its own needs. The settlers, not
unacquainted with manufacturing procedures, took readily to a larger
scale of manufacturing as their population grew and as their markets
expanded. Despite the availability of natural resources, the demands
for the necessities of life, and the pioneers' ready aptitude for manufacturing, the actual process was slow because the quantity of ready
money in the West was limited. The majority of settlers had migrated
because of their unfavorable economic conditions in the more settled
areas; consequently they had little or no available money when they
arrived in the West. Their small surplus was usually exhausted by the
time they were permanently located. Thus Pittsburgh's industrial
development was handicapped by lack of capital, inexperience in
finances, and especially by the already existing economic groove. Eastern contacts had been made early and these were not easily broken
because the East had credit and the advantage of priority. But despite
these handicaps, Pittsburgh stuck to her policy of encouraging local
manufacturing, and newspapers pleaded with the people to cast off
their dependence on foreign importations and to patronize their home
products.

Commerce was stimulated immeasurably by the demands of the
emigrants who passed through Pittsburgh on their way to "the West."[9]
Pittsburgh, probably the best-publicized of all river towns, was the
closest point of transfer to the Ohio River. The emigrant's visit was of
considerable commercial importance to the inhabitants of Pittsburgh
because the majority of emigrants from the East came overland and
made preparations at Pittsburgh for embarkation down the river.
Household supplies and agricultural implements were purchased; food
was secured both for the trip down the river and for later use because
a crop required months of care before an adequate supply could be

8 *Pittsburgh Commonwealth*, November 5, 1806.
9 The West has been a beckoning light throughout American history. "A country whose
fascinations spread a charm over the mind almost dangerous to civilized pursuits . . .
phantom like it flies before us as we travel, and our way is continually gilded before
us as we approach the setting sun." New Orleans *Commercial Bulletin*, July 24, 1833.

guaranteed. Some ideas of the significance of this business can be obtained from various newspaper accounts. In 1794 the number of emigrants who passed through Pittsburgh was estimated at 13,000.[10] In 1795 the number was even larger and the editor of the *Gazette* reported that:[11]

> The emigration [sic] to this country this fall surpasses that of any other season and we are informed that the banks of the Monongahela, from M'Kees Port to Redstone, are lined with people intending for the settlements on the Ohio and Kentucky. . . . As an instance of the increasing prosperity of this part of the state, land that two or three years since was sold for ten shillings per acre, will now bring upwards of three pounds.

Fortunately for Pittsburgh, large numbers of immigrants continued to come either in waves, or in small groups, almost up to 1840. The extent of immigration can be recognized by the fact that from 1800 to 1840, nine new states were formed in the West and South and admitted to the Union. Economic depressions in the East stimulated westward migration and each depression sent out its wave of settlers. The West was looked upon as "an assylum [sic] of the oppressed" instead of a thing disagreeable and uncomfortable and "something to scare children."[12] No matter where "the West" happened to be at the moment, immigrants were always welcome, for "man is the only growth that's wanted here."[13]

The increasing commercial activity, produced by supplying the demands of the transients, gave an additional stimulus to industrial development. The demands for agricultural implements and building tools produced rapid expansion of the iron industry. A large part of the agricultural necessities was purchased at the forks of the rivers and carried away by the departing settlers. The industries which developed in Pittsburgh were not the complicated affairs of the old industrial section but industries which could be operated in or near the home and which did not require much capital. The immigrants also aided Pittsburgh by paying cash for their supplies and the merchants felt the thrill of having money once again in their strong boxes, even though the amounts were small. Merchants also anticipated future sales because they knew where the settlers were going, and they were not slow to realize that there a potential market was being created if they could only continue to supply the settlers with manufactured goods.

---

[10] *Pittsburgh Gazette*, February 7, 1795. Extracts of a letter to a commercial house in Baltimore, dated November 6, 1794, reported that 13,000 emigrants had passed over the Wilderness Trail and that the total had been obtained by persons authorized and paid by the government to keep score. The editor of the *Gazette* added that "the number by way of Pittsburgh cannot have been much less, if indeed any less at all."
[11] *Ibid.*, November 21, 1795.
[12] *Ibid.*, May 4, 1819.
[13] Fordham, Elias P., *Personal Narrative of Travels in Virginia, Maryland, Pennsylvania, Ohio, Indiana, Kentucky, and of a Residence in the Illinois Territory, 1817-1818,* edited by Frederic A. Ogg, (Cleveland, 1906), 119.

Not all the immigrants who came to Pittsburgh were transients; many stopped at the forks of the Ohio.[14] Pittsburgh's natural resources and economic possibilities attracted skilled laborers to the areas in ever increasing numbers. The number and variety of laborers can be seen from a list of master-workmen which was compiled by Zadok Cramer in 1802:[15]

5 Bakers	3 Gunsmiths
14 Boot and shoe makers	2 Hatters
9 Blacksmiths	2 Hair Dressers and Perfumers
1 Brass founder	2 Nailers
1 Book-binder	6 Masons
6 Brick layers	2 Plasterers
4 Brick makers	2 Potters
1 Brush maker	1 Pump maker
5 Butchers	4 Saddlers
8 Cabinet makers	1 Sythe and Sickle maker [sic]
21 Carpenters	3 Ship Carpenters
3 Chair makers	1 Skin dresser
6 Chandlers	1 Stocking Weaver
3 Clock and Watch makers	2 Stone Cutters
1 Coach maker	6 Tanners
2 Coopers	12 Taylors [sic]
4 Cloth Weavers	2 Tin Plate workers
1 Diaper and Carpet Weaver	1 Trunk maker
1 Dyer	1 Upholster [sic]
1 Engraver	2 Waggon makers [sic]
1 Gilder	2 Wheel Wrights
1 Glass cutter	1 White Smith and Tool Maker
4 Glazers	1 Wire screen maker

---

14 The *Gazette* reported that: "The settlement of the lands west of the Allegheny River within the boundary of this state, still engrosses the public attention, and we are informed, from good authority, that upward of twelve hundred persons here crossed that river within this month passed with the express intention of fulfilling the law by making an actual settlement." *Pittsburgh Gazette*, March 5, 1796.
Probably not enough of the immigrants stopped in Pittsburgh, for a letter appeared in the *Gazette* protesting against the emigration westward:
" 'Hills are green a great way off,' is an old saying, yes, and a true saying. I have from circumstance of residence been obliged for many years to observe the hordes of emigrants who have travelled through the western parts of Pennsylvania—to settle in the 'State of Ohio' or 'on Congress lands,' or on lands 'down the river' to use their own language. . . . I have at such times asked the head of the emigrant family, 'Why not buy land in this country when you can procure it on as easy terms as you can down the river?' The answer uniformly was, 'we hear such a name of the near state—we can raise so much corn there with so little labor.' etc., etc. . . . It is, however, latterly observable, that this manna is working its own cure, and will soon cease. Persons accustomed to the oak, chestnut, and hickory timbered land of the eastern parts of Pennsylvania, and the advantages of the Philadelphia market begin to discover, that if they remove to the westward, they ought to settle as near as possible to *Pittsburgh* because it is the *next best market in America* (a few of the cities on the Atlantic excepted) . . . and can acquire land of superior fertility to that they before owned *at as low or a less price*, than *lands* in Ohio cost. Without noticing the *diarrehas* and *fever* which rage every spring and fall in the country low down the Ohio, and is unknown here, emigrants now reflect before they decide on the place of their permanent residence." *Pittsburgh Gazette*, March 26, 1813.
15 Cramer, Zadok, *The Pittsburgh Almanack for the Year 1802*, (Pittsburgh, 1802). Pittsburgh had always encouraged skilled laborers, and even as early as 1789 John Scull, the editor of the *Gazette* wrote: "We want people, we want sober and diligent tradesmen; hatters, button makers, weavers, etc., will be more welcome and will effectually promote our prosperity. . . . I wish this state would give a bounty of forty shillings to every mechanic or laborer who arrived in it from Europe. Population and industry are the true causes of national greatness." *Pittsburgh Gazette*, April 25, 1789.

With the arrival of labor, Pittsburgh possessed the necessary concomitant prerequisites for manufacturing, which, combined with agriculture, gave Pittsburgh a commercial right in her own name. Commerce cannot be of much account if a community does not produce marketable commodities. The editor of the *Missouri Gazette* described the need of the West that had been a common characteristic of each and every frontier, Pittsburgh included:[16]

The emigration to the West continues to be constant and increasing. It is a subject of regret, however, that correct advice and information is not possessed by emigrants before they start on their journey. Mercantile men in the present state of the country, receive but little encouragement. The number of them is already sufficiently large, and the supply of goods received by the present dealers is sufficient for the wants of the country. It is not every branch of mercantile business that succeeds well. We are young people, and we trust, will never be overstocked with goods. The necessary results of such a state of things would be similar to that in Ohio and Kentucky. Experienced farmers, and useful mechanics and artists are wanted in the country, and those receive liberal encouragement, and cannot do wrong in emigrating. Carpenters, shoemakers, blacksmiths, tanners, and a variety of other branches might be named as offering superior advantages. Professional gentlemen will find the west as well supplied as the east and south. Superior talents and information would be encouraged, but we have a sufficient of mediocrity already.

The army expeditions to the northwest and to the southwest used Pittsburgh as the focal point of departure and aided Pittsburgh's development in much the same way as the emigrants. Numerous expeditions against the Indians in the 1790's increased the general business, for practically all the supplies came through Pittsburgh.[17] Later, in the War of 1812, the northwest army was also provisioned by Pittsburgh merchants.[18] For a time it appeared that the primary circulating medium of exchange in Pittsburgh was to be army certificates, and, despite the fact, that the army contractors of the East took the lion's share of the army's custom, the frontier traders found that the mere presence of an unproductive and non-competing group meant business for them. More people came to Pittsburgh in one year than other frontier communities saw in a lifetime. Naturally business in general was stimulated, and Pittsburgh had an incentive that was tangible and active.

Pittsburgh, fortunately located, aided by a rapidly growing market, and possessing natural resources which could be manufactured into articles greatly demanded, faced a commercial development with almost limitless possibilities. Today, Pittsburgh belongs primarily to Pennsylvania and to the East; but prior to 1850 she was more united to the Mississippi Valley, and moreover, benefited by the connection.[19]

---

[16] *Missouri Gazette*, November 9, 1819.
[17] *Craig Papers*, Quartermaster's Reports.
[18] *Pittsburgh Commonwealth*, March 10, 1812; November 25, 1812; *Pittsburgh Gazette*, January 1, 1813; August 14, 1812.
[19] Channing, Edward, *A History of the United States*, 5 Vols., (New York, 1932), V. 80.

A huge local commerce extended throughout the valley and followed westward after the trail breakers; Pittsburgh's manufactured products were in demand throughout the West because they were cheaper than eastern goods. The Allegheny Mountains, which so effectively separated Pittsburgh from the seaboard, were really a blessing in disguise because Pittsburgh's manufacturing development would have been seriously retarded had the mountains not acted as a sort of protective tariff.

By 1800 Pittsburgh had 63 shops, 23 of which were general stores, six shoe shops, four bakeries, and four hat shops.[20] The general stores handled a great variety of goods and were usually connected with Philadelphia firms. But local manufacturing had begun to take hold; in 1802 Cramer reported that one brewery, two glasshouses, a paper mill, several oil mills, fulling-mills, ironworks, powderworks, saltworks, sawmills, and gristmills had been established. By 1800 Pittsburgh was ready and eager for a place in the developing economic scheme. In a little over fifty years she had grown from a mere military post to a good sized town; the frontier had moved West, and Pittsburgh was sufficiently strong to have well-defined economic aspirations of her own. Pittsburgh's commercial development cannot be attributed to any one influence or advantage, but rather to a group of factors which worked intermittently. At the turn of the century, Pittsburgh was the product of circumstances, in a strategic location, with natural resources, and an increasing and ingenious population that was equipping and settling not only in the Pittsburgh area, but in the entire Mississippi Valley.

[20] Douds, Howard C., Merchants and Merchandising in Pittsburgh, 1759-1800, (Master's Thesis, University of Pittsburgh, 1936), 29.

II

Pittsburgh, Provider for the West

THE COMMERCIAL development of Pittsburgh was inextricably interwoven with and dependent upon the settlers' demands and the resulting progress in manufacturing. At the beginning of the century a nascent manufacturing movement existed. Zadok Cramer, one of the earliest advocates of home industries in Pittsburgh, produced the following report of Pittsburgh's manufactures in 1802:[1]

In the town of Pittsburgh there is one extensive brewery; in its vicinity, there are two glass works, the third for the finer kind of glass is erecting; one extensive paper mill, several oil mills, fulling mills, powder works, iron works, salt works, saw and grist mills, boat yards. . . .

Such, fellow citizens, is your spirit of enterprise. Your manufacturies are going up around you as the weeds growth in a rich garden. Your exertions cannot be too much applauded. And, though Europeans may be jealous of your covering the seas with your Allegheny and Monongahela ships of war, they will do you the justice to admire your adventurous dispositions exhibited in so new a country.

Although from this summary, manufacturing may seem to have been insignificant, at least a beginning had been made. Pittsburgh, out of sheer necessity, started to manufacture first, because she was isolated from the eastern markets by a chain of mountains which were more effective than a protective tariff in aiding infant industries; and second, because she, like any other frontier post, was poverty ridden; money was extremely scarce and even money for taxes was hard to raise.[2]

Domestic manufacture had been forced upon the first American frontier for the same reasons, and each succeeding frontier more or less followed a similar pattern. Self-sufficiency was a necessity and not an inherent virtue. In this simple frontier society where the population was limited, existence was the primary object and class distinction was very slight. But, as the starving period passed, society became more complex and the peoples' wants increased. Pittsburgh, past her hand-to-mouth stage of existence, was beginning to have a surplus to send to market. Had the East been accessible, probably Pittsburgh's history would have been another epoch in the expansion of the Philadelphia market. Instead, Pittsburgh had a development of her own, and for some time afterward she considered Philadelphia as a rival rather than an established fountainhead.[3] The isolation that had been a disadvantage during the period of settlement proved to be

---

[1] Cramer, *Almanack, 1802.*
[2] Habermehl, John, *Life on the Western Rivers,* (Pittsburgh, 1901), 5.
[3] *Pittsburgh Commonwealth,* November 5, 1806.

a valuable incentive to economic independence. Not that complete independence was ever desirable but, at least, Pittsburgh was relieved from a binding dependence which stifles and delays, and in the end, destroys local industrial development.

Manufacturing of the domestic type began simultaneously with settlement in frontier Pittsburgh. Almost all of the everyday needs were supplied in each individual household, and the supply was adequate as long as the frontier stage existed. The primary products needed were food, shelter, and clothing, as well as the tools and implements necessary to produce these primary commodities. Food and shelter, the most pressing needs, were readily secured because the soil was fertile and the natural resources were satisfactory.

Milling was probably the earliest established industrial pursuit since flour was an absolute necessity. According to the standards of the day, whiskey was almost as much a necessity as food.[4] Whiskey had been made for home consumption as soon as the grain crop exceeded the requirement for food. Expansion was rapid both in the milling of flour and the manufacture of whiskey, articles which could be traded with profit. Flour and whiskey, thus, were in active demand, and could be readily marketed, the first to the South and the second both to the South and East. Flour and whiskey, moreover, were products of the frontier which could stand the freight rates. After the initial effort of clearing the land and the planting of crops and harvesting, there was time for other home pursuits, for the business of maintaining life allowed for no regulation of hours or division of labor. Stock raising was a natural concomitant of agriculture, and while the Pittsburgh market was never so successful as that of Cincinnati, the supply met the demand.

Shelter was roughly secured for immediate protection, but since the building program of any frontier was heavy, lumber, shingles, and stone were in constant demand. A sawmill was almost as important as the inevitable gristmill, neither of which manufactories could take place in individual households. Window glass, nails, and the manufacture of simple tools were the earliest auxiliary industries.

Clothing was not the industrial factor that it is today, because fashion had no place when life itself was at stake. Although replacement was frequently needed, clothing was simple but adequate; and materials were coarse. Flax was grown to be made into coarse country linen; wool was a supplementary material; and linsey-woolsey was a frontier staple.[5] Much of the demand was filled by domestic manufacture, but factories were started early to take care of the extra

---

4 Cramer, Zadok, Pittsburgh Almanack for the Year 1804, (Pittsburgh, 1804), 21. Cramer estimated the value of the distilling business at $32,000.
5 Cramer, Almanack, 1804, 21. Textiles were valued in 1803 at $46,825 which included the 41,500 yards of linen, 7,500 yards of linsey-woolsey, and 8,500 yards of cotton.

demands. The hat and cap industry became an important factor and was one of the earliest of the established type to be successfully introduced in Pittsburgh.[6]

Almost equally important with the primary commodities were the products by which the frontier maintained its position. Guns and ammunition were of prime importance, both for fighting and for securing food. Agricultural implements needed replacement and repairs; and as soon as surplus crops were produced, containers were demanded, thereby requiring the manufacturing of barrels, casks, and bottles. The numerous home utensils, pots and pans, cranes, spinning wheels, looms and furniture necessitated the manufacturing of iron and wood products. The demand for these commodities increased as the region was settled and the population grew. Various vehicles of transportation were demanded early by emigrants and even by settlers. These transients who passed through Pittsburgh to the West required boats for carrying themselves and their goods to their new homes. Even Pittsburghers or settlers in the immediate region found boats essential to transport their goods to markets. The boat building industry in 1803 was valued at $40,000 and was the third largest industry in the city.[7] A faint beginning at wagon building had been made by 1803, but the demand was small due to road conditions. In the same year the largest industry created by overland travel was the manufacture of saddles and bridles. Four hundred and fifty pairs of saddles and one thousand five hundred bridles were manufactured in Pittsburgh in 1803 and the value of the articles was placed at $9,500.

As Pittsburgh began to take on the appearance of a settled community, interest was directed towards the manufacture of the finer things in life. Paper was needed for printing, since Pittsburghers now had time to read; tobacco was manufactured; brass and tin articles were replacing the cruder utensils; soap was manufactured in factories by 1803; candle making was going out of the home. There was also a demand for rugs. Pittsburgh began rather early to emerge from the homespun stage.

Food, shelter, clothing, and the sustaining products were demanded in constantly accelerating amounts, and as the demand grew, factories gradually appeared. Domestic manufacture, as the basis of production, gradually declined in importance and was replaced by the factory system. The earliest manufactories were neighborhood affairs. One man put up a flourmill or a sawmill, or even a combination of the two, and did the work for the entire area. Glass and iron factories had an early beginning in Pittsburgh because these industries were not adaptable to domestic manufacture. Other industries started because

---

[6] *Ibid.*, 21, lists the value of hats and caps manufactured at $14,675.
[7] *Ibid.*, 21, iron and textiles were larger, iron industries in 1803 were valued at $56,-548, and textiles were valued at $46,825.

of the increased demand and because the natural resources and enterprise were present to make them a reality. Once started, the factories stayed, and by 1810 Pittsburgh was already assuming the appearance and importance of a manufacturing center.[8]

The earliest surviving estimated summary of manufacturing in Pittsburgh was made by Zadok Cramer in his *Almanack for the Year 1803*.[9] The total value of Pittsburgh manufacture was estimated at $358,908.[10] The iron industry even in 1803 was the most important. It produced castings and bar iron to the amount of 180 tons and 40 tons of nails. The total value of the iron manufactures was $56,548.[11] Textiles were second in importance with a value of $46,825.[12] Linen was the type of cloth produced in the largest amount; cotton was second but its total amount was in no way comparable to that of linen.[13] The manufacture of cotton goods was a modern innovation at this time and indicated a decidedly new trend in textiles. For some unaccountable reason the public began to demand this new fabric, preferring it to wool or linen,[14] and Pittsburgh was keeping up with the times even in 1803. Boat building was third in value of products manufactured, the total estimated at $40,000. The following industries are those which produced goods in 1803 valued at $10,000 or over:[15]

Iron	$56,548	Liquor	$32,100
Textiles	$46,825	Brick and Stone	$17,500
Boat Building	$40,000	Brass and Tin	$15,600
Leather	$34,165	Hat and Cap	$14,675
Wood	$33,900	Glass	$13,000

No estimate can be made on the number of the laborers employed at this time, nor the number of establishments which manufactured these products. But some idea of the numbers can be seen by comparing the figures for 1802 and 1807. In 1802, classes of master-tradesmen in Pittsburgh, numbered forty-six different groups,[16] while in 1807 the classes of master-workmen had increased to seventy-nine.[17]

---

[8] Jones, Samuel, *Pittsburgh in 1826, Containing Sketches Topographical, together with a Directory of the City, and a View of its Various Manufactures, Population, and Improvements*, (Pittsburgh, 1826), 49.
[9] Cramer, *Almanack, 1804*, 21.
[10] *Ibid.*, 21. Pittsburgh manufactures were given at $266,403, while the total value of country products by which a barter was carried on, was estimated at $92,505, or a total value of the two being $358,908. Cramer estimated the value of articles manufactured "as upwards of $350,000." Totals of manufacturing are estimates by various individual authors of almanacs and directories and consequently are given in general terms. It must also be remembered that the area included under Pittsburgh varies—some writers include the whole of Allegheny County while others will include only parts of the county. Cramer in his 1804 *Almanack* uses both Pittsburgh and an unknown area from which are drawn "country products." Attention is drawn to Appendix I where figures are given for the estimated value of manufactures for the year 1836. Two writers published directories for approximately the same time yet the figures vary widely.
[11] *Ibid.*, 21.
[12] *Ibid.*, 21.
[13] *Ibid.*, 21. Linen, 41,500 yards; cotton, 8,500 yards; linsey-woolsey, 7,500 yards.
[14] Channing, V, 407, asserted that "the development of the demand for cotton throughout the world is one of the extraordinary phenomena of the 19th century."
[15] Cramer, *Almanack, 1804*, 21. For complete chart see Appendix I.
[16] Cramer, *Almanack, 1802*.
[17] Cramer, *Navigator, 1808*.

Somewhere between these two lay Pittsburgh's employment figures for 1803.

In 1810 the United States marshal made a report on the manufacturing establishments in Pittsburgh and in Allegheny County for the *Census Report* of that year. The figures from this source are more reliable and more complete than any preceding account. By 1810 "big business" in Pittsburgh had changed considerably; but the iron industry remained first in total value of articles produced, and a study of both local and county surveys indicates that iron was produced in Pittsburgh proper. The most notable increase was in the glass industry for it rose from tenth place in the business line-up in 1803 to third place in 1810. Textiles fell from second place in 1803 to tenth in 1810; but this decrease is not as significant as it seems, for the 1803 figures included also the estimated amount of rural or domestic produce.[18] The manufacture of leather goods, which included the tanning process as well as the manufacture of saddles, boots and shoes, rose to second place in 1810.[19] The distilling and brewing industry in that year also showed that it was a significant rural enterprise as well as an industry of Pittsburgh proper. The following chart shows Pittsburgh industries in 1810, in order of the value of goods produced, both in comparison to Allegheny County in 1810, and to Pittsburgh in 1803:[20]

PITTSBURGH 1810

Iron	$94,890	Hats and Caps	$24,507
Leather	81,378	Brick and Stone	22,400
Glass	63,000	Wood	19,674
Boat Building	43,000	Soap and Chandlers	14,500
Brass and Tin	25,500	Textiles	14,248

ALLEGHENY COUNTY 1810

Textiles	$146,977	Glass	$63,000
Milling	136,160	Hats and Caps	28,204
Liquor	117,878	Wood	27,895
Leather	110,950	Brass and Tin	25,500
Iron	94,890	Maple Sugar	18,274

PITTSBURGH 1803

Iron	$56,548	Liquor	$32,100
Textiles	46,825	Brick and Stone	17,500
Boat Building	40,000	Brass and Tin	15,600
Leather	34,165	Hats and Caps	14,675
Wood	33,900	Glass	13,000

---

[18] Textile manufacture for the entire country ranked first in the report, being valued at $146,977, thereby indicating that Pittsburgh did not supply the area with textiles. *Third Census of the United States, 1810,* (Philadelphia, 1813).
[19] Cramer's *Pittsburgh Almanack, 1812,* 52; Lyford, Williams S., *Western Address Directory for the Year 1836,* (Baltimore, 1837), 62.
[20] *Third Census of the United States, 1810;* Cramer, *Almanack, 1812,* 52; Cramer, *Almanack, 1804,* 21.

From this chart it can be seen that iron, glass, boat building, brass and tin work, and the soap and chandler industries were decidedly products of Pittsburgh proper. The milling and liquor industries for Pittsburgh proper were not evaluated, and it is concluded that these industries, as well as the major part of textile production, were carried on by the farmers of the surrounding area, rather than being localized in Pittsburgh. Maple sugar was exclusively a rural product.[21] Each industry—except boat building—had a decided increase, and only two maintained the same position in relation to valuation in 1810 as in 1803, namely, the iron industry and brick and stone manufacturing.[22] Thus, it can be said that by 1810 Pittsburgh really had begun to manufacture those basic products which she needed.

From 1810 to 1816 Pittsburgh manufactures grew from infancy to a point of over-expansion. Close observation revealed all the handicaps of a too-rapid growth. The reasons for this growth were partially due to natural increase, but principally because European powers had drawn America into their quarrels. The European struggle, extending intermittently from 1789 to 1815, gave the United States an opportunity to secure a great share of the carrying trade up to 1807. From 1796 to 1807 an almost incredible prosperity developed for American merchants, shippers, manufacturers, and even farmers. Gradually, both England and France began to retaliate upon American commerce; but even when spoliations, sequestrations and confiscations were at their height, the Americans continued to find the trade profitable if one vessel in three landed its cargo.[23] Anglo-American relations between 1795 and 1805 had been, on the whole, growing in harmony, but then English shipowners began to bring an ever-increasing pressure upon their government to put an end to American commerce which seemed to them to be jeopardizing their prosperity. English restrictions provoked French retaliation, and American commerce was caught between the two.

The British pressure became more evident in the winter of 1805-06, and Jefferson reverted to the policy of commercial restrictions, thereby hoping to bring England to terms. The Non-Importation Act became law April 18, 1806,[24] and the United States became actively involved

---

[21] In 1803 maple sugar was produced to the amount of 15,000 pounds, and was valued at $1,800.
[22] See Appendix I for complete chart.
[23] Channing, IV, 352.
[24] *Annals of Congress*, 9 Cong., 1 Sess., 1259; The American Non-Importation Act of April 18, 1806, provided that from and after the 15th day of November next (extended at various times, until date was finally set for the second Monday in December, 1807), no articles of which leather, silk, hemp, flax, tin, brass, or wool is the material of chief value, shall be brought into the United States from any port or place within the British Empire except the cheaper grades of articles made from tin, brass, or wool. Furthermore, no glass whatever, no silver or plated wares, paper, nails, spikes, hats, ready-made clothing, millinery, playing cards, beer, ale, porter, pictures and prints shall be brought into the United States from the British Empire and none of these goods produced within the British Empire shall be brought in-directly from any other foreign port.

in the commercial warfare that was then raging in Europe. English and French depredations on American commerce continued to increase; and since England was fighting for self-preservation, her actions were ruthless, and near the end of 1807, war between the United States and Great Britain seemed inevitable. Jefferson, realizing that the country was unprepared for war, and being essentially peace-minded, devised the Embargo Act, hoping to exert sufficient commercial pressure upon Great Britain to put an end to her impolitic actions. This measure became law on December 22, 1807, and went into effect immediately.[25]

The second attempt to exert pressure on Great Britain was no more efficacious than the first, but it did aid American industrial development. Formerly, American manufacturing had been retarded by keen competition, both from American shipping interests and from foreign manufacturers. Now, the high prices of imported goods increased by the necessity of evading the Non-Importation Laws, gave manufacturers everywhere the needed encouragement and forced the people to buy American products. Old factories were reopened and new ones sprang up everywhere. The expansion of manufacturing throughout the United States continued during the entire period of commercial warfare; and when actual hostilities broke out, the process was even accelerated.

Pittsburgh industries, begun earlier because of isolation, felt the stimulation of European commercial warfare and of governmental restrictions on American trade. Pittsburgh's first reaction, however, was one of distrust and suspicion because she could not understand how the Non-Importation Act could aid "our own manufactures." The only possible effect that would result, as far as Pittsburghers could observe, was that the Act would "embarrass our merchant and jeopardize our peace," because if the goods did not come from Great Britain they would come from some other country. Pittsburgh merchants considered the law a device for protectionism, asserting that the articles prohibited were not those which were imported in the largest quantities, and that those omitted should have been included.[26] Their attitude may have been influenced because the huge local demand for cotton was a sensitive matter to Pittsburgh industrialists, and they berated and scolded all parties involved.

The distrust of governmental restrictions of commerce gradually receded in the face of newspaper articles advocating home industries, and industrial progress alleviated their opposition to the restrictive

---

[25] *Annals of Congress*, 10 Cong., 1 Sess., II, 2814-15, 2839. This act continued in force (technically at least) until a new act on March 1, 1809, substituted non-intercourse with Great Britain and France rather than embargo on all shipping.
[26] *Pittsburgh Commonwealth*, November 12, 1806. "If it had not been for a bravado, to what purpose were the following articles inserted in this famous prohibitory act— cloathing, [sic] ready made, milinery, [sic] playing cards, beer, ale, porter, paper, etc., they might as well have prohibited bricks, Portland stone and Thames' water, for any injury it would do to England, or good to America."

measures. The East was reminded that wool and linen had been worn before cotton, and that the western country would soon be able to manufacture cotton goods for itself "before the present stock on hand is exhausted. They could do it now, if the time now used in card playing and whiskey drinking were devoted to spinning and weaving."[27] In the next sentence, it was asserted that the Pittsburgh textile manufacturers, Kirwin and Scott, could supply all of Allegheny County with yarn and that the Pittsburgh weavers could make sufficient cloth, "but they do not spin or weave so much, because cotton cloth *is not so good unless it be carried* 3000 miles at least. Being packed up in the hold of a ship, it becomes more valuable." But the editor had hope and he was convinced that Pittsburgh manufacturing would soon be supplying local demands:[28]

. . . and then the importations of Walpole Smith and his fellow merchants, who know no *God* but *Gold,* and no *Bible* but their *Ledger* will be convinced that the farmers and mechanics of America have sense enough to see their superiority, and not to submit to be fleeced of their hard earning to support merchants. . . .

The cries for economic independence grew louder with each succeeding outrage, and all known devices were tried to encourage "our useful manufactures." Processes and substitutes were proposed and the newspapers contained numerous suggestions on how to cut down on imports and, at the same time, encourage home manufactures.[29]

The paper restrictions of the pre-war era worried the struggling manufacturer, goaded him into thinking, but did not accomplish much other than to prepare the way for economic independence, effected by the actual declaration of war against Great Britain. The war forced the American people to depend on one another and opened up various channels of trade which would otherwise have remained closed for years.

Pittsburgh industries were stimulated by war itself because much of the fighting took place in the Northwest, and military supplies once again flowed through Pittsburgh.[30] Local manufacturers supplied a large amount of both manufactured articles and food products. Furthermore, the western bitterness towards the East was temporarily forgotten; good times, high profits, and equal opportunity made possible a degree of cooperation heretofore impossible because of Pittsburgh's unfavorable balance of trade with the seaboard.

---

[27] *Ibid.,* February 25, 1807.
[28] *Ibid.,* February 25, 1807.
[29] Cramer in his *Pittsburgh Magazine Almanack for 1806,* 29, included a recipe for converting the potato into a substitute for coffee. The *Pittsburgh Commonwealth,* November 12, 1806, published an article from *The Aurora* which gave directions on how to make "Cold Blue Dyes" for linen and hempen thread. The Pittsburgh editor added that he hoped that the newspapers in the interior would copy the article; "but from the papers dependent on English mercantile interests we do not expect, and therefore do not ask that public service." As late as 1821, Cramer included the description of a shrub called *Red-root* which could be used for tea.
[30] Cramer, *Pittsburgh Almanack, 1816,* 37.

The decided growth of manufacturing between the years of 1810 and 1815 was far in excess of a normal increase.[31] The most notable development was primarily in the war industries. The most important enterprises of Pittsburgh in 1815 were essentially the same as those of 1810, as is shown by the following chart:[32]

1815

Iron	$764,200	Hats and Caps	$122,000
Brass and Tin	249,633	Textiles	115,500
Glass	235,000	Red and White Lead	110,000
Leather	215,600	Liquor	91,050
Wood	144,900	Tobacco	45,850

PITTSBURGH 1810

Iron	$94,890	Hats and Caps	$24,507
Leather	81,378	Brick and Stone	22,400
Glass	63,000	Wood	19,674
Boat Building	43,000	Soap and Chandler	14,500
Brass and Tin	25,500	Textiles	14,248

ALLEGHENY COUNTY AND PITTSBURGH 1810

Textiles	$146,977	Glass	$63,000
Milling	136,160	Hats and Caps	28,204
Liquor	117,878	Wood	27,895
Leather	110,950	Brass and Tin	25,500
Iron	94,890	Maple Sugar	18,274

The new manufactures which had risen to the "big business" level in 1815 were war industries or those stimulated directly by the war and the Non-Importation Act. Red and white lead, liquor and tobacco, were the most important of the newer industries. Boat building, although not mentioned in the survey, may have been included under wood manufactures because that industry showed a decided increase in valuation; neither were the manufacture of brick and stone included, and the soap and chandler industries were relegated to the "miscellaneous" column. Iron continued to hold first place; brass and tin rose to second place. Glass, however, maintained its position as the third largest industry in Pittsburgh despite the war demands, and from the amount manufactured it is evident that glass had become a principal export article. Textiles rose in the scale, and although woolen cloth

---

[31] Not only was manufacturing developing, but also agriculture was benefited. Cramer in his *Pittsburgh Almanack for 1817* wrote that "the erection of manufacturing establishments have [sic] created markets for the produce of the farmer near his door. Indeed this recent country is already attaining to that state of comfort and independence which arise from the mutual exchange of labour among ourselves without a dependence on foreign countries. Let those honest but wrong headed opponents of internal manufactures, who also contend for the preference of a foreign market because it is cheaper, visit Western Pennsylvania; they will find the agriculture of this country more lucrative than the old Atlantic States because the farmer has a nearer and better market. It is a fact known to every man in this country that our manufactures have already more than doubled the value of real property." *Ibid.*, 1817, 43.
[32] *Pittsburgh Gazette*, January 1, 1820.

was now first in the textile industry, cotton was second and linen had dropped even below the amount produced in 1803.

Pittsburgh manufactures were estimated to have produced goods in 1815 valued at $2,617,833; and although the number of establishments is not given, the number of persons employed was listed at 1,960. Even this increasing supply of laborers was insufficient; the West was introducing machinery to make up the deficiency of manual labor.[33] The introduction of the machine and the extensive use of the steam engine aided Pittsburgh greatly, stimulating a development which meant success for her. Happily, Cramer wrote:[34]

It [manufacturing] has almost rendered us as independent of the eastern states, as those states have been rendered by the war independent of the old world. Not that I consider a total independence of the eastern section, as a desirable thing, no, the more closely we are connected by mutual interests and wants the better, but there ought to be something like an equilibrium, and doubtless there still exists and will ever exist, a sufficient dependence for the purpose of reciprocity.

Pittsburghers' attitude on their economic destiny was vastly improved over that of 1806. In that year, the West was dependent upon the seaboard for its commerce and yet was not in a position to demand trade reciprocity. The *Commonwealth* of November 5, 1806, asserted that, "They [the eastern merchants] would sooner give their money to our natural enemies, the British;" that it was almost impossible to attempt manufacturing; that "a man might as well attempt to ascend the falls of Niagara, as to establish a factory for the employment of twenty hands;" and that the Atlantic states had flooded Pittsburgh with foreign goods. Now in 1815, the merchants and industrialists of the western city were sufficiently independent of the seaboard to insist on a trade reciprocity that seemed essential.

Unfortunately for Pittsburgh, the war came to an end; and the wonderful prosperity collapsed suddenly, for wartime profits are frequently business liabilities after a peace treaty is concluded. The over-rapid expansion which had taken place without too secure a foundation brought an abrupt retrenchment in business; many establishments were forced to close entirely, and others sharply reduced their operations. The war had been directly responsible for the mushroom-like growth of all branches of industries and for the speculative fever which had characterized all commercial pursuits. The fiscal

---

[33] Cramer, *Pittsburgh Almanack, 1817*, 48. "Manufacturers of all articles for which we have the raw materials, and where manual labour can be overcome by machinery succeed well here . . . but where we have to compete with the foreign importation of such manufactures as require many hands, we again flag. . . ." *Ibid., 1817*, 45. Cramer in comparing business establishments for 1807 and 1816 wrote that there were no steam engines employed here in 1807 while in 1816 eight were being used:
    2 driving grist mills
    1 each nail factory
    1 each paper mill
    1 each saw mill
    3 applied to different purposes

[34] *Ibid., 1817*, 36.

measures adopted by the government to carry on the war abetted
the private speculative disposition; heavy loans were made; and the
excessive issuing of treasury and bank notes caused a depreciation in
their value.[35] Money and credit were easy while the war lasted; prices
and profits rose to a high level. Increased demand due to the war and
to the suspension of foreign trade, turned the country's interest from
commerce to manufacturing. Business expansion in Pittsburgh, as
well as throughout the United States, was checked in 1817. Merchants
who had drained their capital in establishing industries did not have
sufficient working funds to tide them over. Again, the British manufacturers began to dump their goods on the American market, and the
prices were so cheap and the goods so attractive that American manufacturers could not stand the competition. Money could not be imported fast enough; banks began to contract their paper currency[36]
and to suspend specie payment; and once the retrenchment policy was
commenced, the bankruptcies and distress became more and more
general.[37]

Manufacturing statistics for the post-war period are more complete
than the earlier accounts and from them the effects of the war on
Pittsburgh can be definitely noted. The "pressure," as the depression
was called, was first felt in the East, and from there, spread westward.
That it had reached Pittsburgh by 1816 is evidenced by the fact that
the council appointed a committee to investigate manufactures in the
city and vicinity sometime previous to January, 1817. The committee
replied[38] that 259 various establishments made reports; that total employment was set at 1,637 laborers, and that the value of goods manufactured was placed at $2,266,366. By comparison with 1815 the
"pressure" had evidently not hit Pittsburgh too severely although the
value of manufactures had fallen 14 per cent.[39] The decrease was in
those industries which produced war materials and which were immediately affected by the cessation of war. Despite this decrease, the
most important industries were essentially the same as in 1815, as is
shown by the following chart:[40]

1817		1815	
Iron	$525,616	Iron	$764,200
Leather	276,860	Brass and Tin	249,633
Glass	240,000	Glass	235,000

[35] Bishop, James L., A History of American Manufacturing from 1608 to 1860, 2 vols., (Philadelphia, 1864), II, 202.
[36] Pittsburgh Gazette, December 22, 1818. The banks in Philadelphia in the last six months had curtailed upwards to eight millions, and the policy was still pursued vigorously. Suspension of specie payment was necessary because the Bank of the United States and all its branches had only $2,800,000 in specie.
[37] Livengood, James W., The Philadelphia-Baltimore Trade Rivalry, 1780-1860 (Harrisburg, Pennsylvania Historical and Museum Commission, 1947), 18.
[38] Cramer, Navigator, 1821, 48-49; Lyford, 64.
[39] In 1819 the council made another report on manufacturing and compared it with 1815. In this report the value of manufactures for 1815 was set at $2,617,833.
[40] Cramer, Navigator, 1821, 48-49.

Brass and Tin	200,000	Leather	215,600
Wood	141,700	Wood	144,900
Textiles	82,080	Hats and Caps	122,000
Liquor	72,000	Textiles	115,500
Milling	50,000	Red and White Lead	110,000
Hats and Caps	44,640	Liquor	91,050
Red and White Lead	40,000	Tobacco	45,850

As compared to 1815 all the industries, except leather and glass, experienced a drop in production. Iron was still the leading industry; glass retained its position as Pittsburgh's third largest industry; and milling was the only new enterprise to reach the big business class, replacing tobacco which suffered a severe and early set-back. Manufacturing, in general, suffered a definite decrease but industry in Pittsburgh was by no means paralyzed in 1817.[41]

A decided change did take place between January, 1817, and January, 1820, however, and the tardy arrival of the depression did not mitigate its effects. The following chart shows the state of manufacturing in 1819 and 1817:[42]

1819		1817	
Iron	$166,500	Iron	$525,616
Leather	85,000	Leather	276,860
Brass and Tin	56,700	Glass	240,000
Hats and Caps	50,200	Brass and Tin	200,000
Wood	48,000	Wood	141,700
Glass	35,100	Textiles	82,080
Liquor	35,000	Liquor	72,000
Red and White Lead	35,000	Milling	50,000
Paper	30,000	Hats and Caps	44,640
Tobacco	27,550	Red and White Lead	40,000

Retrenchment was now commensurate with previous expansion. By 1819 the value of products manufactured fell from the 1815 level of $2,617,833 to $832,000.[43] Five industries, cotton, linen, queen's ware, umbrella and pipe-making closed entirely, while others barely managed to keep operating. Even iron experienced a setback, although it still maintained its foremost position as a Pittsburgh manufacture. But despite this severe check to business, Pittsburgh manufactures, when compared to the pre-war days of 1810, showed improvement. The following chart shows the post-war condition of Pittsburgh's business, as compared with the earlier years of 1815 and 1810:[44]

---

[41] See Appendix I.
[42] Hazard, Samuel, The Register of Pennsylvania, Devoted to the Preservation of Facts and Documents and every other Kind of Useful Information Regarding the State of Pennsylvania, (Philadelphia, 1829), IV, 169; Cramer, Navigator, 1821, 48-49.
[43] The number employed in 1819 was 672, as compared to 1,960 employed in 1815.
[44] Cramer, Navigator, 1821, 48-49; Pittsburgh Gazette, January 1, 1820.

1819

Iron	$166,500	Liquor	$35,000
Leather	85,000	Red and White Lead	35,000
Brass and Tin	56,700	Hats and Caps	50,200
Wood	48,000	Paper	30,000
Glass	35,100	Tobacco	27,550

1815

Iron	$764,200	Hats and Caps	$122,000
Brass and Tin	249,633	Textiles	115,500
Glass	235,000	Red and White Lead	110,000
Leather	215,600	Liquor	91,050
Wood	144,900	Tobacco	48,850

1810

Iron	$94,890	Hats and Caps	$24,507
Leather	81,378	Brick and Stone	22,400
Glass	63,000	Wood	19,674
Boat Building	43,000	Soap and Chandler	14,500
Brass and Tin	25,500	Textiles	14,248

Thus compared to 1815, Pittsburgh had declined as a manufacturing center, but, disregarding the unnatural increase caused by war, and looking back to 1810, manufacturing may be said to have progressed. Textiles and glass were the only industries which had suffered a decline, although the character of "big business" had changed decidedly since 1810.[45] The textile industry was completely prostrated in 1819 because of British importations. Neither cotton nor linen was manufactured, and only a small amount of wool was produced to remind Pittsburgh industrialists of a once promising business. To those who remembered only the war years, the outlook was dark indeed; but in comparison with the pre-war days, Pittsburgh had moved forward, and in the light of history that is the more important.

Pittsburgh was more fortunate than the East when it came to weathering the storm. Scarcity of money, unemployment, and bankruptcies were as common in the West as they were in the East; but the West quickly reverted to older habits and resumed bartering and self-denial. Pittsburgh felt the effects but found readjustment less difficult to make. The newspapers carried numerous accounts of the hard times, but there was always a note of hopefulness and determination. Pittsburgh had known hard times before and had survived, and even in her present difficulties she had no notion of submitting "to the terms of Charles Fox and the London Jews."[46] Merchants hoped that a few years' time and the help of the government would be sufficient to restore

[45] Boat building, brick and stone making, and the soap and chandler business dropped out of the big business class in 1819 and were replaced by liquor, white and red lead, paper and tobacco industries. In comparison to 1815 paper was the only newcomer, and it replaced textiles.
[46] *Pittsburgh Mercury*, June 4, 1819.

prosperity.[47] The West had not yet gotten over the idea that difficulties could be remedied by legislation. On January 1, 1819, the editor of the *Gazette* wished his readers a happy New Year, and consoled them with this rather dubious reasoning:[48] ". . . though trade may be shackled, though specie may be scarce, and bankruptcies plenty, we find ample consolation for our individual misery, in the general prosperity." Pittsburgh benefited by the depression and the benefits were more lasting than the war profits. The hard times in the East turned peoples' faces toward the West; many collected the remains of their fortunes and moved to the frontier.[49] Once again Pittsburgh owed a debt of gratitude to eastern emigration because this influx helped Pittsburgh to rebuild her industries on a firmer foundation, and the depression of 1818-1819 did not leave a permanent scar.

During the next ten years Pittsburgh commerce recovered remarkably. The critical point had been passed; Pittsburgh learned that manufacturing was her main source of wealth; and that without manufacturing, commerce was unreliable. A combination of manufacturing and the control of the carrying trade gave great promise to Pittsburgh's future. The *Gazette*, wise beyond its years, observed that:[50]

These sufferings will more than probable, produce beneficial effects on our country. Mercantile pursuits have become too extensive and monopolizing. Commerce is only useful when it operates as a stimulus on the productive labour of a country; when support for it is sought from other sources, it becomes diseased, and ends by communicating the infection to the citizens at large.

Pittsburgh's manufacturing seemed to have passed the crisis by 1821 and thereafter industries began to revive slowly.[51] By 1826 the value of the products manufactured in Pittsburgh had reached $2,553,549 which was only $64,284 below the level of 1815.[52] The number of laborers employed by industry was 2,997, which exceeded the 1815 number by 1,037, or 53 per cent. By 1826 the iron industry had exceeded the million dollar mark and was by far the outstanding industry. Iron manufacture in 1826 represented over 50 per cent of the total value of Pittsburgh's business. Textile manufacturing had recovered by 1826 from total oblivion to the extent that it became Pittsburgh's second largest industry. Glass, too, made a remarkable recovery; and while the production was not equal to the 1815 level, it was Pittsburgh's fourth largest business. Boat building, due to the invention of the steamboat, returned to the list of the ten leading

[47] *Pittsburgh Gazette*, November 18, 1818; May 4, 1819.
[48] *Ibid.*, January 1, 1819.
[49] *Ibid.*, May 4, 1819.
[50] *Ibid.*, May 4, 1819.
[51] Thurston, George H., *Pittsburgh as It is or Facts and Figures Exhibiting the Past and Present of Pittsburgh, Its Advantages, Resources, Manufactures and Commerce,* (Pittsburgh, 1857), 39. Thurston is of the opinion that the rallying point did not commence until 1825 or 1826, but on the basis of Jones' estimates it appears to have begun earlier, for in 1826 the value of products manufactured almost reached the war level.
[52] Jones, *Directory*, 1826, 49.

industries. "Big business" had altered considerably; manufacturing
had settled down; and specialization had eliminated many minor industries. "Big business" in Pittsburgh in 1826 compared favorably to
1815; the ten foremost industries are given for the two periods to show
similarity and Pittsburgh's recovery:[53]

1826		1815	
Iron	$1,155,094	Iron	$764,200
Textiles	288,032	Brass and Tin	249,633
Leather	245,000	Glass	235,000
Glass	199,804	Leather	215,600
Wood	90,000	Wood	144,900
Milling	72,000	Hats and Caps	122,000
Boat Building	62,000	Textiles	115,500
Brass and Tin	58,000	Red and White Lead	110,000
Tobacco	53,000	Liquor	91,050
Liquor	48,000	Tobacco	48,850

Textiles, milling and boat building industries were the newcomers
to "big business" in 1826. The hat and cap industry never recovered
from the shock of 1819, and thereafter comprised only a minor industry,
usually so unimportant as to be included under miscellaneous. The
lead industry encountered a decline in 1826, but the relapse was only
temporary. In the textile industry in 1826, cotton was supreme.
Over a million yards of cotton cloth were manufactured in Pittsburgh
in 1826 while woolen cloth amounted to only a little over 20,000 yards,
and linen was not mentioned.

No surveys of manufacturing appear to have been made between
1826 and 1836, but from the newspapers and scattered accounts,
manufactures seem to have been increasing.[54] The good times which
existed from 1825 to 1833 were diminishing in 1834. The Jacksonian
manipulation of finances was beginning to take effect. The press
speaks of retrenchment and dull times for business "from the pressure"
produced by the removal of the deposits and the bitter and unrelent-
ing war carried on against the Bank of the United States by the
"Kitchen Cabinet."[55] However, since the business of Pittsburgh in
1835 was estimated to have doubled due to the opening of the Pennsylvania Canal,[56] manufacturing must have felt a similar stimulation.
But no definite conclusions can be reached. The times were charged
with dynamite for the financial status of the country was in a state
of turmoil. Credit had been stretched by the over-expansion in public
improvements and over-speculation in public lands.[57]

William Lyford published in 1837 his *Western Address Directory*

---

[53] Jones, *Directory*, 1826, 49.
[54] Hazard, *Register*, 1834, XIV, 304.
[55] *Pittsburgh Gazette*, April 7, 1834.
[56] *Ibid.*, February 22, 1836.
[57] Kline, Harriet E., Financial and Industrial Aspects of the Panic of 1837 in Pittsburgh,
(Master's Thesis, University of Pittsburgh, 1933), 60.

in which he estimated the value of Pittsburgh's manufactured products at $15,575,640.[58] The iron industry produced goods valued at $6,290-000. Glass exceeded the million dollar mark and was second in size among Pittsburgh's industrial enterprises. Textiles, third in the list, were estimated at one-half million. Manufactures had grown even more in proportion by 1836 than during the war period, and speculation had evidently not been restricted to public lands and internal improvements. Isaac Harris who also published a *Directory for 1837*, observed that many of the business establishments "either partially or wholly suspend their extensive operations" which may be explained by the fact that his survey covered only part of the year 1836 and extended into the early part of 1837.[59] The value of Pittsburgh's manufactures was placed by Harris at $11,606,350,[60] less than Lyford's estimate by almost four million dollars. The ranks of production of both surveys continued to be the same as in 1826; only the value of the products had increased.

Lyford did not make as detailed a study of the individual manufacturing establishments as had earlier compilers, but his conclusions were essentially the same. Harris on the other hand, listed separately the industrial outputs and establishments of Pittsburgh and Birmingham (Southside). Consequently, his statistics for Pittsburgh are smaller than Lyford's estimates.[61]

The two surveys show Pittsburgh's business for 1836 to be as follows:

1836—LYFORD		1836-1837—HARRIS	
Iron	$6,290,000	Iron	$5,878,500
Glass	1,260,000	Cotton	770,000
Cotton	500,000	Glass	430,000
White Lead	241,000	Rope Walks	250,000
Plough Manufacturing	174,000	White Lead	206,000

Both surveys listed *miscellaneous* and each compiler put the small industries under this general heading; Lyford listed *miscellaneous* at $6,000,000 and Harris placed it at $4,000,000. Unfortunately the term, *miscellaneous*, does not give much information; it may mean that the industries were numerous but unimportant as to the amount of production, or the *miscellaneous* column may have been used to facilitate the work of the compiler. The only certain conclusion that can be drawn is that over 25 per cent of Pittsburgh's business in 1836-37 must remain unclassified.

The individual summary of 1836 given by Lyford as compared to

[58] Lyford, *Western Address Directory*, 1836, 94-109. Total number of laborers employed estimated at 2,940.
[59] Harris, Isaac, *Pittsburgh Business Directory for the Year 1837*, (Pittsburgh, 1837), 140-41.
[60] *Ibid.*, 187. Harris also estimated the mercantile business at $13,100,000; the commission business at $5,875,000; the coal trade at $565,200; the grand total of Pittsburgh's business being $31,146,550.
[61] *Ibid.*, 185, lists the total values of manufacturing in Birmingham, the South Side of the Monongahela at $2,522,200. He does not give an individual survey of all the districts.

1826 does indicate progress and development, despite the financial maneuvering of the previous four or five years. The output of the iron industry for 1836 had increased more than $5,000,000 in amount over the output of 1826. Glass, too, showed a remarkable increase, having jumped from $199,804 in amount manufactured to $1,260,000 in 1836. Textiles had not increased as phenomenally as had iron and glass, even though the increase was almost 40 per cent. Not only had manufacturing developed in certain branches, but the total manufactures had increased over $13,000,000 in ten years' time. This huge growth in production led to industrial speculation in Pittsburgh. The picture of Pittsburgh's business, however, is not complete for the year unless notice is taken of the fact that Harris set the figures for the mercantile business at $13,100,000; the commission business at $5,875,-000; the coal trade at $565,200; and the total for Pittsburgh's commerce at $31,146,550 for the year 1836-37.[62] The period from 1826 to 1836 was one of great advancement for Pittsburgh. New markets had been opened by the improved and extended transportation system, thus increasing the demands for Pittsburgh's products.

The panic of 1837, however, interrupted business of all kinds; Pittsburgh's industries suffered with the rest of the country, but the industrialists and merchants did not lose their spirit, and manufacturing was checked only temporarily. One editor observed that:[63]

> The business community of Pittsburgh is the last to despond, and it never quite despairs; yet there is much to excite fears for the future in the ominous state of the several heavy branches of industry, in which we have been for many years successfully engaged. . . . We do not fear for Pittsburgh, however, she will be the first to recover as she was the last to be effected by the pressure, and so soon as anything like a currency is determined on, the clink of the hammers will sound as merrily as ever.

The editor was too optimistic, however, for the "clink of her hammers" did not "sound as merrily as ever," at least, not for some time. Harris' survey of 1839 estimated that the total amount of capital invested in manufactures was $5,848,472.[64] Production had decreased decidedly although not as much as might be expected. According to the survey of 1839, Pittsburgh produced goods valued at:[65]

Iron	$4,946,400	Furniture	$249,400
Textiles	536,400	Drugs and Paint	205,575
Glass	520,000	Leather Department	341,768
Machinery	443,500	Wagons, Carriages	203,450
Hardware	351,500	Hats and Caps	189,560

---

[62] Harris, *Directory*, 1837, 187.
[63] *Pittsburgh Saturday Visitor*, March 24, 1838.
[64] Harris, *Directory*, 1841, 119. The total for manufacturing was not stated, although certain industries were credited with valuations. See Appendix I.
[65] When compared with 1836, the extent of the decrease can be seen:

	1836	1839
Iron	$6,290,000	$4,946,880
Glass	1,260,000	520,000
Textiles	500,000 (cotton only)	536,400

In the 1840's manufacturing rehabilitated itself slowly. The tariff and financial policies of the country were too uncertain to allow for much progress, although these were not the primary factors which prevented extensive growth. Pittsburgh's manufacturers had developed sporadically, surging forward in advantageous eras, halting abruptly in unpropitious times. The abrupt retardations in 1819 and in 1837 checked the bubble-like enlargement and allowed for a steadier and regular development in keeping with the demands. From 1840 to 1850 Pittsburgh manufacturing expanded on a more solid basis. No survey was made of business from 1840 until 1850, but in that year Samuel Fahnestock estimated that Pittsburgh's manufacturing and other business was valued around $50,000,000.[66] Individual statistics for all Pittsburgh industries are not listed separately, and of the few listed, iron and glass had recovered to the 1836 level, while cotton textiles exceeded the 1836 level. Comparing the two periods, their values were:

	1836	1850
Iron	$6,290,000	$6,300,000
Glass	1,260,000	1,000,000
Textiles (cotton)	500,000	1,500,000

For fifty years the iron industry in Pittsburgh exceeded all other branches of manufacturing. Pittsburgh had had acute business reversals, but the supremacy of the iron industry was never challenged.

Manufacturing depends upon sales, for goods are made to be marketed, and the demand sets the pace for the development. Pittsburgh's progress had been indicated by Thurston, who has shown the value of Pittsburgh's manufacturing in relation to the population of the country to which Pittsburgh had contact by the way of the river:[67]

WESTERN POPULATION		VALUE OF MANUFACTURING		PER CAPITA
1800	385,647	1803	$350,000	91.2%
1810	1,073,531	1810	1,000,000	93 %
1820	2,541,522	1817	2,266,366	Short of 90 %
1830	3,331,298	1826	2,553,549	
1840	5,173,949	1836	31,146,550	Over 600 %
1850	8,419,179	1850	50,000,000	About same

Pittsburgh, once only the "gateway to the West," was now a manufacturing center that served as a provider for the West. In addition, there was an exchange of goods between Pittsburgh and the East. Pittsburgh's manufacturing now attracted trade which otherwise might have taken other channels. Commerce was decidedly improved because Pittsburgh had those products which a growing country needs. Home industries were not only a boon to the local inhabitants, but to the western country in general.

---

[66] Fahnestock, Samuel, *Pittsburgh Directory for the Year 1850*, (Pittsburgh, 1850), 148.
[67] Thurston, George H., *Pittsburgh and Allegheny in the Centennial Year*, (Pittsburgh, 1876), 163. See Appendix I for check on manufacturing totals.

III

The Ohio River, an Avenue of Trade

THE INCREASE of Pittsburgh's population, the development of its manufacturing and commerce, and the settling of the West all tended to supplement each other and to expand Pittsburgh's trade area and commercial contacts during the half century from 1800 to 1850. Numerous channels of transportation radiated from Pittsburgh and were essentially responsible for Pittsburgh becoming more and more important as the provider for the West. Pittsburgh might well be likened to the hub of a giant wheel whose spokes extended in all directions. The strength of the wheel depended substantially upon a strong hub and upon the contributing support of each of the individual spokes that join the hub and the rim. As both spokes and hub unite to form a sound wheel, so did Pittsburgh and her trade channels unite to produce an industrial center with a rapidly expanding trade area. Regardless of whether the channels conducted commerce towards Pittsburgh, or carried it from Pittsburgh toward the periphery, they cooperated in strengthening the commercial structure of Pittsburgh.

Not only did the channels of commerce serve as connecting links between the gradually growing commercial city and its markets, but they also became subsidiary and contributing units of the trade area. The rivers, roads, and canals, in addition to serving as conduits of economic goods, themselves stimulated settlement and economic development along their courses. Since they pointed toward Pittsburgh, their economic increment added materially to the commercial increment of the city at the forks of the Ohio.

The longest, most significant of these conduits was the Ohio River, the link with the ever-growing West. While other rivers were significant, they were mere feeders or tributaries of the Ohio geographically, and tributaries of Pittsburgh commercially. Not only was the Ohio River Pittsburgh's leading trade artery to the West but also her outlet to the world market at New Orleans.[1] Pittsburgh was fortunate to have a water route to the West, and for the greater part of the period from 1800 to 1850 she looked to New Orleans as her most important market rather than to the East.

The river was a free and open highway accessible to all who were able to obtain a boat.[2] Nor did the boat present much of a problem,

---

[1] Dunbar, Rowland, "The Mississippi Valley in American History," in Mississippi Valley Historical Association, *Proceedings*, (1915-1916), IX, 65. "If the Mississippi Valley would have been forced to depend upon its over mountain route for contact with its markets, there would never have been any great commercial development, at least not until railroads became more numerous than they are at the present time."
[2] Cramer, *Navigator*, 1821, 21.

for wood was plentiful and a crude craft could be constructed by almost every farmer or merchant. Transportation had not yet become a specialized undertaking, and almost every one who had goods to sell was his own transporter. The types of boats used were almost as numerous as the individuals who used them for sizes and shapes varied and crafts were of no definite specification.

The types of boats used on the Ohio and Mississippi Rivers depended largely on the levels of water and the commodities to be carried. Prior to 1811, all boats were floated or rowed on the western rivers, and the most common types were the flatboats and the keelboats.[3] The flatboat was an oblong ark of varying size from fifteen feet to twenty feet in width and from fifty feet to one hundred feet in length. Long poles, or paddles, were used to aid in keeping the boat on its course, although it was almost entirely at the mercy of the current. The flatboat was little more than a strongly constructed, unwieldy raft designed to carry a heavy load.[4] The keelboat, on the other hand, was a long, slender craft of lighter construction. Its advantage lay in the fact that it was easier to control and could be navigated in shallower water. Likewise, the keelboat varied in size with a capacity that ranged from fifteen to fifty tons, although the average burden was less than thirty tons.[5]

Both the keelboat and the flatboat provided inexpensive transportation; construction costs were low, usually about $1 or $1.25 per foot,[6] and overhead was slight. Wages were a small item because the enterprise was usually of a family nature. The owner of the cargo was the captain of the craft and his sons or friends the crew.[7] The food supply for the journey was taken from home, and the only other expenses were the pilot's fee for navigation over the Falls of Louisville,[8] and the wharfage and duties at New Orleans.

The exporter sold his cargo, and usually his boat, in New Orleans. After seeing the sights of the metropolis, the boatman with his cash, either took passage on a sailing vessel for Philadelphia or Baltimore, or walked home past Lake Pontchartrain, northward to Nashville, and then to Pittsburgh. A return cargo was rarely taken upstream because navigation against the current was slow, tedious, and expensive. As a result, upstream trade was only one-tenth as great

---

[3] Also known as Kentucky boats, barges, arks, broad beams, broad horns, sneak boxes, and rafts. Hulbert, A. B., *The Ohio River*, (New York, 1905), 232.
[4] The tonnage carried varied as much as did the size. Switzler reported that flatboats were designed to carry from 200 to 400 barrels. U. S. *House Ex. Docs.*, 50 Cong., 1 Sess., XX, no. 6, pt. 2, 186. Fordham in his *Personal Narrative*, reported that they could carry 700 barrels. An anonymous letter in Cramer's *Pittsburgh Magazine Almanack* for 1814 reported that barges carried from 40 to 80 tons.
[5] Baldwin, Leland D., *The Keelboat Age on Western Waters*, (Pittsburgh, 1941), 45.
[6] Cramer, *Navigator*, 1821, 29. Cramer estimated that a family boat cost about $35— "exclusive of this expense, is the price of a cable, pump, fireplace, perhaps $10 more."
[7] After the volume of business became larger, boating became specialized and goods were sent by regular boats and professional boatmen.
[8] This item of expense was not absolutely required, although the risks involved for the amateur boatman were great, and the $2 fee was considered a wise expenditure, especially when the water was low. U. S. *House Ex. Docs.*, 50 Cong., 1 Sess., XX, no. 6, pt. 2, 187. After 1830 a canal was built around the falls, and tolls were collected.

as the downstream trade. Manufactured articles were purchased in Philadelphia instead of New Orleans and transported overland to Pittsburgh, thus forming a triangular trade which continued even after the introduction of the steam boat.

The year 1811 was a memorable year in the transportation history of the Ohio and Mississippi valleys. The steamboat *New Orleans* made a safe voyage from Pittsburgh to New Orleans in the fall of that year. The event was spectacular and exciting, but, as for immediate results, the experiment was neither a perfect success nor a complete failure. The *New Orleans* had proven that steam could be used for motivation, but the cost of steamboats and their newness retarded their general use for five years.[9] Fortunately, the stimulating economic effect of the war years encouraged experiments and business demanded a two-way trade with New Orleans, as well as a more efficient system of transportation. From 1811 to 1816 nine steamboats were built, each a decided improvement over the preceding one; but despite the technical progress made, steam navigation was not considered practical until 1817 when Captain Shreve of the steamer *Washington* made the trip from New Orleans to Louisville in 25 days.[10] By 1830 the steamboat was the undisputed leader in the river trade.

Important as the invention of the steamboat was to later western economic and social development, there was an appreciable trade previous to 1811. The commodities shipped to New Orleans increased annually in volume and variety. By 1800 Pittsburgh was shipping flour, whiskey, bar iron and castings, glass, salted pork and beef, copper and tin wares, cordage, apples, cider, peach and apple brandy. Pittsburghers were ready to sail with the spring floods, hoping thereby to reach New Orleans before the market was over-crowded. In 1801 the total value of exports by river was $3,649,322, of which Pennsylvania and the territory northwest of Ohio sent $485,000.[11] In 1802 the total value of produce reached $4,475,364, of which Penn-

---

[9] U. S. *House Ex. Docs.*, 50 Cong., 1 Sess., XX, no. 6, pt. 2, 188. Robert Fulton had successfully proven the principle of steam navigation in 1808 on the Hudson River. Appreciating the importance of the western waters, Fulton was anxious to experiment with the boat on the Mississippi River because of its strong current. An agent, Nicholas Roosevelt, was sent ahead to Pittsburgh to make arrangements for the building of the new boat, which was completed and launched on its maiden voyage at Pittsburgh in September, 1811. The *New Orleans* reached Louisville on October 1, but when the water at the falls was found to be too low for crossing, she returned to Cincinnati, and thus proved that the steamboat could navigate up stream as well as down. By November the river had risen, and the *New Orleans* crossed the falls safely. On December 24, 1811, the boat reached the city of New Orleans, and from that time until 1814, when she hit a snag and sank, the *New Orleans* carried freight in the Natchez trade. In 1811 the boat cleared $20,000 net profit.

[10] The *Washington* also broke the monopoly which Fulton and Livingston had obtained from the State of Louisiana, whereby they had exclusive rights to navigate steamboats on Louisiana waters, or, in other words, the control of the important terminus of western trade. The United States court swept away that monopoly in 1817 when it declared that the Mississippi River was the heritage of the whole people, and the State of Louisiana could not control it or give rights thereon to anyone. U. S. *House Ex. Docs.*, 50 Cong., 1 Sess., XX, no. 6, pt. 2, 188.

[11] *Ibid.*, 183. The shipments for the districts of Kentucky and Mississippi alone equaled $1,626,672, while the total amount shipped by the American possession amounted to $2,111,672.

sylvania exported $700,000.[12] The total amount of freight received at
New Orleans by way of the river in 1801 was 38,325 tons, and in 1802
the amount rose to 45,906 tons.[13] In 1808 the produce from the river
was valued at $8,062,540, while in 1815-16 the amount had increased
to $9,749,253. The effect of the steamboat apparently can be noted
in the increased value of the products received in 1817-18, although
the increased number of floating vessels detracts from the validity of
the conclusion. The next year, however, does show an increase in the
number of steamboats employed and a decrease in the floating vessels.
The steamboats employed on western waters had increased from 36
in 1817-18 to 191 in 1818-19, and floating vessels had decreased from
1,670 in 1817-18 to 1,532 in 1818-19.[14] The total value of the products
received at New Orleans in 1817-18 was $13,501,036 and the total ton-
nage reached 100,880 tons. The next year the receipt for products was
listed at $16,771,711 and the tonnage set at 136,300 tons. During the
year of 1825 New Orleans listed the arrival of 502 steamboats and
valued the receipts at $19,044,640; freight received amounted to 176,-
420 tons. By 1830 the number of steamboats that arrived annually at
New Orleans had increased about 46 per cent, or to 989 boats, and
the total value of produce reached $22,065,518. The amount of freight
for 1830, likewise, increased in proportion reaching a yearly total of
260,900 tons. Five years later, 1,272 steamboats arrived annually at
the port of New Orleans, and the total tonnage reached 437,100 tons
valued at $39,237,762. By 1850 the annual number of steamboat ar-
rivals had reached 2,918 and the value of produce was set at $96,897,-
876. Unfortunately, Pittsburgh's share in this trade cannot be recorded
specifically, but the newspapers indicate that Pittsburgh continued to
use the New Orleans market and that the trade was increasing year
by year.

But these amounts received at New Orleans were small in comparison to the amounts actually sent from the various river ports. The
river, although easily accessible to Pittsburgh merchant-exporters, was
beset by innumerable dangers and impediments to navigation. These
handicaps that retarded navigation correspondingly retarded commerce. No account of trade can be complete unless the losses sustained
on the way are, at least, indicated; the mortality rate was especially

---

[12] *Ibid.*, 183. The value of goods received at New Orleans for 1801 and 1802 are as
follows:

	1801	1802
American Territories	$2,111,672	$2,634,564
Pennsylvania & territories northwest of Ohio..	485,000	700,000
Kentucky, Tennessee, and Mississippi	1,626,672	1,522,064
Mississippi Territory	—	412,500
Spanish Possessions	1,537,650	1,840,000

[13] *House Ex. Docs.*, 50th Cong., 1st Session, no. 6, pt. 2, 184.
[14] Flatboat arrivals in New Orleans in 1817-18 increased over 50 per cent of the previous
year, while steamboats increased but 33 per cent. In 1818-19 the number of flatboats
decreased slightly, while the steamboat arrivals increased almost 400 per cent. After
1819 flatboat arrivals decreased sharply while steamboats increased steadily. *Ibid.*, 183.

high during the flatboat era when probably one-third of the crafts were lost.[15] The Ohio and Mississippi Rivers were filled with snags of all sorts. Snags were caused primarily by large trees falling from the banks into the water and then becoming firmly entrenched by the roots in an upright position. Thus, a few innocent looking branches floating on the surface of the water were frequently solid barricades and meant ruin to the unsuspecting vessel. The boatmen called this type of snag "a planter." Another variation of the same type was the "sawyer", which was also a large tree embedded in a less perpendicular manner and which appeared and disappeared by turns, depending on the pressure of the current.

Driftwood formed an additional serious obstacle, especially if impeded by a barricade into a matted, solid mass. The Mississippi River particularly was spotted by these "wooden islands" which, over a period of years, became larger and, consequently, more serious obstacles.[16] The current itself was treacherous in many places; eddies and whirlpools kept pilots constantly on the alert. In flood stage the river was generally rapid and choppy, steering being almost impossible for boats that depended on the current entirely, while in low water levels all the obstacles were magnified and exposed. Sand bars and rocks were additional obstacles to navigators in both high and low water and both took their toll of river crafts. Shipping news was filled with stories such as these: "The *Hero,* Hewes, from New Orleans for Shippingport ran against a rock eight miles below Hurricane Island, stove in her bow and sunk. A part of her cargo has been saved."[17]

The logs of ships also presented a picture of physical difficulties often underestimated. These logs were printed in the shipping news of all river town newspapers and merchants scanned them anxiously, especially if their cargo was overdue. For example, the *Columbus* reported that on her way from New Orleans to Louisville she "assisted the *Olive Branch* in getting off the Bar at Thompson's Point;" two days later she "got up to the *James Ross* aground at Petit Gulf, stopped by her two hours."[18] The most formidable obstacle on the river, however, were the Ohio Falls at Louisville,[19] which required precautionary measures. The Falls were solid rock formations two miles long and

---

[15] DeBow, J. D. B., *DeBow's Review,* (New Orleans and Washington, 1846-61), III, 240.
[16] Fordham, *Personal Narrative,* 82. Moses Austin reported in his *Journal* that "pass'd a large sand Barr [sic] with near a mile of Driftwood on which we see Men examining the Drifts and Bends of the River for flower [sic] lost from the Kentucky Boats 18 of which we were informed had been lost above Walnutt [sic] Hills in March and early in April." *Austin Papers,* (ed. by Eugene C. Barker) in American Historical Association, *Reports,* 1919, II, 74.
[17] *Louisville Public Advertiser,* February 20, 1822.
[18] *Ibid.,* April 10, 1822.
[19] Cramer, *Navigator,* 1821, 22. Cramer reported that the Falls were the greatest impediment to river trade "for unless vessels happen to hit the time of the highest stage of water, they are either detained, perhaps to the next season, or if they attempt a passage over them, a wreck in part or in whole may be the consequence, in either case, putting in jeopardy property to an amount that few individuals can bear the loss of."

with a drop of 22 feet. Three channels, or chutes, enabled local pilots to take boats over the dreaded section.[20] During low stages of the river, however, steamboats could not negotiate the Falls. Consequently, boatmen either waited until the river rose or carried their goods around the Falls,[21] and transferred them to boats on the other side. Both procedures cost money and time. Drayage around the Falls cost seventy-five cents per ton, and, as a result, the boatmen usually waited hopefully for a higher water level.[22] Such delays were almost equally as costly because perishable goods spoiled, or, when the water did rise, all boats reached New Orleans at the same time, thereby glutting the market. Shipping news took particular notice of the Falls and repeatedly the same dreary account was printed: "the *Paragon* and the *Car of Commerce* arrived from Cincinnati, with full cargo, bound for New Orleans—both detained for want of sufficient water to pass down the Falls."[23]

Ice, likewise, was a serious handicap in shipping. Boatmen anxious to reach market ahead of their competitors often set out too soon after the ice had broken in the river. Under shipping news such a comment was frequently inserted: "The ice is still running, but the boats both, at this place and Shippingport are making active preparations to depart."[24] Consequently, much damage was caused by floating ice to all classes of boats. As the *Louisville Public Advertiser* reported:[25]

The *Gen. Pike,* on her way to Cincinnati, is reported to have been injured by ice. Considerable losses have been sustained during the past week, by the destruction of keel and flat boats above this place, by the floating ice. In some instances the boats were abandoned by the whole crew, and in others, in spite of all that could be done the greater part of the cargoes were lost.

Nor did the ice injure only floating vessels; ships wintering in ports were almost equally vulnerable. The *James Ross* wintering in St. Louis had been severely crushed by ice and the damage was so extensive that "the boat is done for."[26] Unfavorable weather conditions also wrought havoc on the early types of river craft. High winds and squalls occasionally would destroy the defenseless crafts by the hun-

[20] Baldwin, *The Keelboat Age on Western Waters,* 68. The Kentucky assembly provided for the appointment of a Falls pilot as early as 1797 and his fee was fixed at $2.00 per boat. Other pilots were also available on the Indiana side.
[21] Gephart, William F., *Transportation and Industrial Development in the Middle West,* (New York, 1909), 107; Ambler, Charles H., *A History of Transportation in the Ohio Valley,* (California, 1932), 91.
[22] Sometimes boats were delayed as long as three months.
[23] *Louisville Public Advertiser,* March 2, 1822.
[24] *Ibid.,* February 6, 1822.
[25] *Ibid.,* December 29, 1821.
[26] *Louisville Public Advertiser,* quoting the *St. Louis Enquirer,* March 19, 1823. The article goes on to say that only the machinery and engines could be saved.

dreds.[27]   The uncertainty of the uncharted rivers and the shifting of the currents made navigation largely a matter of good luck, although experience with river characteristics helped boatmen to detect danger signals and to avoid pitfalls.

A good summary of the boatmen's problems exists in the advice written by Moses Austin to his son, Stephen:[28]

General rules to be observed in descending the Mississippi River in opposition to every other advice do you observe the following rules first, never run late at Night but always make a landing under a Willow Point in time, it's always better to loose [sic] a few hours than be exposed at Night. Never land under a high bank and large timber. When you Intend to land begin in time to pull your boat in shore and always before the boat striks [sic] turn her stern down Stream. Never trust your boat to float unless you have a man on the look out—lett [sic] this rule be always strictly observed, too much care cannot be taken in Descending, this river, when you make your Boat fast at Night see yourself that the Cable is properly made fast—Never suffer any water to be in your boat a [t] Nigh [t] always put to land in Winds I advise you always to Keep out from the bends of the rivers, and, guard against Points of Islands, having observed this much I must committ [sic] you to the Care of the being that govern us all.

The standard guide book for western navigators for more than a quarter of a century was Zadok Cramer's *Navigator*.[29] This little book described the rivers from Pittsburgh to New Orleans, pointed out the danger spots and gave advice on how to navigate.   Cramer warned traders that navigation on the Ohio was difficult in low water from Pittsburgh to old Mingo town, or a distance of 75 miles, but that from Mingo town to the Mississippi River, barges and keelboats of less than 200 tons burden would have no difficulty.[30] The best times to navigate the Ohio, wrote Cramer, was in the spring and autumn; the spring season usually commenced at the breaking up of the ice about the middle of February and continued good for three months at least, while the autumn season commenced about October and continued until the first of December.[31] Cramer warned the reader that the summer months

[27] *De Bow's Review*, III, 240. Referring to Moses Austin's *Journal*, 69: "Day prov'd [sic] windy and raney [sic] was obliged to land. . . . Got under way about Daylight but was obliged to make a landing about 10 o'clock the wind blowing a tornado the whole Day from the South . . . the River still filled with Islands and Drift wood with bad shore and Short bends—about 10 O'Clock passed near the shore when the Bank gave way and large tree fell into the River—Cloudy and like for rain with high winds made but bad Days Run came to Shore on the American side. . . . Morning Cloudy and still like for rain about 10 O'Clock was boarded by two Canoes of Arkansaw Indians who had three Barrells [sic] of flower [sic] on board taken up on the River lost by some Kentucky Boats 8 of which these Indians informed us had been drownd [sic] about 12 O'Clock the Winde [sic] became so high that we was [sic] obliged to land and remane [sic] the whole Day with rain and thunder. . . . Cloudy like for rain about 10 O'Clock a Barrell flower [sic] seen on Spanish Shore two men from Mr. Clarks boat of Pittsburgh took it in—it was branded with Frankford S. Tine . . . there was seen on the shore in Sundry places a number of Barrells [sic] but the Wind together with the state of the River prevented us from Landing." *Austin Papers*, II, 69-73.
[28] *Ibid.*, I, 203.
[29] *Pittsburgh Commonwealth*, March 17, 1812. The *Navigator* had to be thoroughly revised as a result of the earthquake of December 16, 1811. A letter described the effects of the disaster to the Mississippi River, and reported that navigation was extremely difficult. *Pittsburgh Gazette*, January 31, 1812.
[30] Cramer, *Navigator*, 1821, 20-21.
[31] *Ibid.*, 1821, 33.

from July to October were unsuited for navigation because of the low-ness of the water, and although occasional heavy rains sometimes per-mitted boats to sail, the risks were greater than usual.

Steamboats met with the same disaster as did the flatboats and the keelboats, and, in addition, they were subject to the additional dis-asters of explosions and fires. Steamboats, too, were more vulnerable to snags because they required a greater depth of water. From 1822 to 1827 the losses in the Ohio and Mississippi rivers by snags alone amounted to $1,362,500.[32] From 1827 to 1832, during which period quite a number of snags were removed, the losses were greatly reduced and did not exceed $381,000.[33] From 1833 to 1838 the Secretary of the Treasury reported that 40 steamboats had been snagged on the Missis-sippi and the damage totaled $640,000.[34] Between 1840 and 1846 over 225 steamboats were lost on the western waters. The following chart shows the total steamboat losses from all causes from the year 1811 to 1850:[35]

1810 to 1820	3
1820 to 1830	37
1830 to 1840	184
1840 to 1850	272
Boats the dates of whose loss is unknown....................	576
Total in forty years	1,070
Tonnage	85,256
Cost	$7,113,940

The annals of western trade are filled with the gloomy accounts of these heavy casualties. Newspapers carried the stories, and the losses of property and lives were felt by all commercial interests. The sink-ing of the steamboat *Alexandria* will illustrate. The *Alexandria* left New Orleans at 10:30 A. M., Monday, March 5, 1823 with an over-load of freight and passengers, but she proceeded along without any mechanical difficulties except that "a driftwood got in contact with one of her wheels and stopt [sic] her headway for a few minutes."

---

[32] These figures include losses to all types of river vessels.
[33] U. S. *House Ex. Docs.*, 50 Cong., 1 Sess., XX, no. 6, pt. 2, 198. The government first undertook to improve the navigation of the Ohio and Mississippi Rivers in 1829. After nine years of supplication by the western people, Captain Shreve was employed to remove the snags which had created the greatest losses. He used a double steamboat, the bows of which were protected with heavy beams plated with iron. A heavy head of steam was put on, and the snags were run down. In 1832 not a single boat was lost by snagging, although again in 1846 the record was very gloomy. In that year alone 120 steamboats were lost by the following causes:

Snagged	46	Destroyed by fire	13
Sunk	38	Shipwrecked	10
Burst Boilers	16		
Collision	15	Cut down by ice	7

[34] In 1839 the total loss of boats from snags, fires, explosions, collisions, etc., was 40, of which two were snagged, seven struck rocks and other obstacles, and the total loss was $448,000. *Ibid.*, 198.
[35] U. S. *House Ex. Docs.*, 50 Cong., 1 Sess., XX, no. 6, pt. 2, 208. Insurance rates on the western rivers were exceptionally high, and during the early years of steamboat-ing, the rates varied from 12 to 18 per cent of the value of the cargo. Hall, James, *The West: Its Commerce and Navigation*, (Cincinnati, 1848), 44.

About 11 o'clock that night she encountered another floating drift-wood, which, although the shock was so light that it did not cause any excitement, "knocked off three of her boards on her larboard side, from under the first birth next to the wheel."[36] The captain discovered the leak and turned around in order to run her on a sand bar. Upon reaching the sand bar the cargo was partially unloaded before the boat sank to her upper deck. But despite the heavy losses, boats continued to ply the western rivers and New Orleans was considered a profitable market. The people of the valley were almost completely dependent upon the river, and consequently, they struggled to conquer and to control it.

But physical difficulties were not the only encumbrances to Pitts-burgh commerce. The uncertainty of the right to navigate the Mississippi; to enter New Orleans with goods; and to deposit them there, restricted commerce until 1803. The treaty of 1783 had divided the United States at the Mississippi River between the United States and Spain. Unfortunately for the western merchants, New Orleans was located on the wrong side of the river, and thus was under the control of Spain. The fact that the whole export trade of the West was subject to Spanish decrees was a continuous source of irritation to the inhabitants of the entire Mississippi and Ohio valleys. That these people had little surplus to send to market did not deter them from objecting to Spanish domination,[37] for they were determined to have New Orleans as an outlet; driven by necessity, the people became desperate. Their surplus might be small, but large or small, the West demanded the free navigation of the Mississippi as a right, with vehemence that was lusty and forceful. James Madison understood the value the frontiersmen placed on the Mississippi River for he wrote to the American minister at Madrid that "the Mississippi River to them is everything—it is the Hudson, the Delaware, the Potomac, and all the navigable rivers of the Atlantic States formed into one stream."[38]

Between the years of 1783 and 1803 the Mississippi question was a bitter issue. In 1784 the river was closed to American commerce and the period of exclusion lasted for four years. A Spanish royal order of December 1, 1788 modified the exclusion and decreed that the people of the Mississippi Valley might bring produce to New Orleans, subject to an import duty of 15 per cent; upon an additional six per cent export duty, the produce might then be shipped to any of the ports with which

[36] *Louisville Public Advertiser*, January 4, 1823, quoting the *Baton Rouge Gazette*. The article goes on to tell that one of the passengers stabbed the mate with a sword when an argument arose over his cargo which had not been rescued.
[37] The reason that there was no surplus was because of the fact that before 1790 the frontiersmen were busy providing for their own consumptive needs; while after 1790, when a surplus was accumulating, the Federal armies in the field depended upon the region for supplies. The increasing number of immigrants also needed supplies for the first few years, and the Ohio Valley people were kept busy supplying a rapidly growing home market. Downes, Randolph C., "Trade in Frontier Ohio" in the *Mississippi Valley Historical Review*, (1929-30), XVI, 472.
[38] U. S. *House Ex. Docs.*, 50 Cong., 1 Sess., XX, no. 6, pt. 2, 182.

New Orleans was permitted to trade.[39]   Despite these handicaps western trade began to expand and to assume a semblance of order; by 1795 the foundation of American commerce at New Orleans was already established.[40] Diplomatic negotiations between the United States, Spain, and England resulted in the Pinckney and Jay treaties, and the frontier looked forward to a brighter future. Unfortunately, the Pinckney treaty did not entirely dispose of the Mississippi problem until 1798, and the delay gave rise to misunderstandings and confusion. Nevertheless, during the troubled years from 1795 to 1800 the river trade of the western settlements continued to flourish. The western peoples, however, were not satisfied and insistently they demanded a free outlet to the ocean.[41] The frontier traders had discovered that they needed something more than the assured right to navigate the river, for this they had; yet they felt the need for a more adequate system of deposits than was provided by the Pinckney treaty.[42] The merchants feared the right of deposit provision because Spain had the upper hand entirely. The United States had no voice in the question of changing the right of deposit at all, for if Spain decided to close New Orleans, Spain had the unrestricted choice in a new selection of a port or might even suppress the right entirely.[43] This fear of an alteration was not merely imaginary on the part of the West, because just as the shipbuilding and exporting interests of the Ohio Valley were getting firmly established "they received a shock that was felt around the world."[44]

On October 16, 1802, the three years clause of the Pinckney treaty lapsed and the Spanish Intendant formally refused to allow Americans to deposit their products; furthermore, he gave them 40 days to leave Spanish territory pending the transfer of the colony to France! The worst fears of the Americans had come true, and the resultant feeling was a combination of rage and perplexity as to the reason why Spain was playing the cat's paw to Napoleon.[45] The termination of the right of deposit was, without a doubt, one of the most important provocative measures in the whole history of international rivalry in North America. It has been said:[46]

Although foreign relations provided that generation of America with constant succession of surprises, it is doubtful whether any event of the period—even Jay's treaty or the XYZ affair—caused a greater sensation than the closing of the deposit.

[39] The 15 per cent import duty was reduced to 6 per cent in 1793.
[40] Western commerce had been stimulated because the regular imported French goods had been cut off due to the war between Spain and France.
[41] Pelzer, Louis, "Economic Factors in the Acquisition of Louisiana," in Mississippi Valley Historical Association, *Proceedings*, (1912-13), VI, 177-78.
[42] After the treaty of San Lorenzo the right of navigation was never questioned, either by the Spanish court or the colonial officials. Whitaker, Arthur D., *The Mississippi Question*, (New York, 1934), 89.
[43] *Ibid.*, 89.
[44] Ambler, *A History of Transportation in the Ohio Valley*, 93.
[45] Whitaker, *Mississippi Question*, 189.
[46] *Ibid.*, 189.

Both the *Pittsburgh Gazette* and the *Tree of Liberty* carried the news prominently although no indication of any planned action was given.[47] In the Ohio Valley the effects were immediate and paralyzing. "Silence reigned in the boatyards; agriculture came to a standstill and credit became demoralized, goods valued at almost two million dollars having gone into the interior during the previous year, most of them on promises to pay."[48] Whether the effects were as serious as this statement would lead one to believe is a disputable question, but it is a fact that the West was saved from the worst consequences of the closing of the deposit. About this time New Orleans was faced with a serious food shortage, and as hunger knows no law, the Spanish Intendant permitted the Americans to bring in their foodstuffs.[49] This raised a cry of resentment in the *Pittsburgh Gazette*:[50]

> We look upon it as adding insult to injury. They will permit you to carry on a trade with which they cannot dispense without starving, but the stamina of your commerce is trampled on. Why did not your government lay an embargo on all provisions from the Upper Country? The business would then have been soon adjusted. As long as they open their mouths they will have to keep their ports open for provisions.

Perhaps the seriousness of the deposit question was mitigated a little, but the idea of the retrocession of Louisiana to France shocked the frontiersmen, and talk of descending the river to settle the question for all time became louder. The West had lost its love for the French during the years 1801-02 because they suspected that the French had dictated the closing of the deposit and that this was only a taste of what the United States would suffer when the new neighbors arrived.[51] Even before the formal announcement of the retrocession, rumors of the French menace were constantly appearing in the Pittsburgh papers, and if the fear psychology stalked trade in 1802 as it does today, the effects were disastrous. Such was evidently the case for it was reported that:[52]

---

[47] *Pittsburgh Gazette*, December 3, 1802; *Tree of Liberty*, December 4, 1802. The *Gazette* published the extracts of a letter by "express from New Orleans": "Yesterday (October 18) the Intendant closed the port against American vessels coming with cargoes to sell. . . ." The *Gazette* also carried a copy of the proclamation.

[48] Ambler, *A History of Transportation in the Ohio Valley*, 92; *Pittsburgh Gazette*, January 21, 1803.

[49] *Pittsburgh Gazette*, March 25, 1803, "Conformably to the resolve of the Council of Finance, held this day, I permit the introduction into this capital of Flour, Salted Meat, and Other Provisions, brought in flat-boats and other vessels from the American settlements on the Ohio, *Under the condition* that on landing of the same, the duty of 6 per cent as established by the royal order of the 24th of April, 1794, relating to said articles, will be exacted. And whatsoever may not be consumed in the province, will be subject to the customary duties on exportation, which is to be effected solely in *Spanish vessels,* for the foreign ports with which by the existing royal orders, this colony is allowed to trade." Before this, the Spanish Intendant permitted only flour and cotton to be admitted on payment of 6 per cent duty, until the news of the proclamation would be spread. Western goods could still be transferred directly from flat boats to American vessels anchored in the river, because the right of navigation was not interfered with.

[50] *Pittsburgh Gazette*, March 25, 1803.

[51] *Ibid.*, August 2, 1802.

[52] *Ibid.*, August 2, 1802.

Flour was selling at $2.50 per barrel at vendue and other articles of produce equally low, except whiskey, which was brisk at one dollar per gallon—that the French had not yet arrived in Louisiana, but were daily expected—that dispatches had been received by the Spanish commanders, which it was thought related to the arrival of the French, and which created lively sensations in the Mississippi territory; it being thought they would make troublesome neighbors.

In another open letter dated June 22, 1802, a gentleman wrote that:[53] "We are all in anxious suspense, ignorant of what is to be our fate." Pittsburgh was convinced that for the peace and security of the valley only one line of action was possible. Why wait for the slow process of doubtful negotiation? "Now is our time to act with dignity, success is certain."[54] After the official news of the transfer appeared in Pittsburgh on February 3, 1803, the talk of war became stronger:[55]

The reptile Spanish act in a most hostile manner toward our citizens and commerce. With degrading remarks that the people of the United States have no national character—that they are divided, weak, quarrelsome people, without energy that they have nothing to fear from them. Such language is too insulting. . . . I trust 700,000 persons will not wait for Mr. Jefferson to go through all the forms, ceremonies, and etiquette of the courts of Spain and Bonaparte, before they determine whether it will be best to drive the miscreants from their waters or not. I say start and drive them with the spring flood, and then negotiate. We can now get the whole province without the loss of one drop of blood, and let the French get there it will be otherwise. . . . Good God! Can all western America be dead to their true interests?

The effects of the double announcement threw the business of the entire valley into confusion. Commerce was hampered and trade suspended because of a scarcity of cash in New Orleans.[56] The principal holders of specie had hoarded it in order to be prepared for the worst when the French should arrive. Prices were at a new time low; and although the imports from the river were abundant, there was

---

[53] *Ibid.*, July 30, 1802. "We were some time dazzled with the hopes that the United States were negociating [sic] for this part of the river, and as the report was pretty current, it furnished an excellent opportunity of ascertaining the sentiments of the people. I was so pleased to perceive the universal prevalence of satisfaction." Also "the people in office are in general consternation, confident of the retrocession being agreed upon. All are proposing to secure their property from the fraternal rapaciousness of their dear allies." Numerous references to the transfer were made in the newspapers, *Ibid.*, April 9, 1802; June 18, 1802; July 9, 1802; July 16, 1802; August 14, 1802; December 31, 1802.
The most ominous one appeared on June 18, 1802:
"The Louisiana business, by a late political document which I have seen, which is not only official but from high authority in England, presents but a gloomy menacing aspect towards the United States. It is fact, that as soon as the St. Domingo and Guadalupe business is arranged, General Bernadotte will proceed to that country with about 150,000 men, military and others, among which are to include every Jacobin and refractory man in France, whom Bonaparte is tired of and wants out of the way. To those are to be added all the rebel negroes of the two islands taken in war or who surrendered. This settlement is to be called a military colony, and their commander will immediately solicit the friendship and alliance of Kentucky, Tennessee, and the neighboring countries that are separated from the Atlantic States; The Indians in that quarter have already been invited. This business will perplex our administration, and will most unquestionably depress our friends, and ultimately, in all probabilities will produce a state of war."
[54] *Pittsburgh Gazette*, July 30, 1802.
[55] *Ibid.*, February 3, 1802. The royal order had been signed at Madrid, July 3, 1802, *Ibid.*, March 11, 1803.
[56] *Ibid.*, March 18, 1803; April 22, 1803; July 29, 1803.

no demand for them.[57] With the tightening of the money bags, war talk on the American frontier became impassioned, and it was even rumored that the Intendant was hoping for an American invasion and that "he is secretly instructed by the Minister of his Catholic Majesty to pursue this measure."[58]

The right of deposit was unexpectedly restored to the Americans[59] on May 18, 1803, and still the French had not appeared; Pittsburgh was informed of the fact one month later. But the rejoicing over the re-establishment of the right of deposit was paled when on July 15, 1803, the *Gazette* brought the greater news of the Louisiana purchase. The Republican *Tree of Liberty* celebrated the occasion by printing the news in heavy print[60] and boldly stated that "the cession of Louisiana . . . at once puts a stop to the bellowing of the federalists, and obliges them to praise the administration." The Americans, however, were not under any false impressions as to their own importance in bringing about the purchase, and both the Federalist and Republican presses admitted that circumstances had been favorable for the purchase.[61] After 13 years of more or less continued agitation, the West was finally assured of its outlet.

The Louisiana purchase, however, did not result in the expected increase of business; in fact, the tonnage reports of New Orleans did not show any startling change. The receipts of produce by the river for the first four years after New Orleans became a port of the United States were as follows:[62]

1803 . . . . $4,720,015   1805 . . . . $4,371,545
1804 4,275,000   1806 4,937,323

Nevertheless, the purchase of Louisiana was a great event, even if the immediate results were slight. A commercial revolution did not take place when the United States gained possession of the Louisiana territory, although the western interests appeared to think that their troubles would cease if the Spanish were ousted. The Spanish, without a doubt, had placed restrictions on the river trade of the United States, and, after the purchase of Louisiana, business did assume a freer and more healthful aspect; but even under the Spanish restrictions the river trade had been carried on with New Orleans to the fullest

[57] *Tree of Liberty*, May 14, 1803; *Pittsburgh Gazette*, May 27, 1803. "Times are bad at present here. . . . Flour in the last month was nine dollars per barrell [sic]—for new flour—now it is offered for five and a half and is coming down in great quantities. Adventurers from your country are likely to suffer unless they have purchased lower than usual."
[58] *Ibid.*, May 27, 1803.
[59] *Pittsburgh Gazette*, June 26, 1803. In the *Gazette*, April 29, 1803, there appeared an interesting letter to James Madison from Marquis Casa Yrujo, dated April 19, 1803, in which Yrujo wrote that the King knew nothing of Intendant Morales' order which closed the deposit at New Orleans. The King, he said, ordered the port to be opened "until the two countries shall come on an agreement for another place." The order was sent by express to New Orleans.
[60] *Tree of Liberty*, July 16, 1803.
[61] *Pittsburgh Gazette*, July 29, 1803; *Tree of Liberty*, July 16, 1803.
[62] U. S. *House Ex., Docs.*, 50 Cong., 1 Sess., XX, no. 6, pt. 2, 178-213.

extent of its possibilities. The benefits of the Louisiana purchase, therefore, were not realized immediately, and trade did not increase by leaps and bounds. The growth was gradual, and other factors, such as the Embargo of 1808, the War of 1812, the invention of the steamboat, and increased emigration all contributed to the West's later economic success. Receipts did increase and the increases were steady, but the Louisiana purchase did not revolutionize the commercial aspects of the valley nearly so much as the steamboat. The purchase of Louisiana might be compared to the foundation of a building. The foundation being solid and firm, the height was determined by later circumstances. The Mississippi question finally was settled, and America was free to build.

What part did the Ohio River Valley and, especially, Pittsburgh play in this building process? Unfortunately, it is impossible to state the exact amounts of trade contributed by Pittsburgh and other towns; but it has been estimated that the Ohio Valley in 1821 was responsible for almost 50 per cent of the total receipts at New Orleans, and that the entire Mississippi Valley made up the other 50 per cent.[63] Pittsburgh's share of this trade was probably about 15 per cent, and the possibilities are that this estimate is too conservative. This estimate is based upon the fact that from 1800 to 1830 emigration was directed to the Ohio Valley thereby causing a rapid increase both in population and production.[64] The bulk of western trade during this period was from and to the Ohio Valley. After 1830, however, the percentage of trade from the Ohio Valley decreased although the total amounts continued to increase. This was due to two causes, first, the new trend of emigration to a region further west[65] and, second, the internal improvements program which was making possible a more direct West-to-East trade from the Ohio Valley.

The population trend, however, had the more important effect on the valley's trade. The agricultural, or frontier produce, after 1830 came from a different region (i. e., the lower Mississippi), and Pittsburgh began to ship iron, coal, and manufactured goods instead of these products both to New Orleans and to the region newly settled. Thus,

[63] U. S. *House Ex. Docs.*, 50 Cong., 1 Sess., XX, no. 6, pt. 2, 194. Taking the period of 1822 to 1826 as a basis, the following would be about the proportion of the traffic of the several districts constituting the Ohio Valley: Ohio Basin—49 per cent; Upper Mississippi—9 per cent; Lower Mississippi—42 per cent. In 1816 the same authority estimated that "at least 80 per cent of the articles came from the West, that is, from the Ohio, and the Upper Mississippi above the Ohio." *Ibid.*, 197. As for Pittsburgh's part in this trade it has been stated that "most of the supplies from Pennsylvania appear to have cleared from Pittsburgh and from points on the Monongahela River." On June 10, 1806, for illustration, a certain McGraw entered in New Orleans 1,755 barrels of flour which he had brought from the Monongahela district on eight barques or flats. Galpin, William F., "The Grain Trade of New Orleans, 1804-1814," in *Mississippi Valley Historical Review*, XIV, (1927-1928), 501.

[64] By 1802, the population of the West had already grown to one-half million, or ten times as many people as had been there after the Revolution. Whitaker, *Mississippi Question*, 152.

[65] U. S. *House Ex. Docs.*, 50 Cong., 1 Sess., XX, no. 6, pt. 2, 205. The trend of emigration from 1830 to 1850 was to the lower Mississippi region and after 1850 to the Upper Mississippi region.

the origin and character of the Ohio-Mississippi trade had changed, but, as yet, no one was the loser. "In other words, the western trade, while not growing less, did not increase as fast as that section advanced in population and production. . . ."[66] The western products received at New Orleans did not decrease; instead they constituted a smaller percentage of the city's total trade, and New Orleans was fast becoming the cotton port of America. The settlement of additional land after 1830 was a benefit to New Orleans because new settlers also used the Mississippi River to ship their products to market, and also a benefit to Pittsburgh because Pittsburgh supplied them with much-needed manufactured goods. The fact that Pittsburgh had an industrial development independent of her commercial activities assured her an important position which the whims of trade and new population trends could not destroy. The Pittsburgh merchants followed the settlers and sold to them Pittsburgh iron, nails, textiles, and window glass.

One of the most radical changes in the economic life of Pittsburgh came with the building of the Pennsylvania State System. Hereafter, Pittsburghers looked to the East for a trade outlet, not because they preferred the canals, but because Philadelphia offered certain advantages such as credit, a direct route to Europe, and a return cargo of merchandise which the West demanded. Furthermore, after 1830 geographical factors, too, began to assert themselves, and a definite alignment was being made which greatly affected the Ohio Valley. The industrial North began to form a complementary arrangement with its western food basket by means of a belated system of internal improvements. The South, meanwhile, had begun to specialize in cotton and sugar, and being lulled by an economic system and a kind of medieval philosophy, enjoyed life and mortgaged her future to the money-grabbing Yankees. New Orleans was a decidedly southern port both in geographical location and in business activities; cotton and sugar became year by year increasingly important items of trade,[67] and, consequently, the gradual reduction of western produce was not even missed.

Not only was the Ohio Valley, in general, undergoing a vast economic change, but Pittsburgh especially was progressing and specializing. An entirely different place from the Pittsburgh of 1800, the Pittsburgh of 1825 had made a name for herself in industry and commerce. No longer did she need to worry about a market for a small surplus of agricultural products, for now she was a producer of manufactured goods and her products were in demand throughout the Mississippi

---

[66] *Ibid.*, 205.
[67] *Ibid.*, 205. Cotton began to monopolize the port of New Orleans. In 1816 the value of the receipts of cotton was barely 12 per cent of the total value of receipts. From this small beginning cotton receipts rose to 75 per cent of the total receipts, thus explaining why the western produce was not missed. *Ibid.*, 191.

and Ohio Valley. Instead of having only New Orleans as a market, the Pittsburgh merchant found customers in the growing river towns, once areas of lonely wilderness and Indian hunting grounds. Consequently, a great internal commerce was built, in addition to the New Orleans trade. The Ohio Valley was a section distinctly homogeneous, and "the interests of each were the interests of all."[68] Pittsburgh supplied the river towns with manufactured products from her own factories as well as from the East, and took in return the raw materials which these towns had to sell. As the process of specialization developed, both in the Ohio Valley and in the Mississippi Valley, the importation became greater and commerce increased in volume as well as in variety.

Pittsburgh became the northern focal point in the Ohio Valley trade. She was the entrepôt of the East to West trade and also the head of the Ohio navigation. Louisville played a similar role at the southern end of the valley. Thus, Pittsburgh and Louisville were complementary, and an active trade developed. In 1837 the total number of vessels which arrived in Pittsburgh was 1810, with freight amounting to 32,532 tons. Of this number 525 arrived from Louisville, 76 from St. Louis, 15 from New Orleans, 1,004 from all other ports below Louisville, and 190 from the Allegheny and Monongahela Rivers.[69] Although Louisville was the most frequently mentioned port of call, too much emphasis must not be laid on the fact, because an occasional boat after calling at Louisville might then proceed to New Orleans. Such a procedure was possible, but not likely for the large majority of boats, especially after the steamboat became larger and after trade became more highly developed. The differences in the depths of the two rivers made necessary difference in sizes of boats. On the Ohio keelboats and flatboats were in more general use, especially when the water became too low for the steamboat; smaller and lighter draught steamboats were likewise used, while on the Mississippi the boats, as a rule, were larger.[70] Not only did the water level restrict the boats to a certain area, but also the canal at the Louisville Falls was the

---

[68] Fish, Carl R., "The Decision of the Ohio Valley," in American Historical Association, *Report*, (1910), 158.

[69] *Pittsburgh Mercury*, January 31, 1838. The departures are of a similar nature:

```
Total Boats.................. 1764 with cargoes of 52,373 tons
For New Orleans ..............   19
For St. Louis ................  109
For Louisville ...............  523
For all other ports ..........  940
For Allegheny and Monongahela..  173
```

[70] Harris, *Directory*, 1837, 178. Harris reported that the average value of steamboats engaged in the Ohio trade was $15,000 and that the boats "that ply from Louisville and below that point are worth on an average about $25,000. Some Pittsburgh boats costs from $20 to $30,000, however, and some boats in the Mississippi trade cost as much as $75,000."

final determining factor. The canal, though small in size, charged high tolls. Pittsburgh boats would not make the long run to New Orleans if a closer market of equal advantage were available. A study of the shipping news of New Orleans and Louisville strengthens this conclusion. More space was devoted to the Pittsburgh trade in the Louisville papers than in the New Orleans paper; in New Orleans the Pittsburgh trade was evidently considered only a part of the great river trade,[71] and her market reports were of little concern to the New Orleans cotton exporters who were more interested in market prices and freight rates for the East and for Europe.[72] Pittsburgh's river trade increased as the valley became more and more settled and as the frontier moved farther west. Previous to 1825, however, the statistics for the river trade are scattered and incomplete but after 1825 the figures are more accurate.[73] Statistics for Pittsburgh's share in the river trade are available for the latter half of the period because a wharfmaster was appointed by an act of council on January 7, 1825, and he was required by the ordinance to keep a record of the tonnage which arrived at the Monongahela wharf.

In 1825 the total amount of goods shipped to and from Pittsburgh was 22,440 tons.[74] Of this total 7,190 tons were imported and consisted largely of cotton, tobacco, sugar, molasses, and hemp. The exports amounted to 15,250 tons, and consisted chiefly of merchandise

---

[71] No special mention of Pittsburgh was made. Cotton, sugar and tobacco occupied most of the space in the shipping news, although general mention was made of western products. Way, R. B., "The Commerce of the Lower Mississippi in the Period, 1830-1860," in American Historical Association, *Reports,* (1916-1917), X, 66.

[72] *New Orleans Commercial Bulletin,* June 5, 1833.

[73] For some time the need for a wharfmaster had been urgent because traffic conditions on the wharf were anything but satisfactory, and the appointment of a wharfmaster with sufficient power to regulate the wharf business was a welcome improvement.

The ordinance provided that each time a vessel whose tonnage exceeded five tons landed at any of the public wharves or landing places within the city for the purpose of loading or unloading, the owners of said vessels were to pay the wharfmaster five cents for every ton contained in the measurement ("which wharfmaster shall make") ; and if the boat remained in port for a period exceeding 48 hours, Sundays excepted, the charge was to be one cent a ton for each 24 hours. The ordinance further authorized the wharfmaster to direct traffic, and the masters who refused to go to the directed place were to be fined $20 and costs.

To simplify the problem of loading and unloading, the Monongahela beach was divided into specialized zones, and all traffic was obliged to follow the directions of the wharfmaster. The money which was collected by the wharfmaster was to be appropriated for five years for the improvement of the public wharves and landing places. This ordinance was a long overdue civic measure, but more than that, it provided a more or less official source for a study of Pittsburgh's commerce. The wharfmaster was required to keep books and to record the arrival and departure of vessels engaged in the freighting business to and from Pittsburgh, and as far as was "convenient" he was to keep an account of the freight of each vessel. Unfortunately, the records themselves do not appear to have been preserved, but a yearly report of trade does appear in the City Treasurer's *Report.* The Treasurer's *Report* on the financial condition of the city included all the sources of income; and as the wharfmaster was required to turn over to the city treasurer two-thirds of the fees collected, his reports were included in the *Annual Reports* of the city of Pittsburgh, published the first part of each year in the local newspapers.

The wharfmaster's reports dealt only with the tonnage imported into Pittsburgh, so that the total amounts reveal only half of the picture. For the complete ordinance, see *Pittsburgh Gazette,* February 4, 1825.

[74] Jones, *Directory,* 1826, 89.

and Pittsburgh's manufactured goods.[75] By 1830 the total amount of river trade had increased to 29,550 tons. The imports had doubled in the five-year period, totalling 14,410 tons.[76] Exports, too, had increased, but not nearly so much as had the imports; the total amount of exports was reported to be 18,200 tons. By 1835 the river trade had reached 63,333 tons, of which 21,800 tons were imported and 41,533 tons were exported. In 1840 the total amount of tonnage received at the Monongahela wharf reached 130,803 tons. After 1840 figures are not available for the total amounts of trade or for the amounts exported, but it may be assumed that because of Pittsburgh's great industrial development and the improved transportation facilities eastward, the exports from Pittsburgh were not decreasing.[77] In 1845 the amount of freight received at Pittsburgh reached 241,974 tons, and by 1848 the total was 381,539 tons. The following chart shows the tonnage received at Pittsburgh:[78]

Year	Tons	Year	Tons
1825	22,440*	1838	78,923*
1826	——	1839	136,469
1827	46,434½*	1840	130,803
1828	——	1841	——
1829	——	1842	——
1830	29,550*	1843	178,992
1831	46,903*	1844	228,751
1832	42,030	1845	241,974†
1833	37,022‡	1846	292,537
1834	53,502‡	1847	393,195
1835	63,221‡	1848	381,539
1836	74,734‡	1849	——
1837	99,739*	1850	——

* Includes imports and exports.
‡ Included exports and imports but totals of the two do not equal total tonnage given. Newspaper figures may be in error; totals should be
    1833—38,002   1834—49,026   1835—63,333   1836—63,637
† Incorrect addition in total as quoted; if all component parts are correct, the total should be 242,174 tons.

[75] *Ibid.*, 87. Jones reported that the value of Pittsburgh's exports from April 1, 1825, to April 1, 1826, was as follows:

Iron	$398,000	Whiskey 4,200 bbl.	
Nails	210,000	@ 22c per gal.....	$29,832
Castings	88,000	Bacon, 860,000 lbs. ...	51,820
Steam Engines	100,000	Dry Goods exported to	
Cotton Yarns & Cloth..	160,324	N. and W.	480,000
Glass	105,000	Groceries & foreign	
Paper	55,000	liquors to N. & W...	525,000
Porter	18,000	Saddlery & Other Mfg.	
Flour	10,500	in leather	236,000
Tobacco & Segars [sic]	25,800	White lead	17,000
Wire Work	8,000	Miscellaneous exports..	214,000
Axes, Sythes, [sic]			
Shovels, Sickles	49,000		$2,781,276

[76] Chart compiled from the *City Accounts* showing import and export trade:

	Imports	Exports		Imports	Exports
1830	 14,410	18,200	1835	 21,800	41,533
1831	 18,358	22,229	1836	 21,303	43,333
1832	 14,087	22,014	1837	 23,402	40,842
1833	 16,897	21,105	1838	 25,994	23,451
1834	 21,294	27,732	1839	 63,943	84,915

[77] *Pittsburgh Gazette*, January 22, 1848. A report on the Ohio River trade stated that the exported cargo was "at least equal in amount," while Ambler, *A History of Transportation in the Ohio Valley*, 172, estimated that the exports were larger. See Footnote 76,
[78] Compiled from the Treasurer's *Reports* of the City Accounts as found in various Pittsburgh newspapers and directories, 1825-1851.

What were these goods that Pittsburgh received from the Ohio Valley? What did she export in return? According to the manifests,[79] or bills of lading, which every ship carried, the boats departing from Pittsburgh carried an entirely different type of cargo than those coming in to Pittsburgh. Dry goods formed the bulk of the articles exported, although iron, porter, whiskey, hardware, merchandise, queen's ware, coal, and salt are listed separately and were exported in large amounts. Too frequently the only description given was "freight." The articles most frequently imported in large quantities to Pittsburgh were sugar, cotton, tobacco, pork, feathers, coffee, lead, pig metal, and rags. Other items frequently shipped but not in such large amounts were flour, ginseng, brooms, copper, whiskey, hemp, books, starch, hides, merchandise, flax seeds, dried fruits, and various other items of saleable goods. Raw materials and agricultural products formed the bulk of trade. Manufactured articles were both imported and exported although the amounts are in no way comparable. New Orleans was almost exclusively an export point; manufactured goods from the East were shipped overland to Pittsburgh. By 1833 the export manifests were no longer included in the shipping news, but a study of Pittsburgh's manufacturing development supports the conclusion that the articles shipped from Pittsburgh did not radically change from those shipped in 1823, although the amounts increased yearly.

By 1836 the cargoes, too, were omitted from the shipping news, but a general picture of the import trade in 1844 can be obtained from a summary made by the editor of the *Pittsburgh Gazette and Advertiser.*[80] The summary is given for the period March 7, 1844 to December 1, 1844; and although the period does not represent the entire year, the months of January, February and December were frequently low trade months because of the winter season closing the Ohio River.

---

[79] These manifests were printed in the port news of the *Pittsburgh Gazette* (various titles) in more or less detail. The earlier manifests were more informative, and the original plans had been to classify these manifests and to total the amounts of the various products; but due to the great variety of containers and the lack of standard measurement, this was impossible. For example, the *Fairy Queen* from Louisville carried as cargo, *Pittsburgh Gazette*, November 25, 1833:

25 bales hemp	53 sacks feathers
7 bales tobacco	1 keg red lead
31 sacks rags	1 bag feathers
16 sacks rags	5 sacks feathers
2 crates rags	9 cabins: 20 deck passengers

or the cargo of the *Boston, ibid.,* December 10, 1833:

279 pig lead	50 sacks alum salt
6 bales cotton	10 sacks feathers
lot rags and sundries	26 barrels iron scraps
6 barrels dry peaches	1 box merchandise
6 hogsheads, 32 bales, 3 boxes tobacco	17 sacks dry peaches

The *Pittsburgh Gazette* from November 23, 1833, to December 31, 1833, printed the manifests which contained the following measurements: boxes, carboys, pounds, packages, bundles, tierces, barrels, bales, sacks, kegs, hampers, casks, crates, bags, hogsheads, trunks, "lot of," "sundry small lots," tons, pieces (or numbers of). Weights and measures must have been a sore problem to transporters. In 1833 there were twenty-two different types of measures in the trade imported into Pittsburgh, and, consequently, a summary of the manifests was out of the question.

[80] *Pittsburgh Gazette and Advertiser,* December 12, 1844.

With this in mind, the returns may be considered almost a complete picture. The trade may be classified into three groups: agricultural products and provisions, extractive products, and manufactured articles. The most important group, as far as volume was concerned, was the agricultural class, and under this class, provisions formed the bulk of the trade. Bacon and pork were sent to Pittsburgh in large quantities, both for home consumption and for re-export. Lard and lard oil found a satisfactory market at Pittsburgh. Cheese and butter from Ohio also reached Pittsburgh *via* the river. Of the agricultural products, potatoes and apples constituted the largest single items. Feathers, hay, oats, coal, cotton, and hemp were other items of major importance.[81] Only a small quantity of wheat was imported, suggesting that the Pittsburgh market was supplied from other sources.[82] The following chart shows the agricultural products and provisions imported by way of the river from March 7, 1844 to December, 1844:[83]

Apples, green	barrel	13,822
Apples, dry	barrel and sacks	1,365
Barley	sacks	1,351
Bacon	hogsheads	15,962
Bacon	box	474
Bacon	barrel	3,444
Bacon	tierces	556
Bacon	pieces	83,132
Beef	barrel	876
Bristles	barrel	111
Butter	barrel	705
Butter	kegs	6,620
Cheese	casks	1,287
Cheese	box	29,569
Corn	bushel	6,480
Cider and Vinegar	barrel	583
Cotton	bales	8,009
Cloverseed	barrel and sack	259
Eggs	barrel	166½
Feathers	tons	4
Feathers	sacks	10,776
Flaxseed	sacks and bushels	3,084
Hay	ton	285
Hay	bales	108
Hemp	bales	4,864
Hops	bales	119
Lard	kegs	12,427
Lard	tierce and barrel	2,810
Lard oil	barrel	2,636
Lemons	box	286
Oranges	box	208

[81] Tobacco, which has been classified under the heading of manufactured products, should be mentioned here, for it is probable that much of it was in leaf form. There arrived in Pittsburgh during this time, 17,855 hogsheads and 3,520 boxes and kegs of tobacco.
[82] Flour (see manufactured goods) was an important trade item. The Pennsylvania Canal attracted the flour trade of the Ohio Basin.
[83] *Pittsburgh Gazette,* December 12, 1844.

```
Oats ..........................bushel ....................... 22,658
Pork bulk .....................pounds ....................... 607,259
Pork bulk .....................tierces ....................... 57,860
Pork ..........................barrel ....................... 1,237
Potatoes ......................bushel ....................... 18,076
Potatoes ......................buckets ....................... 10,406
Peaches, dry ..................sacks, bbl. ................... 4,101
Rice ..........................tierces ....................... 262
Raisins .......................box ........................... 81
Rye ...........................bushel ....................... 1,589
Tallow ........................packages ..................... 348
Timothy seed ..................sacks, barrels ............... 521
Wool ..........................sacks ....................... 10,356
Wheat .........................bushel ....................... 2,415
```

The extractive products did not find Pittsburgh the best market and, consequently, the amounts listed are rather small. The reason for this is that by 1844 the frontier had moved farther west, and Pittsburgh was no longer the only gateway to the West. The items imported show that Pittsburgh maintained trade connections, however, especially with St. Louis and the lead region of the Missouri Valley. Lead, salt, and hides are the three most important items. Pot and pearl ashes, although greatly demanded in Pittsburgh, were not supplied by the Ohio River, and the amounts imported were small.

The following chart shows the extractive products imported *via* the river from March 7, 1844 to December 1, 1844:[84]

```
Alum ..........................barrels ....................... 154
Beeswax .......................casks ......................... 514
Copperas ......................barrels ....................... 402
Deer Skins ....................packages ..................... 751
Fur and Robes .................packages ..................... 1,877
Fish drums ....................barrels ..................... 194½
Ginseng ....................................................... 1,189
Hides .........................pieces ....................... 5,985
Lead ..........................pigs ......................... 21,040
Oysters .......................barrels ....................... 18
Pearl ash .....................casks ......................... 184
Potash ........................casks, barrels ............... 1,288
Saleratus .....................casks ......................... 301
Salt ..........................barrels ....................... 13,458
Scorchings ....................casks ......................... 1,527
Sand ..........................barrels ....................... 70
Snakeroot .....................barrels, sacks ............... 160
Tanner's oil ..................barrels ....................... 55
```

Manufactures also formed a large part of Pittsburgh's trade. The extent of this business can be seen from the following chart which shows the amounts of manufactured goods imported into Pittsburgh by way of the river from March 7, 1844 to December 1, 1844:

[84] *Ibid.,* December 12, 1844.

Bonnet boards	bundles	640
Blooms	tons	131
Blooms	pieces	3,924
Blooms	dozen	4,648½
Candles	boxes	7,986
Crackers	barrels	140
Castor oil	barrels	243
Corn meal	barrels	463
Coffee	bags	2,329
Flour	barrels	81,159
Fire bricks	thousand	459½
Fire bricks	tons	6
Glass	boxes	28,480
Hoop poles	thousand	193
Iron bars	tons	334
Iron scrap	barrels	144
Linseed oil	barrels	588
Leather	bundles	745
Lime	barrels	350
Liquor	packages	163
Merchandise	packages	8,771
Molasses	barrels	7,219
Nails	kegs	9,253
Pig metal	tons	16,582
Pitch	barrels	6,204
Paper	bundles	7,523
Rags	sacks	4,288
Rosin	barrels	417
Staves	thousand	385½
Soap	boxes and barrels	4,230
Sugar	hogsheads	2,974
Sugar loaf	boxes and barrels	681
Starch	boxes	710
Steel	bundles	66
Tin plate	boxes	1,012
Tar	barrels	175
Tobacco	hogheads	17,855
Tobacco	boxes and kegs	3,520
Tea	chests	281
Whiskey	barrels	7,360
Ware	crates	430
Sugar imported since Jan. 1	hogsheads	5,577
Molasses imported since Jan. 1	barrels	13,314

Of this class the most important single item imported was iron in its various semi-manufactured forms. Pittsburgh was already famed as a manufacturer of iron but she needed the raw material. Sugar and molasses were imported for the Pittsburgh market alone. Flour of the lower Ohio Valley did find Pittsburgh a good market, and the amount imported was large. Tobacco of the Upper Valley also traded through Pittsburgh. Glass, too, came to Pittsburgh, evidently for re-export, for glass was not needed at Pittsburgh. Coffee and tea were apparently the only foreign products imported by way of New Orleans.

Merchandise was the largest item, second to iron, imported *via* the river. However, merchandise of the river trade does not mean the same thing as merchandise by way of the Pennsylvania State System. The Ohio River merchandise, with the exception of coffee, tea, sugar, and molasses were less complicated manufactured articles, and they seem to be the products of one or many cities' labor, which were sent to Pittsburgh to be converted finally into Pittsburgh manufactures.

By 1850 Pittsburgh was no longer entirely dependent upon New Orleans as an outlet for her surplus products, although she did look to that city for certain foreign importations such as coffee, tea, and general groceries. Continuing settlement and the natural increased purchasing power of the Ohio Valley now took care of Pittsburgh's surplus, and internal improvements and the assured supremacy of the East in European contacts also permitted Pittsburgh to look eastward as well as to the South. Louisville and the intervening settlements in the Ohio Valley north to Pittsburgh cooperated and were bound together geographically and economically. Trade rivalries existed, but the markets were large enough for all, and specialization had not developed sufficiently as yet to make any one city completely dominant. Where specialization had developed other necessities were neglected. Pittsburgh, in order to develop her manufacturing, needed foodstuffs and raw materials. Cincinnati specialized in pork products, but she needed products of the entire valley in order to prosper; if she were to send pork to Pittsburgh, she depended on Pittsburgh to supply manufactured articles in return. Pittsburgh had gone a long way since the harrowing days of flatboats, Spanish decrees and international complications for the control of the Mississippi River. The Janus-faced commercial city was now able to take full advantage of her location, not depending completely on either the southern or the eastern connection, but benefiting by the interplay of their joint influences.

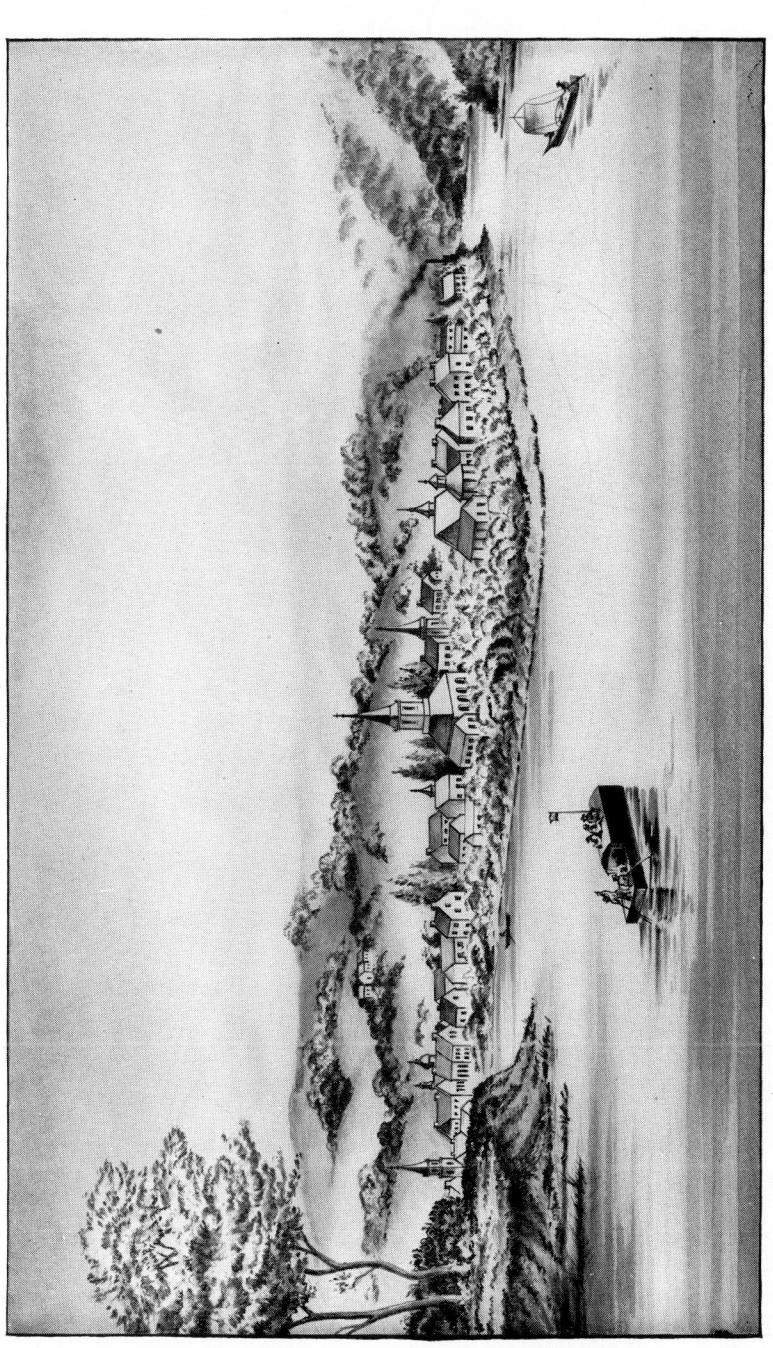

VIEW OF PITTSBURGH IN 1817

Redrawn from a sketch in possession of Carnegie Library, Pittsburgh. Courtesy *Steel Facts* magazine, American Iron and Steel Institute

IV

The Allegheny and the Monongahela Rivers, Avenues of Trade

THE ALLEGHENY and Monongahela rivers were also vitally significant spokes in the hypothetical wheel because each river in itself provided subsidiary market routes which became increasingly valuable as the western section of Pennsylvania became more and more settled. Previous to 1810 the economic development of entire Western Pennsylvania had been extremely sporadic and individualistic. Each farmer-merchant-exporter struggled to establish himself by whatever method seemed expedient at the moment. Each town or settlement was little more than an exporting post, and business was usually restricted to getting a cargo ready for the New Orleans market so that money might be secured to pay taxes and to pay for the importations of salt, iron, and a few textiles. Pittsburgh, Franklin, Meadville, Waterford, McKeesport, and Brownsville, as well as intervening settlements on both rivers, were in the same position—all looked to New Orleans. Pittsburgh's manufacturing and commercial leadership, achieved between 1810 and 1820, was fortunate for the settlements along the Allegheny and Monongahela rivers. Much of their produce which formerly had to be transported over a thousand miles to market could now be sold or traded for merchandise in Pittsburgh. Commercial jealousy and rivalry apparently never existed between the Pennsylvania river towns and Pittsburgh. A feeling of oneness united them, and, as a result, each benefited the other and was mutually dependent in return.

In the days before good roads and railroads most towns considered themselves fortunate to have access to one navigable stream, but Pittsburgh had command over three. Thus, Pittsburgh was able to concentrate on manufacturing without being handicapped for lack of a market or raw materials. By way of the Allegheny River, Pittsburgh was able to supply the entire northwest section of Pennsylvania and a small part of western New York with merchandise. The Allegheny trade was considerably extended by the river's numerous tributaries. One of the most important is the Kiskiminetas River which enters the Allegheny about 45 miles above Pittsburgh. In itself the Kiskiminetas trade was important because the river was navigable for 40 or 50 miles; it had good portages to the Juniata River, and also connected with the Conemaugh River.[1] French Creek is also a significant tribu-

---

[1] Cramer, *Navigator*, 1821, 17.

54 PITTSBURGH'S COMMERCIAL DEVELOPMENT

tary of the Allegheny River, by means of which Pittsburgh had access
to Erie.[2] Equally as important as the Allegheny River was the Monongahela River, which opened the southwestern portion of Pennsylvania
and even part of western Virginia to the Pittsburgh market. The
Monongahela River gave McKeesport, Brownsville, Morgantown and
all intervening settlements a natural outlet at Pittsburgh.[3] The largest
tributary of the Monongahela River is the Youghiogheny River. This
stream enters the Monongahela at McKeesport and was navigable under normal conditions for large flatboats and keelboats. Both rivers
tapped the valuable iron and coal regions and were important not only
as markets for Pittsburgh merchandise but also vital to Pittsburgh's
industrial development.

The trade on the Allegheny and Monongahela rivers was carried by
the usual variety of craft. The invention of the steamboat did not
have an immediate effect on the trade of either stream, except that
when flatboats and keelboats were driven off the Ohio and Mississippi
rivers they entered the Allegheny and Monongahela trade. Both
streams also possessed the usual hazards, and, consequently, the
trade was encumbered in much the same way as that on the Ohio,
except on a smaller scale. Under ordinary circumstances the boats of
the pre-steamboat period were much safer on the Monongahela and
Allegheny than on the Ohio and Mississippi rivers. The greater number of casualties took place when the river was at flood stage because
boatmen, anxious to reach the market as early as possible, often set
out too early and, as a result, ran unnecessary risks. The Allegheny
and Monongahela river craft were of various sizes, but usually of 25
tons or less;[4] no accurate statement of capacity can be made, however, because the level of water and the purpose of the exporter made
the boats of many different burdens. On the whole, the boats generally
were of a smaller class than those on the Ohio, although boats of 40
tons burden have been used on the Allegheny.[5]

The volume of trade on both rivers was large. The total volume of
commerce for any particular year, however, cannot be ascertained
from the reports. The records of the Allegheny wharfmaster's reports
are usually mere notations of the amount of fees received; newspaper
accounts are scattered and incomplete; consequently, the reports of
the Monongahela Slackwater Company covering the decade of 1840
to 1850 are the most significant available records of trade on either of
the rivers. Despite the lack of tonnage figures, a general estimate of

[2] French Creek entered the Allegheny at Franklin, 80 miles northeast of Pittsburgh.
The stream was navigable to Fort Le Boeuf (Waterford) and from there a 15 mile
portage to Erie. Later the Waterford-Erie Turnpike made transportation much easier.
The opening of the Erie Canal in 1825 proved serious competition for Pittsburgh.
[3] The opening of the National Road in 1819 worried Pittsburgh merchants considerably
because merchandise could then be brought from Baltimore.
[4] Kussart, Mrs. S., The Allegheny River, (Pittsburgh, 1938), 59.
[5] Pittsburgh Gazette, April 24, 1837.

the trade of these two great rivers can be drawn. The earliest valuation that apparently was made on the Allegheny trade appeared in the *Gazette* on March 19, 1824. The paper reported that "upward of" 50 flatboats had arrived in Pittsburgh "last week" containing goods "upward of $100,000 worth of property—Bar and Pig Iron, Salt, Flour, etc."[6] In the next year during the April freshet, goods arrived from the Allegheny Valley valued at one-half million dollars and the report was made that:[7]

The shores of the Allegheny alone are covered with arks and flatboats, upwards of one hundred in number, richly freighted for this market. Within the last week, there arrived safely by this channel, on a moderate calculation, 7,000 barrels of salt and 500 tons of pig metal besides other merchandise.

In 1830 the French Creek trade to Pittsburgh was estimated at $100,000 and consisted of agricultural products, salt, staves, bark shingles, cherry and walnut lumber. The average freight of each boat was set at 27 tons, and each boat and cargo was estimated to have a value of $500 at Pittsburgh.[8]

In the late 1830's the Allegheny trade was greatly facilitated by the establishment of regular steamboat service. The steamer *New Castle* proved that the Allegheny River could be navigated by steam, and by April 24, 1837, the boat had already made three trips to Franklin.[9] Furthermore, in addition to carrying 16 tons of freight (and 60 passengers), she towed a 40-ton keelboat loaded with 20 tons of freight. The boat negotiated the rapids between Pittsburgh and Kittanning quite successfully, although the keelboat did not succeed so well, and the editor of the *Gazette* explained that the keelboat had been badly constructed. The *New Castle* had been purchased by a company of iron manufacturers and traders of Venango County, Pittsburgh, and Kittanning, and was intended exclusively for the Allegheny trade "when stages of water will permit."[10] The *New Castle* continued to make regular trips between Pittsburgh and Franklin during the spring of 1837. In fact, the steamboat had proved so successful that plans were made for a second boat, and it was estimated that the trade was even larger than three boats could carry.[11] The success of the *New Castle* finally convinced Congress to provide for a survey to be made of the Allegheny River from Pittsburgh to Olean. Pittsburghers had been campaigning for several years to have the river cleared so that larger boats could be used with safety.[12]

6 *Ibid.*, March 19, 1824.
7 *Pittsburgh Mercury*, April 25, 1825.
8 *Hazard's Register*, V, 1830, 238, quoting the *Erie Gazette*.
9 *Pittsburgh Gazette*, April 24, 1837. The editor concluded by the remark that "thus you see the head of steam navigation is rapidly travelling upstream." The remark was evidently intended for Wheeling because Pittsburgh and Wheeling carried on a long-drawn-out quarrel for the honor of head of river navigation.
10 *Ibid.*, April 25, 1837, quoting the *Franklin Intelligencer*.
11 *Ibid.*, May 18, 1837.
12 *Ibid.*, January 1, 1834; April 4, 1836.

During the next year two new steamers, the *Pulaski* and the *Beaver*, were added to the Allegheny trade and service was extended to Warren, extending shipping for the entire distance of the river within the Pennsylvania limits.[13] By July 4, 1838 the *New Castle* had made a total of 23 trips as compared to seven trips in 1837, and the *Beaver* and *Pulaski* 14 trips.[14] No definite account was kept of the tonnage but the editor estimated it at 2,000 tons.[15]

In 1839 the trade of the Allegheny River had increased to the extent that four steamboats plied regularly between Pittsburgh and Warren.[16] Two steamboats were also added in 1839 and were constantly employed conveying coal to the iron works. During the spring a "new boat" was finished and joined the *Pulaski, Beaver, Elizabeth,* and *Forrest* in the transportation of goods to and from Pittsburgh. About 125 round trips were made up to Warren, so the trade must have justified the increase.[17]

During 1844 the Allegheny wharfmaster reported that he had collected wharfage on 132 steamboats, 78 keelboats, and 854 flatboats.[18] The year 1845 was a low water year and trade for a time was suspended. Pittsburghers renewed their efforts to have the river improved (the 1837 Congressional survey had not produced any results), and the success of the Monongahela which had been slackwatered by this time was pointed out as a fine example of what might be done. The editor concluded by saying that low water "cuts down a wonderful market" and that if Congress will not help, then private enterprise will have to undertake the project.[19] During the suspension it was estimated that $100,000 worth of pig metal alone was withheld from market.[20] The river was again at a low level in July, 1847; and at that time 22 keelboats were engaged in trade, carrying flour, bacon, molasses, sugar, tea, and dry goods to the towns and country along the river. The boats carried an average load of 14 to 20 tons, and the time required for a trip from Pittsburgh to Warren was 12 days up and four days to return.[21] The 1847 season, on the whole, must have been good, for the wharfmaster reported that he had collected $2,320.16 in fees.[22] The next year the wharfage amounted to $3,350.25.[23]

The magnitude and importance of the Allegheny trade can also be illustrated by the amount of lumber which was sent to Pittsburgh. Lumber was one of the largest and most valuable export items of the

---

[13] *Pittsburgh Mercury,* April 25, 1838, quoting the *Armstrong Democrat.*
[14] *Ibid.,* July 4, 1838, quoting the *Venango Democrat.*
[15] *Ibid.,* July 4, 1838.
[16] Harris, *Directory,* 1839, 10.
[17] *Ibid.,* 10.
[18] *Pittsburgh Gazette,* January 14, 1845.
[19] *Ibid.,* May 20, 1845 ; June 23, 1845.
[20] *Ibid.,* May 26, 1845.
[21] *Pittsburgh Gazette and Advertiser,* July 30, 1847. In 1837 the *New Castle* had made the trip to Franklin in 38 hours. *Ibid.,* April 25, 1837.
[22] *Ibid.,* January 10, 1848. In 1845 the wharfage had amounted to $634.71.
[23] *Ibid.,* January 10, 1849.

Allegheny Valley, and year by year the trade increased. The Allegheny region was covered with large fine trees of white pine and hemlock, "noble trees" three to five feet in diameter, tall and straight "without limbs to near the top."[24] Allegheny lumber rafts were famous throughout the entire Mississippi Valley and no one market had a monopoly of the trade. The amount which Pittsburgh received has been estimated at 25 per cent of the total output.[25] The lumber trade had the advantage of an early start and probably originated about 1795 when Major Craig sent Marcus Hulings "with three bags of money and some other articles" to purchase boards from the Seneca Chief, Cornplanter, who had established a sawmill along the river.[26] Thus, by 1795 Pittsburgh had begun to buy lumber, despite the fact that Fordham prophesied that: "America, however, is not the land of prospects. There is too much wood; and, when on the barren peak of some rocky hill, you catch a distant view, it generally is nothing but an undulating surface of impenetrable forests."[27] In 1812 Pittsburgh purchased about $70,000 worth of Allegheny lumber or about 7,000,000 feet. The lumber, shingles, and lath were sent to market on huge rafts which were then broken up and sold along with the cargo. The usual time of the lumber trade was in the spring when the rivers were high; five or six men comprised the crew.[28] As early as 1825 the editor of the *Conewango Emigrant* estimated the lumber output of Warren County alone at 20,000,000 feet of pine boards and planks; 10,000,000 shingles, and large amounts of various other lumber products; all together valued at $35,000. But he lamented the fact that "unfortunately for the county of Warren, the lumber business has been and continues to be carried to excess"; "that the market was depressed because of an overly large quantity; and that agriculture has been neglected."[29] Nevertheless, the lumber trade continued, and the following chart, compiled from the Board Measurer's *Annual Report*, shows the amount of lumber which was inspected in Pittsburgh:[30]

Year	Feet	Year	Feet
1826	3,792,429 feet	1834	
1827	5,020,492 feet	1835	9,000,000 feet
1828		1836	7,028,814 feet
1829	4,112,064 feet	1837	4,831,416 feet
1830	5,188,602 feet	1838	4,093,934 feet
1831		1839	9,850,494 feet
1832	6,004,575 feet	1840	5,777,373 feet
1833		1841	

24 Cramer, *Navigator*, 1821, 18-20.
25 *Pittsburgh Gazette*, January 22, 1848.
26 Craig, *History of Pittsburgh*, 274.
27 Fordham, *Personal Narrative*, 152.
28 *Pittsburgh Gazette*, August 13, 1824; Baxter, Frances, "Rafting on the Allegheny and Ohio" in *Pennsylvania Magazine of History and Biography*, LI, (1927), 27. The raftsmen were reputed to purchase freely and to frequently spend almost all their earnings before leaving Pittsburgh, *Pittsburgh Gazette*, April 10, 1848.
29 *Ibid.*, May 13, 1825, quoting the *Meadville Messenger*.
30 Compiled from the *Pittsburgh Mercury* and the *Pittsburgh Gazette*, 1827-1851.

1842	....		1847	.... 22,960,108 feet
1843	....		1848	.... 19,049,310 feet
1844	.... 10,108,693 feet			
1845	.... 27,312,836 feet		1849	....
1846	....		1850	....

A second important Allegheny trade item, which was directly responsible for the Pittsburgh-Allegheny trade, was salt. The history of the river trade and the salt industry are intimately related and interdependent. The salt trade started only one year later than the lumber trade, and the original promoter was an outstanding Pittsburgh citizen, General James O'Hara. Early in 1796 General O'Hara visited Niagara and found that salt could be brought to Pittsburgh from the Onondaga Salt Works at Salina (Syracuse) cheaper than from Baltimore.[31] As Quartermaster General of the United States Army, O'Hara supplied the garrison at Oswego on Lake Ontario, consequently he had a number of keelboats on the Allegheny River to carry the supplies to French Creek; these he used to bring back salt. He likewise utilized the barrels that had been filled with army supplies which helped to reduce the price of the salt. The Onondaga salt was sent by wagons to Oswego, then by boat to the Falls. Another wagon took it to Schlosser, where it was transferred to a boat to Black Rock, transferred again to another vessel on Lake Erie, then carried by wagon to French Creek, where it was shipped down the Allegheny to Pittsburgh.[32]

Despite the difficulties the trade was a success from the beginning and the original price was reduced from $12 to $9 a barrel. In December, 1805, during a freshet in French Creek, 11 flat bottom and six keelboats passed Meadville. The flatboats each carried an average of 170 barrels of salt and the keelboats 60 barrels, making a total of 2,230 barrels; later in the same month 22 Kentucky boats passed loaded with salt.[33]   In 1808 Cramer estimated that: "There are about 4,000 or 5,000 barrels and sometimes more of Onondaga salt brought down [Allegheny] to Pittsburgh annually, worth per barrel $9, making an average of about $40,000 worth of traffic in this one article."[34]   The salt trade continued to grow and Pittsburgh considered herself fortunate to have had a reduction in the price of so urgently needed an article. In the fall and spring of 1809-1810 the amount of salt shipped to Pittsburgh was between 12,000 and 14,000 barrels, valued at $105,000.[35] Cramer, however, reported:[36]

So great a quantity . . . may not again be expected from that quarter, since the owners of the Kanawha salt works say that they can deliver at this place

[31] Craig, History of Pittsburgh, 284.
[32] Pittsburgh Gazette, August 9, 1845.
[33] Kussart, The Allegheny River, 66, quoting Crawford Weekly Messenger, December 12, 1805; January 1, 1807.
[35] Ibid., 1810, 20.
[36] Ibid., 20.

any quantity at from $5 to $6 per barrel, a price at which it is thought impossible to deliver Onondaga salt, owing to the great distance it has to come and the frequent reshipments. . . .

Cramer was correct in his observations, and the competition from the Kanawha Salines, abetted by the War of 1812, destroyed General O'Hara's salt trade. But the Allegheny River did not suffer a permanent loss.

In 1812 and 1813 William Johnston "under circumstances the most discouraging and against the remonstrances of the neighborhood, who ascribed his undertaking to folly and madness" began to bore wells in the Conemaugh River, and he found "enough brine to furnish salt for one million inhabitants."[37] Other enterprises were also undertaken on the Kiskiminetas River, and by 1817 there were four large establishments yielding 25 to 50 bushels of salt per day, and the price was reduced to 50 cents per bushel, or $2.50 a barrel.[38] By 1826 the region contained 35 salt works and the price was then reduced to twenty and twenty-five cents per bushel.[39] According to the Salt Inspectors' *Annual Report*, Pittsburgh received the following amounts:[40]

1826	12,102 barrels		1839	34,335 barrels
1827	13,252		1840	29,581
1828	—		1841	—
1829	8,420		1842	—
1830	6,730		1843	28,610
1831	—		1844	15,175
1832	20,041		1845	27,765
1833	—		1846	—
1834	24,381		1847	34,078
1835	18,273		1848	48,523
1836	17,466		1849	—
1837	19,400		1850	—
1838	28,661			

These figures do not include all the salt shipped to Pittsburgh because salt inspections were not required, but the reports do show part of the trade increase. Pittsburgh was greatly benefited by the development of the Allegheny salt trade and industry for one of the indispensable articles was thus supplied at greatly reduced prices, and Pittsburgh was released from total dependency on an outside source. The Allegheny trade would have been significant for this single contribution to Pittsburgh's economic development but lumber, pot ashes, iron and agricultural products contributed to make the trade still more valuable, and as a growing market for Pittsburgh merchandise the economic position of the Allegheny Valley is apparent.

---

[37] *Ibid.*, 20.
[38] Cramer, *Pittsburgh Magazine Almanack, 1817*, 40.
[39] *Hazard's Register*, 1828, I, 29. Paper read before "The Pennsylvania Society for the Promotion of Internal Improvements," January 10, 1826.
[40] Compiled from Pittsburgh newspapers, 1826-1851.

The Monongahela River, likewise, played an increasingly important rôle in the economic development of the Pittsburgh area. The river was very early a vitally active avenue of trade, and the volume of business carried on that river increased proportionately as the western population increased. The steady development of the Monongahela region, too, was handicapped by the uncertainty and precariousness of navigation, the time for marketing being dependent upon the season and the wiles of the river. Ice or low water tied up all the river's trade; freshets caused the markets to be glutted and methods of transportation put heavier financial burdens upon the surviving trade. This state of affairs had to be accepted while the trade was in its infancy and the markets were small and local; but with the rapid growth of Pittsburgh manufactures, and the increasing demand for coal, lumber, and agricultural products, this condition was too risky for good business. The Monongahela region needed a dependable outlet, especially for the coal trade which began to assume some importance in the 1830's.

Nothing definite was done, however, to improve the Monongahela River even in the balmy days of Pennsylvania's internal improvements program. Not until March 31, 1836 was an act passed authorizing the Governor to incorporate a company which would install lock navigation on the Monongahela River, and the Monongahela Navigation Company was organized under this provision on February 10, 1837.[41] In April, 1837, an engineer was engaged to begin the survey of the river, but in that year difficulties began which continually harassed the undertaking for years. The panic of 1837, which upset the monetary system of the country, made additional internal improvements out of the question. Furthermore, the river was too high to permit a survey. Despite the difficulties and delays, the contracts for Locks and Dams No. 1 and No. 2 were let on December 17, 1838, and the work on the additional locks and dams which would permit continuous and steady navigation for 55 miles to Brownsville was placed under contract on July 15, 1840.

Conditions, contrary to anticipations, continued to grow worse. The year of 1841 was an extremely difficult one. Due to financial embarrassment the Company suspended work on Locks and Dams No. 3 and No. 4. In the spring of 1841, the Bank of the United States was unable to meet the second installment of $50,000; the Commonwealth failed to pay its subscription for a like amount, except by an issue of State bonds which were disposed of at a great sacrifice; and individual subscribers could not make their payments for money was scarce. Topping all these handicaps, however, was a general public feeling of opposition which balked the Company at every turn.

This combination of adverse circumstances entirely overwhelmed the

---

[41] Monongahela Navigation Company, *7th Annual Report*, (1846), 3.

prospects of the Company for the time being and all work was suspended.[42] Sufficient funds could not even be raised to keep the two locks which had been opened on October 18, 1841, in running order, and a breach in No. 1 Dam had turned the expected improvement into a hazard to navigation. A $40,000 debt added to the difficulties. The creditors were demanding payment. Suits and judgments piled up, until finally the sheriff intervened and sold the personal effects of the Company. The work was only half completed; the Company was deeply in debt; and it appeared that the project would have to be abandoned.

In the fall of 1843 the State sold at auction all the stocks which it held in various public works, including the stock of the Monongahela Navigation Company. A group of Pittsburgh business men under the name of Moorhead, Robertson and Company, believing that all stock would sell much below its value, agreed to buy the stock of the Monongahela Navigation Company which had been held by the State. This Company then put in a bid to finish the Slackwater to Brownsville, taking in payment bonds payable in ten years,[43] and thereby making possible a safe and continuous outlet for the trade of Allegheny, Fayette, Washington and Green counties. The navigation was opened November 3, 1844, and ten days later it was celebrated with appropriate ceremonies.[44]

After eight years of continual struggle against almost overpowering odds, the river improvement was at last completed to Brownsville. The original plans had intended that the Slackwater System should extend to the Virginia line, but that was not realized before 1850. The Slackwater to Brownsville had cost less than $500,000 despite all its misfortunes "about equal to fifteen or twenty miles of our great canals and railroads and maintained at an expense not exceeding the pay of a mere Board of Canal Commissioners."[45] The *Annual Report* presented January, 1846, to the stockholders brought the welcome news that:[46]

The Monongahela Slackwater Improvement is completed; and has been in successful operation for one season. It has fully realized the anticipation of its most sanguine and ardent friends, and has even during the brief period since its completion yielded great benefits to the public and secured a notoriety and popularity which it has not been the fortune of other and similar works to attain for many years.

The president's report was not exaggerated; the Improvement was successful from its first year of operation and the traffic continued to grow. In 1845 a total of 27,257,870 pounds of freight exclusive of sand, hoop-poles, wood, staves, posts, boards, timber, bricks, and coal

---

[42] *Ibid., 5th Annual Report,* (1844), 3.
[43] *Ibid.,* 4.
[44] *Ibid., 6th Annual Report,* (1845), 10.
[45] *Ibid., 7th Annual Report,* (1846), 17.
[46] *Ibid., 6th Annual Report,* (1845), 1.

arrived at Pittsburgh; and 12,961,959 pounds of freight, exclusive of the above articles, were shipped eastward from Pittsburgh.[47] The total tolls amounted to $28,579.70.[48]

An analysis of the Slackwater tonnage reveals two interesting and significant conclusions. First, that numerous commodities were included in the total tonnage of that trade, and secondly, that the amount of annual tonnage of each commodity increased appreciably. The traffic of the Monongahela Slackwater falls into five general classes—(1) agricultural products and provisions, which includes fruits, grains of all kinds, bacon, butter, lard, feathers and wool; (2) extractive products, such as coal, ores, salt, stone and wood; (3) manufactured goods, which were largely the result of labor expended on the extractive products of the region rather than the result of the introduction of a machine culture, including such articles as flour, whiskey, shingles, lath, staves, brick and glass; (4) livestock, which included hogs and horses, really very unimportant traffic so far as the Monongahela was concerned; (5) eastern merchandise, which meant revenue for the Company, and provided more goods at cheaper prices for the western country.

A study of these various classes reveals that under the agricultural group, of the thirteen items included, potatoes formed the only two-way trade article.[49] In 1845 the number of bushels of potatoes sent to Pittsburgh amounted to 16,090 bushels, which, if continued at that rate, would have formed an important article of commerce. In 1846, however, the amount fell to 318 bushels, and, as a westward trade item, potatoes never attained any importance because the Monongahela region found a better market for potatoes elsewhere. On the other hand, the amount shipped eastward from Pittsburgh grew from the insignificant amount of 403 bushels in 1845 to 6,770 bushels in 1850. Since they were not Monongahela potatoes, another era had evidently found the eastern markets more accessible by way of the Slackwater.

Six items alone represent the most important agricultural articles shipped to Pittsburgh. These in order of total tonnage, are apples, oats, wheat, hay, cider and potatoes. All the trade was destined for the Pittsburgh market or for re-export by another route, and, with the exception of potatoes, the Monongahela shows no records of carrying these items eastward. The agricultural products destined exclusively for the eastern market were, in order of importance, bacon, butter (and lard),[50] feathers (and wool), dried fruits, beeswax (and ginseng) and potatoes. These enumerated products, furthermore, were not exclusively the surplus of the Monongahela Valley but had been

---

[47] See Appendix II; compiled from the *Annual Reports*, 1846-1851.
[48] See Appendix II; compiled from the *Annual Reports*, 1846-1851.
[49] See Appendix II, compiled from the *Annual Reports*, 1846-1851.
[50] Articles in parentheses have totals included in preceding item.

gathered elsewhere in the Ohio Valley for shipment to Baltimore. This does not mean, however, that the Monongahela region had no such surplus to be shipped to the East, but it does indicate that as an avenue of trade *from Pittsburgh* for agricultural products of other areas, the Monongahela Slackwater was a vital line. Cider, hemp and seeds were minor articles and of slight importance.

The Slackwater must have been a great disappointment as a carrier of agricultural products, for in comparison to the other classes this tonnage was not so great or regular. For years the Improvement had been advertised as an outlet for the supposedly great agricultural surplus, but in reality, if there was any surplus at this time, it was wholly imaginary. Wheat, the most important product, was converted largely into whiskey and flour, and the extractive products, either in the virgin state or improved by labor, were marketable and more valuable.

The real importance of the Monongahela Valley was not based on agriculture but on mining. Due to the vast quantities of coal, the value of which was recognized, and which was beginning to become a large export article, the Monongahela Slackwater Company had been formed to make it possible for the coal trade to develop without too many handicaps. In the analysis of the tonnage, coal is included in extractive products, and it formed the largest item of that division;[51] in the five-year period under consideration its tonnage tripled. In classifying the tonnage which passed over the Slackwater, the extractive products included those articles which were shipped in their natural state, such as coal, ores, stone, timber and wood, plus those which were but slightly altered to make a marketable product, such as salt, sand and boards. The amount of coal recorded in the tonnage report was shipped exclusively to Pittsburgh, being destined for that market or for re-export down the river. Other items which were westward bound exclusively were, in order of importance, sand, stone, iron ore, wood, and posts. Bark was shipped to Pittsburgh for one year only (1845) and then only in small amounts.

The extractive products which had a two-way trade were boards, timber and salt. Each of these had a greater amount shipped to the eastern market, showing that the Slackwater carried off surpluses of boards, timber and salt from the Pittsburgh area, and that Pittsburgh commanded a market either in Baltimore or in the way-trade along the National Road. The extent of this surplus is seen at a glance in Appendix II. Copper ore is the lone article of this class which had an exclusive eastward passage, but it was only of slight importance.

The extractive class of the Monongahela tonnage was of far greater importance than the basic products and formed the backbone of the Company's business. The Monongahela Improvement cannot be given

---

[51] See Appendix II; compiled from the *Annual Reports,* 1846-1851.

credit for inaugurating the coal trade, but it did facilitate the marketing process, thereby aiding in the rapid growth of the coal export trade. Ever since its beginning the coal trade had clung to the Monongahela River; manufactured articles might seek other channels, but the coal trade belonged to the river.

The most important general class of traffic comprised the manufactured articles. Many of these items were extractive products once removed, and the surplus existed only because the raw materials were so plentiful. Bricks, lime, barrels, hoop-poles, pig iron, shingles, and staves were the work of a growing population who had utilized the raw materials and had converted them into an exchangeable product. Flour and whiskey were very important trade articles and were preferred as marketable products in the manufactured state rather than as grain, thereby reducing the agricultural surplus as such. The Monongahela Valley's importance as a glass center was due entirely to the plentiful raw material and coal plus a cheap, regular outlet to market.

The manufactured class included a greater variety of items than any other group, and this traffic on the Monongahela was more nearly balanced as far as trade movements were concerned. The articles sent to Pittsburgh were, in order of importance, iron, glass, nails, and steamboat hulls. Those articles sent exclusively eastward were tobacco, shingles, lime, molasses, ploughs, and beer. The articles which had a two-way traffic and which were sent in greater amounts to Pittsburgh than to the East were bricks, flour, hoop-poles, staves, and carriages. The amount of whiskey sent to Pittsburgh in 1845 was 5,753 barrels as compared to the 622 barrels sent to the East, while in 1850 the amount sent to Pittsburgh was 3,217 barrels and to the East 4,352 barrels. The eastern-bound products in the two-way trade, whose total was greater than that of the western-bound products, were empty barrels, lath, and pig iron. The manufactured articles formed the bulk of goods transported on the Monongahela during this period. Furthermore, the majority of the items were produced in the valley and were the result of natural resources exploited by skilled labor. Molasses and tobacco were primarily carrying commodities and not native products, but which, because of the advantageous route, were sent through Pittsburgh, contributing to the commerce of that city.

Livestock, which formed the fourth class of articles shipped on the Monongahela, was comparatively unimportant. Hogs and horses were the only animals carried, and the trade was two-way.[52] More hogs were shipped to the East than were imported by Pittsburgh, indicating that the surplus was not entirely from the Monongahela Valley. Horses, too, had a slightly better market in the East.

---

[52] See Appendix II; compiled from the *Annual Reports,* 1846-1851.

The fifth class, or eastern merchandise, was an important trade item beginning in 1846 and its growth was large and steady.[53] The huge increase in 1847 and the subsequent decrease in 1848 do not show a true picture of trade, unless the cause is indicated. A break along the Juniata in the Pennsylvania Canal threw a greater portion of the carrying trade in both directions between the Atlantic seaboard and the Ohio River onto the Monongahela,[54] thereby increasing temporarily the traffic of 1847. Nevertheless, the transportation of eastern merchandise was an important factor in the Company's growth and William Eichbaum's prophecy of 1841 was almost realized:[55]

It (the Slackwater) will bring the navigation of the eastern and western waters into closer proximity than any other route across the Allegheny Mountains and will draw a great portion of the carrying trade both on account of the cheapness of the route, and being less liable to obstructions from ice in the spring and fall than any of the more northern routes.

The only fact that President Eichbaum overlooked was that economically Pittsburgh was more closely bound to Philadelphia than to Baltimore.

The coal trade deserves particular attention because it was the most significant of the commodities carried. The Monongahela Slackwater had greatly facilitated the development of the coal trade, ("almost created it"),[56] and yet the Improvement was in turn made the handmaid of its favorite child. While the Slackwater can hardly be given credit for creating the coal trade, it did aid the trade's growth greatly. In the fall of 1837 a large number of flatboats were loaded with coal at various points along the Monongahela, but when the coal was ready for market, the water on the ripples was insufficient to carry off the boats. The flats were tied up until almost the close of the year, with the constant expense for watching and bailing. When the coal boats finally reached the Ohio, many of them were sunk or destroyed by ice. The losses in this single year were estimated at $40,000.[57]

The coal trade, handicapped heavily by losses on the river, was also unnecessarily taxed for watching and bailing while moored at the coal landings, not to mention the loss from the tie-up of idle capital. During October, 1838, 150 coal boats were tied up at the landings on the Monongahela River for almost three months waiting for a sufficient depth of water. A flatboat usually carried 5000 bushels of coal, and while tied at the landings required one or two men to watch it and to bail out the water. Thus, there were 750,000 bushels of coal, estimated at five cent per bushel, or $37,500 of idle capital. Probably about 200 men were on the payroll for watching the flats. If each man were

[53] See Appendix II; compiled from the *Annual Reports*, 1846-1851.
[54] Monongahela Navigation Company, *9th Annual Report*, (1848), 5.
[55] *Ibid., 4th Annual Report*, (1841), 8.
[56] *Ibid., 9th Annual Report*, (1848), 7.
[57] *Ibid., 2nd Annual Report*, (1839), 36.

paid one dollar daily for 90 days, this tax alone on the coal would amount to $18,000.[58] No wonder that the company engineer reported that:[59] "A trade which can afford to be thus harassed and taxed and still flourish, will readily pay at least a tithe of such expense to insure its safety and regularity, and may be considered a source of revenue to the company." But here the engineer made the same mistake as did the head of almost every other similar undertaking, always anticipating progress that rarely materialized. The gloomy days of the old times were quickly forgotten, and almost from the opening of the Improvement, the coal operators were crying for toll reductions.[60] The fact that the rates of toll on coal were lower on the Monongahela Slackwater than on any other improved or artificial waterway[61] made no apparent difference to the coal operators. During 1848 the *Annual Report* complained that a "systematic effort" had been made to manufacture public opinion against the Company and that the press and local meetings were used to inflame the people's minds.[62] The trade, which in 1837 lost $40,000 due to accidents alone, objected to a little over eight cents per ton for a dependable route to market.

The tolls received from the coal trade were about one-fourth of the total tolls, and yet four-fifths of the labor and expense of the locks were chargeable to that trade.[63] Notwithstanding this fact, however, the legislature on March 21, 1849 ordered the tolls on Locks 3 and 4 reduced for boats intending to pass down the Ohio River; the Board, accepting the order, reduced the tolls on the designated locks 50 per cent, but added that "there was neither justice or propriety in asking the reduction."[64] The Board, at the same time, begged the legislature not to make further reductions until the Company's debts were paid and an 8 per cent dividend could be given to the stockholders.[65] The legislature granted the request. The coal interests were not, however, completely satisfied, and they seemingly remembered only that the river had once been free, forgetting that it frequently could not be used. In the next session of the legislature the perennial question of

---

[58] *Ibid.*, *2nd Annual Report*, (1839), 37.
[59] *Ibid.*, *2nd Annual Report*, (1839), 37.
[60] *Ibid.*, *9th Annual Report*, (1848), 7.
[61] *Ibid.*, *7th Annual Report*, (1846), 9. The following chart shows the rates of toll on various canals as compared to the Monongahela Slackwater:

	Per 1000 Bu.	Per Ton
Monongahela (entire distance of 56 miles) and 4 locks.	2.91	.8
Muskingum Lock Navigation, same distance & quantity	7.36	.20
Green and Barren River (Ky.) " " (est.)	9.00	.25
Schuylkill River (Pa.) " "	11.85	.33
Pennsylvania Canal (Pa.) " "	10.08	.28¼
New York Canal (N. Y.) " "	3.36	—
Erie Extension (Pa.) " "	7.84	.21
Pa. and Ohio Canal (Pa. & Ohio) " "	10.24	.28
Tidewater Canal " "	9.92	.27

[62] *Ibid.*, *9th Annual Report*, (1848), 7.
[63] *Ibid.*, 7.
[64] *Ibid.*, *11th Annual Report*, (1850), 5. Rates were reduced to seven cents per ton.
[65] *Ibid.*, 8.

toll reduction rose again, but this time the coal operators lost, to the great relief of the Company.[66] The amount of coal shipped over Monongahela Slackwater between 1845 and 1850 can be seen from the following chart:

	BUSHELS IN FLATS	BUSHELS IN BOATS	TOTAL TONNAGE—BU	TOLLS
1845	1,944,845	2,660,340	4,605,185	$5,283.79
1846	2,542,475	5,236,436	7,778,911	10,221.28
1847	3,131,130	6,513,997	9,645,127	13,241.94
1848*	3,323,304	6,496,057	9,819,361	12,438.43
1849†	3,378,600	6,329,907	9,708,507	13,533.39
1850	4,472,925	7,825,942	12,297,967	17,023.57

*Low Water on Ohio—no outlet for coal.
† Stationary level due to low water on the Ohio and cholera which paralyzed trade; it is significant to note that the coal trade held its former level.

From a study of the coal tonnage the trade must not have been seriously hampered by the tolls, for the advance made in 1846 was evidence that trade had benefited, and the fact that the trade held its own during the low water and cholera years of 1848 and 1849 is also noteworthy. The tonnage increase of 1850 indicates that the trade was still growing. The chart also points out the fact that the flatboat era, so far as the coal trade was concerned, was by no means over. In 1849, however, the towing of boats superseded the older method. David Bushnell had introduced this innovation in the coal trade in 1845, when he took the *Walter Forward* towing three small barges to Cincinnati, but it was not until four years later that towing to the lower markets was finally accepted as the better method.

The Monongahela Slackwater Navigation Company as an investment was a failure, but as a benefit to trade, it was a decided success. Specifically, the Improvement was directly responsible for building up the coal trade. Generally speaking, the Improvement acted as a feeder to the Pennsylvania State System by tapping the rich area of the Monongahela Valley, and by providing new markets for eastern merchandise. The valley itself was benefited by increased settlement and capital investment, as well as by noticeably increased valuation of land in general.

Both the Allegheny and the Monongahela rivers were valuable contributing factors to Pittsburgh's commercial development, despite the fact that each had another outlet at its source. The National Road for the Monongahela River, and the Erie Canal for the Allegheny, were built in time to absorb the increased production of each river valley respectively, but the natural tendency was to trade through Pittsburgh. The ties of friendship and the economic unity which had drawn the widely separated communities of Western Pennsylvania to

---

[66] *Ibid., 12th Annual Report*, (1851), 5.

Pittsburgh were made stronger and more lasting as each settlement developed. When Pittsburgh became able to manufacture goods, the river towns contributed their raw materials, and the exchange was a mutual advantage. Pittsburgh merchants and manufacturers owe a great debt to both the Allegheny and Monongahela rivers, because they too provided avenues of trade which, in many respects, were as indispensable as the Ohio River or the eastern turnpikes.

V

Eastern Turnpikes as Avenues of Trade

D ESPITE the fact that Pittsburgh had access to the New Orleans market, and also favorable water connections to the north and south of Western Pennsylvania, a way to reach the eastern seaboard was also necessary. Certain purchases were essential to the western region notwithstanding the physical difficulties. Year after year, Pittsburgh labored diligently to establish good roads and to reduce the costs of eastern transportation. The task was extremely discouraging because capital and labor were scarce; the distance was great; and the Allegheny Mountains were not only steep but also wide, consisting of parallel ridges and narrow intervening valleys.[1]

The initial step in building a road to Pittsburgh had been made even before the territory was opened to settlers. A roadway was needed to facilitate military operations in the Ohio Valley where both Great Britain and France were struggling for colonial supremacy. The French actually occupied the disputed territory and had the advantage of control over the only available water route. Consequently, the English were forced to use the land routes in order to reach the French at the forks of the Ohio. In 1755 General Braddock cut a road through the forests to within ten miles of the French fort.[2] Braddock failed to secure his military objective, and three years later General Forbes was sent out on a similar mission. Instead of using Braddock's trail, Forbes cut a new road through the forests and mountains of Pennsylvania.[3] The Forbes expedition succeeded, and the French withdrew from the region. Technically, the British after 1758 were in control of the Ohio Valley, but their tenure was insecure. The succeeding years were ones of military turmoil, and peace was not made final until 1763 when the entire French colonial system in North America was destroyed by the Treaty of Paris. The Revolutionary War followed too closely after the French and English struggles to encourage peaceful development of the valley; but after another twenty years' delay, the political question of supremacy was finally determined.

---

[1] Taylor, John, *The Honest Man's Almanac for 1813*. (Pittsburgh, 1813). Seven mountain ridges which had to be crossed were listed by the Rev. John Taylor viz: Chestnut Ridge, Laurel Hill, Allegheny Mountain, Sideling Hill and the three Kittochtinny Hills.
[2] Braddock's road was also known as the Cumberland Road. The road commenced at Cumberland on the Potomac River and ran westward over the Great Savage Mountain and Little Crossing to the Youghiogheny River at Smithfield, thence to Fort Necessity at Great Meadows, to Connellsville, to Mount Pleasant, and stopped at Turtle Creek, which was about 10 miles from Fort Duquesne or Pittsburgh. See map, Craig, *History of Pittsburgh*.
[3] Lancaster was the outpost of civilization. General Forbes organized his supplies there and proceeded westward by way of Chamber's Ferry, Carlisle, Shippensburg, Fort Bedford (Raystown) and Fort Ligonier.

Out of the general confusion of these conflicts several definite and progressive achievements may be noted for the Ohio Valley. The most important results were that the right to settle in the valley was unquestionably established, and that two roads had been cut through the intervening uninhabited forests. Not to be underestimated were also the facts that the area was well-publicized in the East, and that a military post was maintained at Pittsburgh throughout the period of early settlement. Both of these factors combined to give Pittsburgh the first contacts with the East. Trade with the East resulted even during British occupation because the fort had to be supplied and also because the Indians were found to be good customers. Furthermore, after 1783 settlement was stimulated because of the land grants given to ex-soldiers, and because the East was suffering from the postwar depression.

The two roads which had been opened by the English authorities were more important in the last decades of the 18th century as pathways to the West rather than as avenues of trade, simply because the early settlers in Pittsburgh found the freight rates too high. The cost of transportation usually added about one-third to the prices current in Philadelphia. The system was naturally slow and expensive[4] because goods had to be loaded on packhorses, and each horse could carry only about 150 pounds of freight. Pack trains were usually made up of about 20 horses, and the entire outfit carried about one and one-half tons of goods. Furs and ginseng were the only western products which could actually be sent eastward with profit, for their value was great in comparison to their weight; the few articles imported were salt, iron, and a small amount of textiles.[5] Travel was slow because the road was rough and steep; the trip over Braddock's trail required about 20 days. The time for the journey, however, does not seem excessively long in view of the existing difficulties. Monette described the conditions which were common to all the early mountain trails:[6]

The caravan route from the Ohio River to Frederick crossed the stupendous ranges of the Allegheny Mountains as they rise, mountain behind mountain, in the distant prospect . . . the path, scarcely two feet wide, and traveled by horses in single file, roam over hill and dale, through mountain defile, over craggy steeps, beneath impending rocks, and around points of dizzy heights, where one false step might hurl horse and rider into the abyss below. To prevent such accidents, the bulky baggage was removed in passing the dangerous defiles, to secure the horse from being thrown from his scanty foothold.

Pack horses continued to be used extensively in Western Pennsylvania

[4] Hulbert, A. B., *Historic Highways of America*, 10 vols., (Cleveland, 1904), V, 24.
[5] Durrenberger, Joseph A., *Turnpikes: A Study of the Toll Road Movement*, (Valdosta, Ga., 1931), 14.
[6] Monette, J. W., *History of the Discovery and Settlement of the Valley of the Mississippi by Three Great European Powers . . . to 1846*, 2 vols., (New York, 1847), II, 11.

until 1790;[7] and, although the system itself was highly systematized and efficient as far as was possible under the circumstances, it was not sufficient to produce a high stage of commercial development.[8]

Between 1750 and 1760, however, an event occurred which practically revolutionized road travel. The Conestoga wagon[9] made its appearance in the East, and thereafter wheeled vehicles were employed more and more extensively to carry freight. The use of the Conestoga wagon was delayed in Western Pennsylvania because of the lack of adequate roads, and before the wagons could be used successfully the trails had to be graded and widened into roads. Petitions from Western Pennsylvania were sent to almost every session of the legislature up to 1790, for the Western Pennsylvania settlers were aware of the problems of road building which faced them. They did not receive much legislative consideration, however, because their commercial importance was not realized in the East until after the War of 1812. The eastern capitalists considered the area too vast and uninhabited to encourage the expenditure of much money. Sentiment was too localized and selfish to encourage a general investment where returns were questionable; and the building of a road through a wilderness to reach a few thousand settlers who contributed very little to the general treasury seemed to be unwise, especially when roads through the more thickly populated sections were also needed. Nevertheless, the settlers in the Pittsburgh area continued to dream of cheaper and faster transportation. Finally on September 25, 1785, the legislature passed an act providing for the construction of a road, and two thousand dollars were appropriated to build one hundred miles of the road to Pittsburgh.[10] Thus the Western Road to Pittsburgh, or the State Road of Pennsylvania, came into being. The State Road was a decided improvement over the old military road which had not been designed for commercial purposes. The State Road followed in general the route of the old Forbes Road from Carlisle to Chambersburg, and thence to Bedford and on to Pittsburgh.

Road construction in 1790, however, did not mean the same thing as road building today. A road can hardly be said to have been constructed for it was really only an opening through the forests. Trees

---

[7] *Ebensburg Sky*, November 24, 1836. The writer of an article on the pack horse reported that they were used even as late as 1797 in the Ohio Valley, and an advertisement appeared in the *Pittsburgh Gazette*, August 8, 1795: "Pack horses wanted to go to Chambersburg, for loading, for which a generous price will be given. Apply to Printer."

[8] Durrenberger, *Turnpikes*, 14.

[9] Seymour, Dunbar, *A History of Travel in America*, 1 Vol. edition (New York, 1937), 202. "The precise reason for the name of the vehicle is uncertain. A breed of very heavy horses had already been developed in the valley of the Conestoga, and had commanded wide notice. Probably the wagon was first built in the same region (Lancaster), or else had acquired its name from the type of horse with which it was no doubt associated in its earliest days."

[10] Boucher, John N., *The History of Westmoreland County*, 3 Vols., (New York, 1906), I, 236.

were cut down and stumps were grubbed out; sometimes swampy places were filled with logs, and side hills were dug out. Nothing was done to the road bed; it was usually either a continuous puddle or a heap of dust. More ruts and holes appeared with succeeding traffic, and road maintenance was almost futile.[11] One can imagine the type of road that would result from an expenditure of $20 per mile. The two thousand dollar appropriation was a mere pittance in comparison to the amounts spent today to maintain the same roads. But the significant fact must not be overlooked that the legislature had taken notice of the settlers of Western Pennsylvania and had recognized their need for a road. The money appropriated was well-spent, for even the removal of trees and stumps from the roadway greatly facilitated traffic.

Transportation between Pittsburgh and Philadelphia was much improved, and the results were surprisingly good.[12] Goods were now wagoned and trade increased, although the exact amounts will evidently never be known. Travelers reported that they met numerous wagons and pack-outfits, but definite statistics were not compiled. Authorities differ as to the importance of the overland trade; Kohl-

---

[11] Buck, Solon J., and Elizabeth H., *The Planting of Civilization in Western Pennsylvania,* (Pittsburgh, 1939), 201.

[12] The articles of agreement between Thomas Mifflin and Daniel Stoy provide an accurate description of what constituted a road from Pittsburgh to Bedford. The contract was signed October 23, 1792, and reads as follows:
"Daniel Stoy hath agreed, undertaken and contracted, and by these presents doth agree undertake and contract to and with the said Thomas Mifflin and his successors Governors of the Said Commonwealth in manner following that is to say; that he the said Daniel Stoy shall and will well and truly open and improve that part of the said Road that lies between the forks of Stodler Road and McConnehy's Run being about seven miles and two hundred six perches according to the courses and distance laid down in a draft of the said road hereunto annexed that where digging or bridging is necessary the road shall be made twelve feet wide with convenient places for waggons [sic] to pass and repass and in all other parts the Road shall be made of the breadth of forty feet at least throughout the whole distance thereof, clear of timber and underwood; the said passing places to be at least sixteen feet wide. That he shall and will erect and build ten good and substantial bridges that is to say one over Mc-Conney's run, four between said run and David Penrods, one over Lafferty's run, and four over the branches of Stony Creek, with good and sufficient abutment and maintain the said bridges in good order for seven years from the time of compleating [sic] the same; that he will make good and sufficient cause ways where necessary over runs, gullies, and marshy places, of timber made flat on the upper side, and that the water shall be turned off the Road, by making sufficient ditches for that purpose that he will break down and remove out of the Road all large stones that may be deemed an obstruction to the passage of Waggons [sic] and make the stony places smoth [sic] and even, by breaking the stones and covering the frame with gravel or earth, that he will sufficiently repair the old bridge between Stodlers Road and Adam Helms; that he will reduce the ascents in the Road to an activity sufficiently gradual for four middle sized horses to draw up them on a common waggon [sic] one ton weight at least; that he will do all necessary digging, and in general that he shall and will open and improve the said road, so as to render the same through-out from Stodlers Road to McConnehy's run, a good pass easy commodious and permanent Road: And the said Daniel Stoy for himself his Heirs Executors and Administrators doth covenant promise and agree to and with the said Thomas Mifflin and his successors governors of the Said Commonwealth that he will well and truly in all things perform and execute his agreements undertakings and contract aforesaid; AND the said Thomas Mifflin in consideration thereof covenants promises and agrees to and with the said Daniel Stoy that he shall have and receive the sum of two hundred and fifty pounds to be paid as the same shall from time to time be required for carrying on and effecting the said improvements, and to received and considered as a full compensation for all his expenses and services in executing this contract. IN WITNESS whereof, the parties to these presents have put their hands and affixed their seal the day and year first herein written."
Mss. in Public Records Division, Pennsylvania Historial and Museum Commission.

meier concluded that the costs were prohibitive and that very little produce was conveyed eastward;[13] Durrenberger, basing his conclusion on the great number of early petitions for the incorporation of turnpike companies, is of the opinion that traffic between 1790 and 1800 to and from the interior was considerable.[14] After studying the road manuscripts in the Road and Turnpike Papers, Public Records Division, Harrisburg, the latter conclusion appears to be the more valid. Trade to the East was undoubtedly smaller in amount than the trade to the West; but as the western people paid the high rates on freight from Philadelphia, they were concerned in making improvements so that rates might be lowered. Subscription lists of the stock companies indicate that the people of Western Pennsylvania did subscribe liberally to the building of their roads; and if merchants, traders and ordinary citizens invested their small amounts of capital, the economic needs for better roads must have been pressing. An undated petition addressed to Governor Thomas Mifflin from "The Merchants, Traders and others concerned in the trade and transportation to the town of Pittsburgh and the Western Waters" stated that:[15]

> The means of facilitation [sic] the intercourse to the western waters, and thereby reducing the price of transportation are objects in which all classes of people resorting and emigrating to the western world, are to [sic] deeply interested to remain longer silent upon the subject of complain [sic] here stated.

While Western Pennsylvanians were petitioning for better roads, notable improvements in road building were being made in eastern Pennsylvania. On April 9, 1792, a stock company was incorporated to build a stone turnpike 62 miles in length from Philadelphia westward to Lancaster, and the road was completed in December, 1795 at a cost of $465,000.[16] This new type of artificial road was a radical

---

[13] Kohlmeier, A. L., *The Old Northwest as the Keystone of the Arch of American Federal Union*, (Bloomington, Ind., 1938), 9. "Only a little was conveyed eastward over the Cumberland Road and over the Pennsylvania Turnpike. The cost of transportation to the market was so great that prices in the Ohio Valley were usually so low that there was little incentive to produce a surplus beyond that which could be sold to the newer settlements in the Old Northwest." As late as 1818 to 1824, Kohlmeier estimated that "only about 30,000 tons were carried across the Alleghenies by way of the Pennsylvania Turnpike . . . and most of it went westward," *Ibid.*, 7.

[14] Durrenberger, *Turnpikes*, 117. Cummings also reported that many heavily ladened wagons came great distances and that he met two wagons in Carlisle in 1807 which had come from Zanesville, and that they had made the trip in one month. Thwaites, *Early Western Travels*, IV, 51. Day reported that between 1792 and 1812, thirty companies had received charters and were building roads of one type or another. Day, Sherman, *Historical Collections of the State of Pennsylvania*, (Philadelphia, 1843), 46.

[15] *Mss.* Public Records Division, Pennsylvania Historical and Museum Commission. The petition also stated that the road to Pittsburgh had not been improved, despite the fact that the contracts had been let, and that the road was in such a condition that wagons could not pass, and that the mail was having difficulty in getting through. The petition was signed by all the leading citizens and included such outstanding figures as J. George Wilkins, William Elliot, Ebenezer Denny, John Ormsby, A. Tannehill, William Christy, Adam Burchfield, John Gibson, Nat Irish, etc. The *Mss.* may be dated approximately as having been sent sometime between the years of 1790 and 1799 because Governor Mifflin was in office during that time.

[16] *American State Papers, Miscellaneous*, I, 893.

departure from the old idea of road building; and while the road did not solve the transportation problems completely for the western traders and merchants, it led the way for later development.

The law required the road to be 50 feet wide, of which 21 feet, at least, was to be made an artificial road. The roadway was "to be bedded with wood, stone and gravel, or other hard substance, of an even surface, rising towards the middle by a gradual arch, and in no place to be made an angle of more than four degrees with the horizon." The arch effect was achieved by laying stone 18 inches deep in the middle, and by decreasing the depth to 12 inches on the edge. A summer, or side road,[17] ran parallel to the artificial road.

In 1806 the road was extended to Columbia on the Susquehanna, and a company was also incorporated to build a turnpike from Harrisburg to Pittsburgh.[18] Before anything was accomplished another company was incorporated to build a similar road by way of Huntingdon and the Frankstown Road. Such a program was too ambitious, however, and, as a result, neither company made any progress. Two possibilities may explain this delay; either the trade was too small to support such an investment, or the vested interest delayed that enterprise, despite the fact that the common good was at stake. Indications seem to point to a combination of these two factors; that the vested interests demanded the *status quo,* and that the majority of the people could not support such a heavy outlay of money without the backing of eastern capital.[19] Furthermore, turnpikes were an innovation and required more money to build than was customarily expended. The fact that both roads were already opened may have delayed action, and the newness of the idea of actually laying a road was probably opposed by the stay-at-homes who did not have to travel. Four years passed before action was taken, and then in 1811 the legislature provided for a commission to decide which of the two routes should be built. The commission decided in favor of the

[17] Gallatin, in his *Report on Roads and Canals,* said: "Side or summer roads are found a very acceptable accommodation to travellers, and as they save the wear and considerable expense of the artificial road, they may be deemed, on the whole, economical, provided, however, that good and sufficient drains be kept always open on each side." *Ibid.,* 883.

[18] Ibid., 738.

[19] Dunbar, *A History of Travel in America,* 193. Dunbar stated that "now and then it happened that the proposed transformation of some primitive trail into a better road was actively fought by that part of the public whose material interests would have suffered—at least for a time—by the suggested action. . . . The pack horse system of travel was more important and largely developed in Pennsylvania than in any other colony, and even at so late a date as 1783, the only way of carrying goods from Philadelphia to Pittsburgh . . . was by that method." *A Western Farmer* wrote to the *Pittsburgh Commonwealth,* May 28, 1806, that he favored the Northern route to Philadelphia but that the western farmers had no money. Ellison Perot, President of the Philadelphia and Lancaster Turnpike Company, also mentioned that "the prejudice against the turnpike having, in a great measure, vanished. . . . *"American State Papers, Miscellaneous,* I, 893.

southern route.[20] After fifty years of uncertain roads, Western Pennsylvania was finally promised a reliable road to the East, but the next problem was actually to get the road built. This disparity between the blueprint and the road was great, for the project required a large amount of capital and labor. The State in 1814 was in no position to undertake such a job, nor did the people expect it; neither was private capital available in sufficient amounts to finance the entire road; and as a result, the building program was divided into small units. Five companies were incorporated by the State to build the western section of the turnpike from Pittsburgh to Chambersburg. Each company was an independent project, functioning separately from the other companies, and each contracted to build a certain portion of the road and to keep it in working condition. The following chart shows the number of companies and the time each required to build its section of road:[21]

	LENGTH		BEGUN	FINISHED
Pittsburgh to Greensburg	30½	miles	1814–15	1817
Greensburg to Stoystown	37	miles	1816	1819
Stoystown to Bedford	28	miles	1815	1818
Bedford to Chambersburg	55	miles	1815	1820
Chambersburg	15	miles	1812	1815

The company incorporated to build the extreme western section was the Pittsburgh and Greensburg Company, and since this company and section were intimately related to Pittsburgh, this study will deal specifically with the progress and difficulties of that enterprise.

The Pittsburgh and Greensburg Company resulted from a meeting held in Pittsburgh on December 4, 1813, "for the purpose of considering the propriety of applying to the legislature of Pennsylvania for the incorporation of a company for making the turnpike from

---

[20] Riddle, *Directory,* 1815, 152. The *Directory* listed the roads leading to Pittsburgh and both routes were included:

From Pittsburgh to Philadelphia (The Southern Route):

To Turtle Creek......	12	Carlisle	21
Greensburgh [sic] ...	20	Chambers' ferry	20
Fort Legonier [sic]...	19	Elizabethtown	14
Stoystown	12	Lancaster	18
Ryan's foot Allegheny	17	M'Cllelland's	16
Bedford	11	Downing's	17
Crossings (Juniata)..	14	Admiral Warren	10
Fort Lyttleton	10	The Buck	12
Skinner's	13	Philadelphia	11
Strasburgh	3		
Shippensburgh	10	Total	280

From Pittsburgh to Harrisburg (The Northern Route):

To the Brick Tavern.	18	Waynesburgh	20
New Alexandria	14	Lewistown	10
Armagh	22	Mifflintown	11
Ebensburgh	17	Millerstown	13
Munster	7	Clark's ferry	14
Frankstown	16	Harrisburgh	14
Alexandria	17		
Huntingdon	7	Total	200

[21] Compiled from the *Report to the Senate on Roads, Bridges, etc.* Pamphlets found in Carnegie Library, Pittsburgh.

Pittsburgh to Greensburg."[22] John Wilkins was appointed the chairman of the committee of five who were to work out the plans, and he later became the president of the company. The company received its charter on March 9, 1814, and stock was sold to the public. A total of 1,293 shares at $50 per share was subscribed by individuals and the State held 1,600 shares, thus capitalizing the company for $144,650.[23] The road was 30½ miles in length and cost $151,218.78 to build, leaving a deficit which was covered by a loan of $12,000 from the Bank of Pittsburgh.[24] The road had cost more money than was expected because of the Turtle Creek handicap. Twenty-six miles of road had been either completed, or almost completed,[25] before the contract for the four miles over the Turtle Creek section was let. No one wanted the contract, because a large expensive bridge was required over the creek; and to make matters worse, the steep hills on both sides of the creek created a serious grading problem.[26] Turtle Creek Hill had always been a serious handicap and Harris recalled that: "In olden days it often required two teams of horses to be hitched together, and a whole day to get a wagon or two up Turtle Creek Hill, 12 miles from Pittsburgh."[27] But finally the section was completed, and the simple sentence— "this road is now finished"—found at the end of the company's financial statement for 1817, marked a notable achievement in Western Pennsylvania's development.[28]

Thus, by 1820, a solid road was completed from Pittsburgh to Philadelphia, and the improvement was noticeable in increased traffic and larger loads. Wagons doubled their capacity and still made

---

[22] *Pittsburgh Gazette*, December 10, 1813.
[23] *Mss.* October 4, 1817, found in Public Records Division, Pennsylvania Historical and Museum Commission, Road and Turnpike Papers: Pittsburgh to Greensburg 1815-1824. Individual subscriptions totalled $64,650. Another letter from William Wilkins to Governor Snyder, dated February 7, 1817, reported that "However from this sum should be deducted about thirty shares on which nothing has been or ever will be paid by individuals—except the first instalment." The state subscribed $80,000, thus making a total issue of stock valued at $144,650.
[24] *Ibid., Mss.* dated December 17, 1817.
[25] *Ibid., Mss.* dated February 7, 1817. As each five-mile section (amount usually contracted for by one contractor) of road was completed, the Board of Managers of the Company would inform the Governor and apply for viewers to examine the road. Disinterested persons were then appointed by the Governor to check the road. The same process was used throughout the State, and the Road and Turnpike Papers are filled with reports made by the viewers. The forms are approximately the same: "The commissioners appointed to examine the section of five miles commencing west of Greensburg. . . . Do hereby report to your Excellency, that we have viewed and examined the said section of five miles, and find the same to be made and perfected in a complete and workman-like manner, and according to the true intent and meaning of the acts of the general assembly passed on the 24th day of February 1806, and on the 9th day of March 1814." *Mss.* dated January 10, 1817. Occasionally a report is found which does not approve of the work, as, for example, the Commissioners Report, dated March 6, 1817: "There is one place on the Road consisting of about 30 perches —which is not well graded. . . ."
[26] *Ibid., Mss.* dated February 7, 1817. The Board of Managers estimated that the section would cost about $30,000.
[27] Harris, *Directory*, 1837, 174.
[28] *Mss.* Road and Turnpike Papers, December 17, 1817. By 1820 the entire road was completed to Chambersburg.

better time between the seaboard and Pittsburgh;[29] freight rates fell
from twelve and one-half cents per pound to five cents per pound;
and the annual wagon freight between the Ohio and Philadelphia in
1818 was estimated at one million dollars.[30] The turnpikes cheapened
transportation rates by 50 per cent; consequently, more goods were
transported between the East and the West. Between the years
1818 and 1824 it was estimated that 30,000 tons of merchandise were
shipped annually to Pittsburgh at a cost of five million dollars for
freight rates.[31] One commercial house alone in Philadelphia in 1824
loaded upward of two hundred wagons for Pittsburgh.[32] Year by
year the number of wagons increased, and even after the Pennsylvania State System was completed in 1834, the business continued
to grow. Wagoning really did not compete with the State Works,
but rather supplemented it, because the canals were closed in the
winter and then the roads handled all the East to West freight. From
January to April 1, 1837, the daily average arrivals in Pittsburgh
were about 50 six-horse teams, loaded with groceries and all kinds
of foreign and domestic merchandise.[33] The wagons carried an average load of about six thousand pounds each; thus, in three months,
the total arrivals were estimated at 4,500 wagons loaded with goods
amounting to 27,000,000 pounds. With this increase of trade and
improved roads, rates fell two and one-half cents per pound, or
a total of $775,000 for three months' freighting. In one day, in 1837,
114 wagons arrived in Pittsburgh;[34] and on another day, in 1844,
60 large road wagons were counted on Liberty Street.[35] Thus, it
appears that by 1835 business between the East and West had so
increased that both the roads and the canal had sufficient traffic;
Pittsburgh benefited by having the two avenues, and freight rates
were reduced. When the canal was open the wagons carried great

[29] Breck, Samuel, *Sketch of the Internal Improvements Already Made by Pennsylvania, with Observations upon her Physical and Fiscal Means for Their Extension, etc.,* (Philadelphia, 1818), 11. "Wagons now transport, even in winter, at the rate of 22 miles a day, with four horses, a burden equivalent to 28 barrels of flour, instead of 14, which formerly made the load."
[30] Durrenberger, *Turnpikes,* 34.
[31] *Canal Pamphlets,* I, No. 2, 43, found in Carnegie Library. An article in the *Pittsburgh Gazette,* signed *Allegheny* wrote that the wagoning of goods from Philadelphia to the Ohio cost $730,000 annually which sum did not include "the very considerable por- tion of the goods purchased in Philadelphia for the western market" and then shipped to Baltimore and wagoned over the National Road, because of the cheaper rates. The writer estimated that the cost of wagoning from Baltimore totalled $470,000. The combined cost of freighting was placed at $1,200,000 and travelling expenses were estimated at an additional $300,000, or a grand expenditure of one and one-half mil- lion dollars annually expended between the East and West. *Pittsburgh Gazette,* Febru- ary 26, 1819.
[32] *Pittsburgh Gazette,* March 11, 1825.
[33] Harris, 1837, 172. Niles reported that "Not withstanding the canals of Pennsylvania, the *Pittsburgh Statesman* says—'We are told that on Monday, 83 road wagons were in this city with goods from Philadelphia ; and 64 on Tuesday.' " *Niles Weekly Register,* Volume 48, March 28, 1835, 59. The editor of the *Pittsburgh Gazette* wrote that : "In February and March 1835 there were, it is estimated 70 wagons from Philadelphia and Baltimore arriving daily in Pittsburgh with goods whose aggregate transporta- tion cost figured about $200,000." *Pittsburgh Gazette,* March 13, 1835.
[34] *Pittsburgh Gazette,* March 16, 1837.
[35] *Pittsburgh Chronicle,* February 28, 1844.

quantities of local freight and acted as feeders for the State System.[36]
Yearly statistics for the number of wagons which passed over the
turnpikes are very few in number. The earliest one appears to be
an account furnished by Alexander Thompson:[37]

... who resides on the turnpike road four and one-half miles from Pittsburgh from
which it appears, that from the first of January 1815 to 31st of December 1815,
inclusive, 5,800 road waggons [sic] laden with merchandize [sic], etc., passed his
farm for Pittsburgh. The greater part of these waggons [sic] returned loaded
with cordage, salt petre, etc., to the east of the mountains.

A similar account exists for the year ending May 7, 1818, kept by
Henry Montgomery, keeper of the turnpike gate on Chestnut Ridge
between Greensburg and Stoystown. According to this record 5,108
wagons, drawn by either five or six horse teams passed the gate, but
the direction of travel is not indicated.[38] Traffic over Cove Mountain
on the Pittsburgh Pike between McConnellsburg and Louden, from
December 1, 1817 to November 30, 1818:[39]

Waggons [sic]	9,334
Carriages and carts	621
Waggons [sic] and carriage horses	52,318
Single horses	7,719
Cattle	5,500
Sheep	2,000
Hogs	200

Samuel Jones in his *Directory for 1826* reported that from April, 1825

---

[36] Durrenberger, *Turnpikes*, 117. Durrenberger also reported that before 1830 turnpikes
were usually connected into through lines, but that after 1830 they became feeders for
other systems. The same appears to be true of the wagoning trade.
[37] *Pittsburgh Gazette*, January 27, 1816. This amount did not include the wagons from
the Juniata and other iron works.
[38] *Ibid.*, September 22, 1818. The complete account recorded the following traffic:

```
  7,120  single horses
    350  1-horse carriages
    501  2-horse carriages
  2,412  5-horse carriages
  2,696  6-horse carriages
     38  1-horse sleighs and sleds
    201  2-horse sleighs and sleds
 ------
 38,599  horses since erection of gate
```

Figures for the same traffic are found to differ slightly. According to "The Report
of Commerce on the Internal Improvements" in the *Canal Pamphlets* in Carnegie Library, Volume I, No. 2, 43, the traffic for 1818 was:

	Teams	Horses
6-horse teams	2,698	16,188
5-horse teams	2,412	12,060
4-horse teams	281	1,124
	5,391	29,372

[39] *Ibid.*, December 29, 1818. Livestock was an important item of traffic on the turnpikes
until 1850; cattle, sheep, and hogs were driven to Philadelphia, New York and Baltimore from Western Pennsylvania, Ohio, Indiana, and Illinois. From Pittsburgh to
Philadelphia the trip took about 30 days, for the average distance that the droves
travelled was 10 miles per day. All of this class of traffic, however, did not use the
turnpike because the dirt roads were easier on the animals' feet and they stayed off the
turnpikes to avoid the toll. Durrenberger, *Turnpikes*, 124.

to April, 1826, 3,460 wagons passed the turnpike gates, and that the average weight of goods was four thousand pounds each, or a total weight of 13,840,000 pounds.[40] Jones objected to the overstatements of the cost of freight, and he figured that allowing three cents per pound, as the average price of carriage "which is probably something higher than the general average would bear, the whole amount of the carriage paid during the last, would be $415,200."[41] Jones also estimated the return carriage at about $103,800.[42] The articles purchased by the Pittsburgh merchants, Jones reported further, were the following general items:[43]

Merchandise of various kinds	$1,232,000
Groceries and liquors	813,000
Drugs, stationery, etc.	74,000
Total	$2,119,000

Another yearly report of the traffic passing the west gate of Fort Louden on the Pittsburgh Pike exists for 1834 and consisted of the following:[44]

Broad wheel wagons	6,359	Carts	60
Narrow wheel wagons	374	Riding horses	2,817
Single horse wagons	1,243	Draft horses	42,330
Two horse wagons	779	Cattle	6,457
Carriages	107	Sheep	2,852
Gigs	18	Hogs	40

Figures for 1836 also exist and show an increase for the wagon traffic and "it was remarked that the last two years the transportation on these roads from East to West was greater than it had been at any time before, and the receipts during the last three months evidenced

[40] Jones, *Directory*, 1826, 88.
[41] *Ibid.*, 88.
[42] Trade figures must be carefully checked as to source because the canal advocates were busy compiling statistics to show that a canal was absolutely necessary to Pennsylvania's economic development. Apparently their zeal ran away with them; Jones makes a good point when he said that although he objected to the statement made in the 1825 session of the legislature that $900,000 was spent on freight carriage, he thought that the above figures still warranted internal improvements.
[43] Jones, *Directory*, 1826, 87. Jones pointed out that of the above amounts the following list indicated the amount actually sold:

Merchandise	$932,000
Groceries and liquor	801,000
Drugs, stationery, etc.	62,000
Total	$1,795,000

Thus, a balance for $324,000 was left unsold It appears to be impossible to check these figures; by 1826 Pittsburgh had recovered from a severe depression and business had revived. It is possible that Jones was an advocate of home manufactures and wished to show his disapproval of imported products.
[44] Durrenberger, *Turnpikes*, 118, note.

a still further increase."[45] Despite these facts, freighting news after 1835 was relegated to the background because the newer systems of transportation occupied public attention.

Probably one of the most serious handicaps in the freighting business was the high tolls charged on the traffic. Each turnpike company was permitted by the legislature to collect tolls in order that the company might repay its creditors, and at the same time defray the expensive upkeep. The Pittsburgh-Greensburg Turnpike was permitted to erect five gates[46] and to charge the following rates:[47]

Loaded wagons, broad wheels	4 horses	3¢ a horse every five miles
Loaded wagons, narrow wheels	4 horses	4¢ a horse every five miles
Pleasure carriages	2 horses	12¢ a horse every five miles
Single man and horse		3¢ a horse every five miles

Rates of toll varied with each company, hence no general figures can be stated.[48] To the present generation accustomed to free travel on common highways, the rates seem high, but to the 19th century merchants and travelers the payment was expected. Despite the tolls, turnpikes, on the whole, did not yield dividends sufficient to remunerate their proprietors; in fact, most of them yielded little more than was expended in their annual repairs and some did not even pay expenses.[49]

---

[45] *Pittsburgh Gazette*, April 13, 1837. Account kept by John V. Mollwitz, (Mulvitz) gate keeper at Cove Mountain from January 1, 1836, to January 1, 1837.

There passed the gate:

Broad wheel wagons...................	8,126 having	44,430 horses
Narrow wheel wagons	317 having	1,209 horses
Two horse wagons	726 having	1,452 horses
One horse wagons....................	1,241 having	1,241 horses
Carriages	161 having	322 horses
Gigs	94 having	94 horses
Sleighs and sleds	319 having	459 horses
Riding and drove horses..............		3,303
Horned cattle		6,794
Sheep		3,930

[46] On June 18, 1822, the 5th gate was abolished, the remaining two gates were five mile gates; two were double or 10 mile gates. *Mss.* in Public Records Division, Pennsylvania Historical and Museum Commission.

[47] Pamphlet on *Report to Senate on Roads, Bridges, etc.*, 61, found in Carnegie Library. A letter to the editor from "A Stockholder" advocated that the turnpike should be made free. He reported that the toll for a six horse wagon from Pittsburgh to Chambersburg amounted to $15, and that because of this high rate the trade was being diverted to Baltimore *via* the National Road. He estimated that Pennsylvania lost at least $100,000 annually because of the high toll rates. *Pittsburgh Mercury*, February 14, 1821. In 1822 the loss of the carrying trade to Pennsylvania was estimated at $600,000, or that two-thirds of the carrying trade and travel had gone to the free national road. The article reported that the stockholders were willing to make the Pennsylvania Turnpike free despite the fact that a large debt was yet to be paid. *Ibid.*, March 20, 1822. On June 12, 1833, a turnpike convention was held in Bedford to discuss plans for making the toll rates more equal. *Ebensburg Sky*, July 4, 1833.

[48] Durrenberger, *Turnpikes*, 110, nevertheless, considered a fair average of toll rates for every 10 miles to be as follows:

Cart or wagon whose wheels did not exceed 4 in.	12½¢ for each horse drawing
Cart or wagon whose wheels did not exceed 7 in.	6½¢
Cart or wagon whose wheels did not exceed 10 in.	5¢
Cart or wagon whose wheels did not exceed 12 in.	3¢
Every horse and rider, or led horse	6¼¢
Chair or Chaise with one horse and 2 wheels	12½¢
Coach, Wagon, phaeton chaise 2 horses and 4 wheels	25¢
Either phaeton or chaise with 4 horses	37½¢

Two oxen were counted as one horse

[49] Hazard, *Register*, 1828, I, 407-408.

Turnpikes were not built as an investment, "but they must not, therefore, be regarded as having occasioned an unprofitable expenditure of capital."[50] Stockholders were landowners or merchants and their subscriptions were usually considered as "a contribution to effect some public improvement that would pay its chief returns in an indirect manner rather than in dividends."[51] Merchants needed roads in order that their wagons could get through to market without their merchandise being injured, and landlords wanted to improve the value of their land which was adjacent to the turnpikes. Both were repaid many times, even though the tolls collected on the road did not pay the interest, because as Gallatin pointed out:[52]

They, indeed, when that happens, lose; but the community is nevertheless benefited by the undertaking. The general gain is not confined to the difference between the expense of the transportation of those articles which had formerly been conveyed by that route, but many which were brought to market by other channels will then find a new and more advantageous direction; and those which on account of their distance or weight could not be transported in any manner, whatever, will acquire a value, and become a clear addition to the national wealth.

The toll receipts are a good yardstick to show the yearly amount of traffic. From the amount of toll collected annually by the Pittsburgh-Greensburg Turnpike Company, traffic, after the panic of 1819, appears to have been regular and increasing in amounts. The following chart shows the toll receipts from 1817 to 1828:[53]

1817	$15,942.22½	1823	$9,720.81
1818	17,000.00	1824	10,094.18
1819	8,519.42	1825	10,739.61
1820	8,234.48	1826	11,687.06
1821	7,118.50	1827	11,300.49
1822	9,501.04	1828	10,477.73

According to these amounts the traffic must have been heavy because it would have taken a great number of horses at the rate of three cents per five miles to make up a thousand dollars toll.[54]

Pennsylvania turnpike freighting, in general, was never as highly organized as the transportation on the Pennsylvania State System, or on the Ohio River after the invention of the steamboat. Wagoning required only a wagon and a team, which were usually the possession of most farmers. The normal overland freight was always carried by a class of professional teamsters who made a business of hauling. They considered the road as their possession, and resented intrusion

[50] *Ibid.*, 1828, I, 408.
[51] Durrenberger, *Turnpikes*, 104.
[52] *American State Papers, Miscellaneous*, I, 724.
[53] Compiled from the original *Annual Reports* of the Pittsburgh-Greensburg Turnpike Company, found in Public Records Division, Pennsylvania Historical and Museum Commission.
[54] Toll was paid in cash, or worked out. For example, Robert Stewart who drove the mail coach over the Pittsburgh-Greensburg turnpike "repairs one mile of the turnpike which is allowed in part of his toll." *Mss.* Road and Turnpike Papers.

and improvements as a personal insult.[55] The teamsters ably presented their opposition to the canals when at a wagoner's meeting on February 4, 1824, the following resolution was one of five drawn up to be sent to the legislature.[56]

That the waggoners [sic] of the State of Pennsylvania, had paid with unexampled good faith (except when they could cheat a little!) the heavy tolls, which had been levied by the proprietors of the turnpikes, and are ready and willing to draw any burden, however, heavy, which the public good may demand; but they would be wanting in their duty to themselves and the public, were they, without remonstrance, to submit to speculative projects about canals and water communications calculated to drive them from the honorable pursuits of their early life, and the business of their education—projects which threaten ruin of themselves and dependent families—projects tending to involve their country and their posterity in vast and incalculable mischief.

Evidently the resolution brought no results, for the newspapers did not carry any additional information on the subject.

The turnpikes brought a distinctive improvement in transportation in Western Pennsylvania, and they were forward steps in the development of better connections between the East and West. The heyday of turnpike construction took place between the years 1800 and 1830, and money was generously and widely invested. The net return in actual receipts was usually a disappointment, but the indirect results paid dividends many times more valuable and permanent. That the turnpike would be superseded as a principal artery of trade

---

[55] How much animosity existed between the professional teamsters and the farmers on the Pennsylvania roads is uncertain but on the National Road the feeling ran high, and the "regulars" bitterly resented the "Sharpshooter", or farmer, who put his team on the road in seasons when freight was high and who took it off when the price declined. Searight, Thomas B., *The Old Pike, A History of the National Road . . .*, (Uniontown, 1894), 110-111. A letter from a "pike boy" shows the relationship between the two classes:

"In September, 1844, or 5, my father came home from Uniontown late at night, and woke me up to tell me that there had been a big break in the Pennsylvania Canal, and that all western freights were coming out over the National Road in wagons. The stage coaches brought out posters soliciting teams. By sunrise next morning, I was in Brownsville with my team and whipped off for Cumberland. . . . In Cumberland, we found the commission houses, and the cars on sidings filled with goods, and men cursing loudly because the latter were not unloaded. Large boxes of valuable goods were likewise on the platform of the station, protected by armed guards. After unloading my down load I re-loaded at McKaig & Maguire's commission house for Brownsville at one dollar and twenty-five cents a hundred. We reached Brownsville without incident or accident, made a little money, and loaded back again for Cumberland. On my return I found plenty of goods for shipment, and loaded up at Tuttle's house for Wheeling, at two dollars and twenty-five cents a hundred. In coming back, it looked as if the whole earth was on the road; wagons, stages, horses, cattle, hogs, sheep, and turkeys without number. Teams of every description appeared in view. . . . The commission merchants seeing the multitude of wagons, sought to reduce prices whereupon the old wagoners called a meeting and made a vigorous kick against the proposed reduction. It was the first strike I ever heard of. Nothing worried a sharpshooter more than lying at expense in Cumberland waiting for a load. Two of the "sharps", unwilling to endure the delay caused by the strike, drove their four-horse rigs to a warehouse to load at the reduction. This excited the "regulars", and they massed with horns, tin buckets, oyster-cans and the like and made a descent upon the "sharps", pelting and guying them unmercifully. An old wagoner named Butler commanded the Strikking [sic] regulars with a pine sword, and marched them back and forth through the streets. Finally the police quelled the disturbance, and the "Sharps" loaded up and drove out sixteen miles, to find their harness cut and their axles sawed off in the morning. In this dilemma an old regular, going down empty for a load took the contract of the "sharps" and made them promise never to return on the road, a promise they faithfully kept." *Ibid.*, 143.

[56] *Pittsburgh Gazette*, February 20, 1824.

can be easily understood in the light of the mechanical replacements of the 1840's. But the turnpikes contributed to the general economic development of the country, bridging the gap between the elementary trails and the present rail lines. A generation can build only within its own horizon; and within that limited sphere each one should be judged. Feeble as were the attempts to lower rates and speed up traffic before 1830, the total results should be credited in the light of the general *milieu* of the period. Pittsburgh benefited by each succeeding step in road improvement. The lowering of freight rates, the shortening of the time for transporting goods, and the increasing amount of traffic sent both ways on the roads or turnpikes all tended to raise Pittsburgh's position as a commercial center. Pittsburgh was benefited further by merely being the western terminus of one of the principal trade arteries between the East and the West. Traffic passing through the enterprising commercial center was frequently attracted by Pittsburgh products and the opportunity to trade. As the network of internal improvements became greater, extending Pittsburgh's trade area in all directions, Pittsburgh grew stronger in both her commercial and manufacturing fields. Roads and turnpikes to the East made possible a connection for Pittsburgh which was indispensable. The results were good, but never perfect, and Pittsburgh was still looking for a more satisfactory connection with the East. The Pennsylvania State System was the next attempt; and though it was an improvement over the turnpikes, the desired results were not achieved until the building of the railroads.

VI

The Pennsylvania State System

PITTSBURGHERS were sensitive of their lack of cheap transportation to the East.[1] Despite the fact that the town was fortunately located at the junction of three navigable rivers, Pittsburghers did not consider themselves blessed. Consequently, efforts were never relaxed to improve their eastern connections. As Pittsburgh developed, and as the nation on the whole expanded both geographically and economically, more efficient and more direct trade routes were demanded.[2] The War of 1812 had had far reaching economic effects and especially had it shown the absolute need for internal improvements.[3] The need for better transportation routes was not new, but the ability to build was new. During the 1820's and 1830's the merchants and manufacturers were in a position to demand, and backed with their money, internal improvements throughout the country were started on a large scale.[4] The eastern merchant needed internal improvements to reach the many and increasing number of western customers.[5] He needed a good route to induce the western buyer to come to his shop; at any rate, he needed a route as good as other routes to other shops; furthermore, he needed a safe and short route so that the cost of transportation would not double the original cost of the article to the consumer. The merchants of the leading commercial eastern cities of New York, Philadelphia and Baltimore entered into competition for the control of the rapidly increasing western trade, and from 1820 the heretofore insignificant western trade became more and more desired. For a time, Philadelphia merchants seemed to be unaware that a race was taking place, for Philadelphia had held the enviable position as the foremost commercial city for many years. New York and Baltimore, however, took steps to tap this source of Philadelphia's trade. By building the Erie Canal, New York was able to reach the growing flour trade of the northwest; and Baltimore, aided by the almost toll-free National Road, secured the pork trade of Ohio, as well as the trade of the northern

---

[1] *Pittsburgh Gazette,* February 20, 1841; *Niles' Weekly Register,* Vol. 59, 229.
[2] *Ibid.,* February 20, 1841.
[3] Harlow, Alvin F., *Old Towpaths; the Story of the American Canal Era,* (New York, 1926), 41.
[4] Dunbar, Rowland, "The Mississippi Valley in American History," in Mississippi Valley Historical Association, *Proceedings,* (1915-1916), IX, 65.
[5] Callender, Guy S., "The Early Transportation and Banking Enterprises of the State in Relation to the Growth of Corporations" in *Quarterly Journal of Economics,* XVII, (1902-03), 116-137. The future economic importance of the transmountain region had been foreseen, although prior to 1815 its commercial importance had been slight.

part of the tobacco belt. Philadelphia was in a dilemma (although a Pittsburgh editor called it "dotage"[6]) because the mountains between Pittsburgh and Philadelphia still presented a barrier. Furthermore, Philadelphia had contributed liberally to the building of the various turnpikes and had also invested money heavily in the wagoning business thereon. Gradually, however, Philadelphia began to realize that her State pride was at stake, and more seriously, that part of the trade which she considered as her right was leaking out to Baltimore and to New York simply because the routes to Philadelphia were not equally good.[7] The solution of this problem seemed necessary to Philadelphia's future commercial development.

The question was not settled until 1826, but the determination to do something persisted. The legislature, in December, 1823, appointed a special committee to consider routes, and the committee recommended that surveys be made immediately for a route between the Susquehanna and Allegheny rivers. On April 1, 1824, a board of commissioners was appointed; this board reported early in 1825 that a canal between Philadelphia and Pittsburgh was practicable. The suggested route was from Philadelphia via the Union Canal to the Susquehanna River near Harrisburg, then along the Susquehanna and Juniata rivers to Hollidaysburg; the main ridge of the Allegheny Mountain was to be cut by a tunnel[8] four miles long, and thence to the Conemaugh and the Allegheny rivers to Pittsburgh.

The cost of the canal was estimated at $3,000,000 and the commissioners predicted that the tolls would "support the government and educate every child in the Commonwealth." The Canal Commissioners also pointed out the advantages which would accrue to the people of the region: the proposed canal would provide a good market for the West, and, at the same time, it would raise the price of land which was then selling for less than two dollars per acre. Western Pennsylvania would benefit as had Western New York because of the reduction in transportation costs both in freight rates and passenger rates. Wagons from Pittsburgh to Philadelphia usually carried from 42 to 50 hundredweight and required four to six horses. Allowing that a six-horse team could carry 50 hundredweight, it was estimated that ten such teams would be necessary to carry 25 tons, whereas one canal boat would carry 25 tons and make the trip as fast as a wagon. In other words, "here we have 10 men, 10 wagons and 60 horses, on an excellent turnpike road over the mountains, doing the same work that can be done by one man, one boy, one horse

---

[6] *Pittsburgh Gazette,* May 22, 1818.
[7] Livengood, *The Philadelphia-Baltimore Trade Rivalry, 1780-1860,* 4.
[8] In order to explain what a tunnel was the commissioners described it as "a hole like a well dug horizontally through a hill or a mountain." Pennsylvania, *House Journal,* 1825-26, II, 159.

and one boat on a canal."⁹   The cost of the wagoner's outfit was
estimated at $8,000 and the daily expense was set at $60 while the
estimated cost of the canalboat was "but $260, and the daily expense
but $3."¹⁰   Furthermore, the tolls would be cheaper, for on the turn-
pikes the toll of 60 horses hauling wagons for 100 miles would be
$48 while a canalboat would pay but $25 for the same distance.¹¹
The canal, therefore, would be a benefit to every one, but especially
would it benefit the Pennsylvania iron and salt industries.   The
Canal Commissioners asserted that the Juniata works made excellent
iron which was as good as any iron produced elsewhere, but that the
business was handicapped by the high transportation costs.   The iron
sold at the works for $85 per ton while the cost in Pittsburgh was
$100 to $110.   The Juniata works sent about three thousand tons per
year to Pittsburgh and the transportation tax was from $16 to $20
per ton.   On the canal a ton of iron could be shipped for less than
three dollars per ton.¹²   Thus, a canal seemingly was the correct solution for Pennsylvania because freight charges would be lowered and
western goods would continue to come to Philadelphia.

Internal friction and local selfishness delayed the enterprise, and
the canal question became a legislative tug-of-war.   From the beginning the tier of counties in the northeastern part of the State and
the block of southern counties opposed an East to West route because
such an improvement would not help them in any way.   Philadelphia
was deeply concerned about the prosperous and wealthy southern
counties which, because of bad roads to Philadelphia, were finding
Baltimore a better market.   Therefore, Pennsylvania had to improve
her roads in order to lure back these erring merchants.¹³   Branch
canals were also suggested in order to pacify the anthracite coal
region.   For a while Philadelphia unsuccessfully tried to carry water
on both shoulders.   Meanwhile the "grand canal" of Pennsylvania
was held up while the politicians procrastinated and lost time and
money in branch canals and "log-rolled" local improvements.¹⁴
Finally, after sufficient votes had been bought or traded, the legislature, by an Act of Assembly, February 25, 1826, decided that a main
line of improvements ought to connect the East and the West, and,

⁹ *Pittsburgh Gazette,* March 11, 1825. It was pointed out that in New Hampshire a canal
    not only increased the value of land, but also raised the price of timber.
¹⁰ *Ibid.,* March 11, 1825. "A single year's interest on the outfit of the wagons, would
    nearly fit out two boats with their horses and harnesses."
¹¹ In the *Pittsburgh Gazette,* January 28, 1825, it was estimated that staples would be
    transported to the seaboard at the rate of one and one-half cents per ton per mile
    and that a barrel of flour would be shipped for 45 cents from Pittsburgh to Phila-
    delphia.
¹² *Ibid.,* March 11, 1825.
¹³ McCarthy, Charles, "The Anti-Masonic Party: A Study in Political Anti-Masonry in
    the United States, 1827-1840" in American Historical Association, *Reports,* (1902),
    430.
¹⁴ In order to get sufficient legislative support for the main line local improvements
    had to be bartered. Each section of the State was afraid to help another section and
    each opposed improvements which did not pass its front door, yet all were in favor
    of internal improvement.

after that was accomplished, branch canals should be placed wherever needed. The Pennsylvania State System was to be a combination of canal and railroad, because after a study of two years engineers were convinced that an all-water route, like the Erie Canal, was impossible due to the high elevation of the mountains. The best route was thought to be along the Susquehanna, Juniata, and Conemaugh rivers, so that an adequate water supply would be guaranteed. The Union Canal was to connect Philadelphia with the Susquehanna, using an established route and thereby eliminating additional construction cost. The Allegheny Mountains were to be crossed by a railroad rather than by tunnel. Ground was broken on July 4, 1826, and the work progressed with a certain amount of speed. In this respect the Pennsylvania System was more fortunate than the Erie Canal because a lack of tools and engineering experience retarded the construction of that waterway.[15] Contracts were let on the various divisions and work progressed from both ends simultaneously.

The Western Section of the canal from Pittsburgh to Johnstown was partly opened in 1829, but it was not officially completed until 1830, and the Juniata Division was finished in 1832. The original plan to use the Union Canal had to be altered because the canal was found to be too small to accommodate the boats of the Main Line. Consequently, the State had to make other provisions for a route from Philadelphia to the Susquehanna. As the territory was hilly, and the prospects of a successful canal were problematic, the State undertook to build another railroad in 1828. This railroad was one of the earliest in the United States and the first one in the world to be built by a government.[16] The Philadelphia-Columbia Railroad was opened to traffic in 1834. Work had been started on the Allegheny Portage Railroad in 1831, although it was not completed until 1834. As the canals had been completed before the railroads, canal traffic was permitted, and freight was carried over the mountains by wagons. The Main Line was officially and completely opened in 1834, having required nine years of labor, and having cost the State twelve and a quarter millions.[17] As an engineering feat, the Pennsylvania State System was an unexcelled heroic attempt to overcome physical difficulties. The total distance was 395 miles and the highest point above mean tide was 2,326 feet.

The people of Pittsburgh, as well as Pennsylvania in general, were delighted when the system was completed and all expected great results. For years canal enthusiasts had been busy compiling statis-

---

[15] Harlow, *Old Towpaths*, 99. James Geddes and Nathan Roberts, engineers who had worked on the Erie Canal, directed the building of large sections of the Pennsylvania canals, and Canvass White was the consultant on the Portage Railway.
[16] *Ibid.*, 99.
[17] Pennsylvania *Senate Journal*, 1834,. Appendix to Volume II. The *Annual Report* of the Canal Commissioners for the year ending October 31, 1834, 3.

tics to show the areas from which the Pennsylvania System would draw trade. They expected that the Pennsylvania Route would draw from almost double the amount of population as would the Erie Canal. According to the statisticians, the following areas were expected to use the Pennsylvania route:[18]

One-half of the people of Ohio	50,000
One-half of the people of Kentucky	100,000
Parts of Indiana, estimated at	50,000
Parts of Illinois, estimated at	50,000
Missouri	70,000
Northwest section of Virginia	100,000
Totals	1,020,000

Apparently the figures given are incorrectly reported in the *Gazette* for when added they should total 420,000. The author has assumed that the total of 1,020,000 is correct as it proved the point that the canal enthusiasts were trying to make. Furthermore, Pennsylvania expected her route to excel the Erie Canal because of her more centralized and commercial position and because she, likewise, commanded the Ohio River, the gateway to the West. Figures were produced to show that no great difference existed in the distance between the New Orleans and the Philadelphia markets; and that in some cases, the Philadelphia market *via* the Pennsylvania State System was even closer than New Orleans,[19] and by far the safer and surer way.[20] Pennsylvania figured also that her "inexhaustible beds of coal and iron" would be an additional advantage, although the trump card was to be her theoretically longer navigable season. The Canal Commissioners estimated that the Pennsylvania canals could be navigated five weeks earlier in the spring and three weeks later in the fall, and that the Philadelphia-Columbia Railroad would be open the entire year.[21] At last, Pennsylvania was supposedly adequately prepared to contend with her rivals for the western trade, and, said the Canal Commissioners: "... Pennsylvania has placed herself on an eminence from whence

---

[18] *Pittsburgh Gazette,* January 28, 1825. The same compiler estimated that the Erie drew trade from a population of 610,000.

[19] *Ibid., January* 28, 1825.

From	To New Orleans	To Philadelphia
Cincinnati	1,615 miles	1,000 miles
Junction of Ohio	1,000 miles	1,490 miles
Mouth of Wabash	1,100 miles	1,290 miles
Louisville	1,287 miles	1,178 miles
Mouth of Tennessee River	1,056 miles	1,373 miles

[20] *Ibid.,* March 18, 1834.

[21] Pennsylvania *House Journal,* 1834-35, Appendix to Volume II, 5. *Annual Report* of the Canal Commissioners for year ending October 31, 1834. Unfortunately, the expected longer seasons were few and far between, and the Canal Commissioners usually reported that the spring opening was later than had been expected, or that the opening of one or the other of the divisions was delayed by ice. In 1837 the Erie harbor opened before the Pennsylvania Canal and the New Yorkers were quite amused, much to Pittsburgh's discomfort and chagrin. Pittsburghers made a good face, and retorted that even if the Canal was not open steamboats were navigating the Ohio for six weeks previously. *Pittsburgh Gazette,* March 28, 1837.

she may view without any apprehension of successful rivalry, the emulous exertions of her sister states in similar enterprises."[22] The Western Division had opened on March 8, 1834, and the Allegheny Portage Railway went into operation ten days later.[23] Pittsburghers were especially pleased to hear that:[24]

The *Canal* and Railroad are now in full and successful operation. Goods arrived yesterday, in eleven days from Philadelphia. We believe the calculation is to deliver them in ten days, when the arrangements are all completed.

We have been informed that the New Yorkers have contracted to deliver goods at Portsmouth, on the Ohio, by the way of the New York and Ohio Canal and Lake Erie, for two dollars six and one-half cents per hundred when their Canal is opened. By the Pennsylvania Canal, goods will be delivered at Cincinnati for two dollars and five cents. By the first of May, this will probably be reduced to a dollar eighty cents.

In the *time of transportation,* we possess a still more decided advantage, merchandise will be delivered from Philadelphia to Cincinnati, in *14 or 15* days. From New York to Cincinnati it will require *25* days and frequently much longer. The *risk,* by the Lake, is very great—by the Pennsylvania Canal and Railroad, almost nothing.

The New York Canal will not be opened for more than three weeks yet . . . in that time, steamboats may proceed to St. Louis or Nashville, and return to Pittsburgh; and in the same time, merchandise may be delivered at the Sault of St. Marie, or Chicago. Our prospects in relation to these great improvements, are truly encouraging, if they are not obscured by the folly and madness of General Jackson.

Pittsburgh, after almost fifty years of waiting, had a cheap and short route to the East. The *Blairsville Record* proudly announced the arrival of the *La Fayette* loaded with 30 tons of dry goods at Pittsburgh. The boat had traveled the 103 miles from Johnstown in a little more than one day and two nights and had required only four men and six relays of two horses. The newspaper reminded its readers that before the time of the Canal 15 wagons, 90 horses, and 15 drivers would have been necessary to transport such an order because the goods were light and bulky, and that it would have taken four days and four nights to cover the distance.[25]

The complete opening of the Pennsylvania State System had been the one bright spot in an otherwise gloomy commercial world, for the depression of 1834 had its disastrous effects on western as well as eastern cities. But the Pennsylvania System was busy and business was increasing. Three companies were engaged in transporting goods over the Allegheny Portage and about 110 cars were in use. The

---

[22] Pennsylvania *House Journal,* 1835-36. Appendix to Volume II, *Annual Report* of the Canal Commissioners for the year ending, October 31, 1834, 5.
[23] *Ibid.,* 1834-35, 5.
[24] *Pittsburgh Gazette,* March 18, 1834; March 26, 1834. A note informed the public that the Pennsylvania System opened forty days sooner than the Erie Canal had opened the previous year (April 17) and that it could have "opened sooner but for work on the aqueduct."
[25] *Pittsburgh Gazette,* April 18, 1834.

amount of goods passing westward daily was estimated between 80 and 100 tons; and although the eastward trade was not so large, it was increasing. In 1833 only one boat per day had arrived at Hollidaysburg, while in 1834 the average had jumped to four.[26] According to a Harrisburg paper, five hundred canal boats were registered and in constant use upon Pennsylvania canals, and 15 locomotives were engaged on Pennsylvania railroads.[27] Small wonder that Pennsylvanians were satisfied with their public improvements!

Compared with modern standards, travel over the Pennsylvania State System was slow, cumbersome and expensive, but it was a great improvement over the early roads and turnpikes. The time required for a trip from Philadelphia to Pittsburgh varied with the seasons and the amount of traffic on the road, but the variance was not so great as previously; and, under ordinary circumstances, five or six days was usually the time required for freight.[28] As for the cost of transportation, a substantial reduction took place over the older system and, as the Canal Commission had promised, goods could be transported from the West just as cheaply to Philadelphia as to New Orleans. By the Act of February 26, 1826, the Canal Commissioners were authorized to collect toll on the State improvements, and the act was supplemented by the resolutions of the legislature on June 11, 1832, and February 21, 1834, for the appointment of collectors on the Columbia and Portage Railroads.[29] The toll system was as equally complicated as the other aspects of the State System.[30] First, each vehicle paid a separate rate for the privilege of passing on each of the railroads, viaducts, bridges, and canal outlifts; second, each article of the cargo also paid a different rate based on the market

[26] *Ebensburg Sky,* May 22, 1834, quoting a letter from the Pennsylvania *Reporter.* The letter also stated that the Portage should have a double track. This appears to be the earliest of the suggested improvements, enlargements, or changes which haunted the State System. The building program was never completed, because something had to be repaired or replaced annually.
[27] *Niles' Weekly Register,* Vol. 45, June 7, 1834, 256.
[28] *Ibid.,* Vol. 48, April 25, 1835, 132. "We are informed yesterday, by a respected merchant of this city, (Pittsburgh) that goods from Philadelphia, by way of the Columbia Railroad and Pennsylvania Canal, arrived here within 6½ or 7 days after shipment and that some lots, which were destined for Louisville, arrived at that place within three days, thereafter making 10 days from Philadelphia to Louisville! ! ! ! ! Comment is unnecessary. This serves to show what can be done."
[29] Pennsylvania *Senate Journal,* 1834-35, Appendix to Volume II, 214.
[30] Pennsylvania *Executive Documents,* 1850, The *Annual Report* of the Canal Commissioners for the year ending October 31, 1849, 15. This situation had been changed in 1846, "By an act of the 22nd April, 1846, it is required 'That from and after the passage of this act, the Canal Commissioners shall, and they are hereby required, to adopt, fix, declare and publish the rates of toll on the public works of this Commonwealth, for the then next ensuing twelve months, or the residue of the year on or before the first day of January, in each succeeding year thereafter.' A construction has been given to this act, which if correct, prohibits the Board from changing the rates of toll during the year for which the list has been published even in those cases where the public interest imperatively demands it. It frequently happens that in order to meet changes in the course of trade, by the rivalry of different routes, and to preserve to the public works of Pennsylvania their just and natural share of transportation, it becomes necessary to alter the rate of toll on some particular article. The Board, therefore, recommends an early amendment of the aforesaid act, so as to give them the power to change the rates whenever in their opinion the interests of the Commonwealth may require it."

value of the article; third, these rates were changed frequently, so that it was necessary to state the month, as well as the year, for which the rates applied; fourth, the toll rates had very little to do with cost of transportation which was charged on the State System; fifth, the individual who sent his goods over the Pennsylvania route did not deal directly with the State, but rather with the transportation companies; sixth, no one seemed to be satisfied with the rates and newspapers continually advocated toll reductions and criticized the Canal Commissioners.

Human beings apparently have always had short memories. In the early days, Pittsburghers had paid 14 dollars to transport a barrel of flour from Pittsburgh to Philadelphia;[31] whereas in 1835 by way of the State System a barrel of flour cost one dollar, twelve and a half cents for the same distance. This same flour in 1835 paid a toll of five cents per mile per one thousand pounds on the canal, and a toll of eight cents per mile per one thousand pounds on both railroads.[32] In 1840 a drawback of 20 cents was allowed on the flour if the barrel was transported over the entire distance from Pittsburgh to Philadelphia.[33] In 1843 the tolls on flour were again reduced to three cents per mile per thousand pounds on the canal and to five cents per mile per thousand pounds on the railroads.[34] The bookkeeping and time required to ascertain the toll a cargo should pay were considerable. The task was further complicated by numerous resolutions of the Commissioners changing various items or removing them entirely. At times, tolls were refunded if a drought or a break in the canal delayed the traffic[35] or, in case of a breakdown, a substitute was provided to avoid losing trade. For example, when the Valley Creek bridge was being repaired in March, 1838, the superintendent of the Philadelphia and Columbia Railroad was ordered to secure a sufficient number of wagons to transport the goods around the bridge.[36] Yet despite this paternalistic policy the Canal Commissioners were flayed year after year by repeated editorials on the high rates charged by the Pennsylvania route, and the western editors tantalizingly pointed out the leakage of trade to New York. When the *Annual Report* for 1845 was published a Pittsburgh editor wrote that "the tables show grounds for serious alarm," because the leading western staples were decreasing. He pointed out that:[37]

[31] Storey, Henry W., *A History of Cambria County*, 2 Vols., (New York, 1907), I, 365.
[32] Pennsylvania *Senate Journal*, 1834-35, Appendix to Volume II, 428-432.
[33] Pennsylvania *House Journal*, 1841, III, 8.
[34] Pennsylvania *Executive Documents*, 1843, The *Journal* of Canal Commissioners, February 7, 1843, 84.
[35] Pennsylvania *House Journal*, 1838-39, III, The *Journal* of the Canal Commissioner, October 16, 1838, 320. "Resolved that the toll paid on the boat *Martha*, of Portsmouth (Captain Cole) and cargo, returning from Farrandsville with coal, be refunded, as the boat was detained more than a month by low water."
[36] *Ibid.*, 221.
[37] *Pittsburgh Gazette and Advertiser*, December 6, 1846.

It might be considered that if, in the aggregate, there was no decrease the route was at least holding its own. But when it is remembered that the products of flour, beef, and pork, cheese and butter, lard, tallow bacon, cotton, hemp, etc. is increasing at a very large percentage annually, and yet the route is actually losing on these articles, the inference is plain.

The reason for this situation, continued the editor, was the "onerous tolls and burdensome regulations"; and the only way to remedy the evil was to reduce the rates substantially (not trifling reductions as has been the case) and to publish the rates early.[38] "Philadelphia," scolded the editor, "may flatter herself that she controls the trade of the West, but if figures do not lie, she is losing what she heretofore possessed." But he concluded, "happily for Pittsburgh, her commerce and manufacturing interests now depend in but a limited degree upon the canal."[39] Numerous such articles might be included but they are monotonously the same and all called for the reduction of rates.

Western editors were not the only persons who agreed on this point, for the Canal Commissioners themselves, as early as 1841, reported that the System was not carrying as much as it should or could carry. But they laid the blame on other shoulders and explained that "there is but one way of accounting for this failure in business and revenue. It is, that the *prices* of *freight* have been so high as to give *other* channels of transportation an advantage and preference over those of Pennsylvania."[40] The Canal Commissioners admitted that the Pennsylvania route was more expensive to maintain than other all-water routes and that because of costly trans-shipping, warehouses, and rolling stock needed, individuals were unable to compete in the transporting business.[41] The transportation was, therefore, tied up in the hands of a few companies who were able to supply sufficient capital to buy the necessary equipment. These companies set the freight rates, contracted with individuals to carry their goods, and they paid the tolls to the State.[42] The merchants had no direct business with the State, and if the companies did not make a similar reduction in the freight rates, the reduction of tolls by the State was of no advantage to

---

[38] This was a good point, and in 1846 the Canal Commissioners were required by law to publish the rates before January 1; before that time rates were published at any time during the first quarter of the year.

[39] *Pittsburgh Gazette and Advertiser*, December 6, 1846.

[40] Pennsylvania *Senate Journal*, 1842, III, The *Annual Report* of Canal Commissioners for year ending October 31, 1841, 42. The Canal Commissioners maintained that the State System could carry four times as much freight as it was carrying.

[41] Pennsylvania *House Journal*, 1843, II, 279. The Canal Commissioners estimated that it required no less than $50,000 capital to put into operation a single daily line between Philadelphia and Pittsburgh.

[42] For example, an advertisement appeared in the *Pittsburgh Gazette*, January 14, 1836: "The Western Transportation Company (Leech & Co's Line) have made extensive preparations for transporting merchandise and passengers on the Pennsylvania Canal and Rail Roads, between Philadelphia & Pittsburgh, to commence at the opening of navigation say about the 1st March next. Their new line by way of Columbia & Philadelphia Rail Road, will pass Goods through the entire distance in Eight Days, to the amount of forty tons daily. . . .'"

the merchant.[43] Although the Canal Commissioners realized that the transporters were under heavy expenditure, they objected to the fact that:[44]

Several proprietors of lines have thought it necessary to combine for the purpose of fixing high rates of freight during the first months of the season, when, by reason of the other routes not being open, ours is necessarily crowded. It is, probably in consequence of this policy on the part of the carriers, that the trade so generally leaves us when other routes become accessible and available. The effects of this practice of charging inordinate rates on the early spring business, are manifestly injurious to trade and prejudicial to the public interest. It raises a suspicion of unfairness against us, and it excites a feeling of opposition from which our business suffers loss, during all the balance of the season. It produces, also an impression that we have no fixed or regular standard of rates, but that our whole line is subject to the capricious changes and fluctuations of seasons and interested collusions.

In short, the greatest need was for a standardized price and the setting of reasonable rates which would be maintained throughout the season. The Canal Commissioners asserted that this could be accomplished only by encouraging individual enterprise, by enabling anyone who owned a boat to load at Pittsburgh or Philadelphia, and then to carry his cargo over the Main Line without breaking bulk, or without the interference of warehouse agencies.[45] The idea of eliminating trans-shipment by carrying boats over the mountains had been the dream of enterprising individuals for many years; section or portable boats appeared to be the solution. The section boat had been invented by John Daugherty and had been used quite successfully on the Pennsylvania System since 1837.[46] These boats were so constructed that they could be divided into three parts, placed on trucks, and hauled over the railroad without disturbing the cargo. An individual who owned one of these boats could carry his merchandise from Pittsburgh to Philadelphia and was spared all the costs of trans-shipment. Having eliminated the need for extensive equipment, the person with small capital[47] could enter the transportation business on the Pennsylvania System without the danger of being forced off the line by a combination of large capitalists who, under

[43] Pennsylvania *House Journal*, 1843, II, The *Annual Report* of the Canal Commissioners for year ending October 31, 1843, 114-115. "Hence it is, that the attempts on the part of the Canal Commissioners to produce an increase of business upon our improvements, by frequent and liberal reductions in the rates of toll, have always failed to produce any corresponding reductions on the part of the transporter, and of course but a slight increase in the trade passing over our improvements." The State furnished all "the engines, fuel, stationary power, engines, firemen, agents, dispatchers, hitchers, switch tenders, etc.," and in return she received less than half the fare of passengers on the Columbia-Philadelphia Railroad. On the Portage the State received seventy-eight cents out of the two dollar passenger fare and it was "probably the most expensive railroad of its extent in the world."
[44] Pennsylvania *Senate Journal*, 1842, III, The *Annual Report* of Canal Commissioners for the year ending October 31, 1841, 43.
[45] *Ibid.*, 1842, III, 26.
[46] *Pittsburgh Daily Gazette*, July 15, 1837.
[47] Pennsylvania *House Journal*, 1843, II, 279. A committee appointed to investigate the subject, reported to the House that $800 would be sufficient capital to "become an effective and successful carrier."

the old system, were the only ones who could afford to keep sufficient stock. To encourage the use of section boats appeared to the Canal Commissioners to be the only solution for high freight rates. Not only would free and equal competition be possible, but the rates would be cheapened and the means and facilities of doing business would be extended.[48] If the State would only provide the means for carrying these boats, the Canal Commissioners were confident that "our public works would be, what they were originally designed to be, a source of revenue to the commonwealth, a public blessing, and a general good."[49]

As a result of these recommendations, the legislature by Act of July 1, 1842, authorized the Canal Commissioners to purchase trucks[50] for the transportation of section boats over the Philadelphia-Columbia and the Allegheny Portage Railroads. Eighteen sets of new trucks of four sections each were purchased and ten of these were placed on the Columbia Railroad and eight on the Portage before the new plan went into effect at the opening of spring navigation in 1842. As predicted, the system met with popular approval and business was brisk. The old lines, however, resented the intrusion and they began to object to this infringement of their "rights." The old transporters objected to the fact that the section boats did not have to pay for motive power, but were charged only one set fee for being hauled over the railroad.[51] In May of 1842 a group of transporters, represented by David Leech, James M. Davis, James Steele and Company, and E. G. Dutilh and Company brought a writ of mandamus against the Canal Commissioners.[52] After a hearing in May, 1843, the Supreme Court decided in favor of the Canal Commissioners, for the courts said that by Act of April 15, 1834, every citizen had a right to attach a car to a public engine and that these relators had the same

---

[48] *Ibid.*, 1843, II, The *Annual Report* of the Canal Commissioners for the year ending October 31, 1842, 112-113, "the experiment already made by the portable boats, clearly proves that the requisite facilities of planes, ships, and trucks, are alone wanted to awaken a spirit of enterprise among the citizens, and to produce an amount of individual competition in the carrying business, transportation upon our public improvements."

[49] *Ibid.*, 113.

[50] *Ibid.*. The *Journal* of Canal Commissioners, July 5, 1842, 568.

[51] Pennsylvania *Executive Documents*, 1843, the *Annual Report* of Canal Commissioners for the year ending November 30, 1843, 61. Persons who used the State trucks did not have to pay for motive power, while the companies using their own cars had to pay $34.08 to the Commonwealth for motive power on a round trip from Pittsburgh to Philadelphia. The transportation companies complained that those who used the State trucks "must, therefore, very soon, obtain the monopoly of the carrying trade." In reality, however, the users of the State trucks paid more for transportation than did the transporters. By Act of July 1, 1842, section boats using the State trucks were required to pay, in addition to regular tolls, (excepting motive power toll on wheels) a charge of 25 cents per 1000 pounds on the Allegheny Portage and 37½ cents per 1000 pounds on the Philadelphia-Columbia Railroad. For example, from the opening of navigation to June 1, 1843, there were 267 section boats transported over both roads. These boats paid $3,063.30 for the use of the trucks, but if the goods had been carried on trucks of the transporters the costs would have been $2,123.04, or a difference in favor of the transporters of $940.26.

[52] Commonwealth ex rel. Leech vs. The Canal Commissioners, 5 W. & S., 388; *Pittsburgh Morning Chronicle*, June 17, 1842; *Pittsburgh Mercury and Manufacturer*, March 18, 1843.

privilege so "what more do they want?" and the case was dismissed.[53] The transporters threatened to go out of business, but, in reality, they accepted the changes and made the best of them.[54] The State won the battle, and rate setting became a thing of the past.[55]

As a result of the introduction of State trucks, freight rates were reduced from five to twenty-five per cent per one hundred pounds over tolls, and the tonnage increased. The Canal Commissioners were satisfied that the State System had been saved and that better times were at hand. The Commissioners explained that:[56]

> Previously, mere reductions of toll had no such effects upon the prices of freight — carriage on goods did not come down in proportion. The means of transportation afforded by the combined companies were limited, and with every increase of produce the freights were raised. In this combination system there was no permanent inducement to bring trade to the Pennsylvania Improvements, nor did any ever come, except that which naturally sought the route at any price, or was thrown upon it by over trading, and occasionally by super-abundant crops . . . past experience has proved that the old system of transportation has availed nothing to the State. It is felt in her present condition, she has been sinking under its influence, and her improvements would have become a wreck, a monument of her folly and imbecility—for she could never have secured the trade of the West by such a system, in the hands of a few companies.

The State increased the supply of trucks almost yearly and carried the growing amount of freight over the railroads. No other radical changes were made during the existence of the State System, although enlargements and facilities were added from time to time. Wire ropes were substituted for hemp ropes on the incline planes, and locomotives rapidly replaced horse power.[57] Improvements were made constantly, and the Canal Commissioners tried every possible method, except to remove the mountains, in their attempt to induce trade to use the Pennsylvania System.

The Pennsylvania System carried a large amount of trade both East and West. Total tonnage was not included in the *Annual Reports*, but the total receipts show almost a continual annual increase, which indicates increased tonnage.[58] The individual items

---

[53] Pennsylvania *Executive Documents*, The *Annual Report* of Canal Commissioners for the year ending November 30, 1843, 69 ; *Pittsburgh Gazette*, July 8, 1843. The editor covered the case and ended up by hoping that this would be the last "assault" of the transporters upon the interests of the State!

[54] *Pittsburgh Mercury and Manufacturer*, July 15, 1843.

[55] *Iron City and Pittsburgh Weekly Chronicle*, June 18, 1842.

[56] Pennsylvania *Executive Documents*, 1843 ; The *Annual Report* of Canal Commissioners for the year ending November 30, 1843, 63.

[57] The *Annual Report* of the Canal Commissioners for the year ending November 30, 1846, 7-8.

[58] The receipts of the Main Line collected at Pittsburgh: (which was one of fifteen offices) compiled from the *Annual Reports* of the Canal Commissioners, 1835-1851 :

1834-35	$16,789.93	1843-44	$45,390.30
1835-36	35,706.96	1844-45	98,270.43
1836-37	48,807.97	1845-46	88,264.41
1837-38	45,026.97	1846-47	133,953.39
1838-39	37,093.83	1847-48	117,229.25
1839-40	43,583.42	1848-49	113,148.63
1840-41	43,115.43	1849-50	146,137.08
1841-42	42,465.46	1850-51	120,407.89
1842-43	44,012.93		

of trade are recorded also year by year, and the volume of traffic
can be seen from these charts. A study of the tonnage reports shows
interesting data other than the amount of trade carried on the State
System. From the *Annual Reports* Pittsburgh's economic development can be plotted for they show which articles were imported
or exported. By noting the types of articles one can almost see Pittsburgh's development as a manufacturing and commercial center, not
only from the kinds of finished products which she exported, but also
by the classes of raw materials which she imported, and the products
which sought an outlet through her trade channels. Furthermore,
from examination of the *Annual Reports*, it is very obvious that
Pittsburgh's development as a manufacturing center was not fast
enough to meet the growing demands of the rapidly expanding western market, for the bulk of fine merchandise continued to be imported
from the East. On the other hand, the trend of specialization already
evident by 1835, and Pittsburgh's pre-eminence as a manufacturer of
iron products are noticeable.[59] Furthermore, from the tonnage records
the business trends of the period can be traced, for imports and exports
are an excellent barometer of business conditions.

The tonnage of the Pennsylvania System was not specialized to
any extent and it may be classified into three subdivisions: (1) the
extractive products, (2) the agricultural products, (3) the manufactured articles. Each class played an important role in the Pennsylvania System's history, and no one class outstripped the others.

By reference to Appendix III it will be seen that 17 different items
formed the extractive products either imported or exported to Pittsburgh. Of these, the two-way items which were carried on the Pennsylvania Canal were ashes, boards, coal, fish and oil.[60] The fish trade
was largely an East to West item and the amounts imported and
exported are not comparable. Pittsburgh was a good fish market,[61]
and in 1845 oysters appeared as a separate item having a similar
development to the fish business. Of the extractive class, ashes, boards,
oil, and coal were not important factors in the canal's tonnage, and,
except for oil, were irregular items of commerce.[62] Ashes were
neither imported nor exported until 1844, at which time and until
1848, they were listed only as an export item. In 1847, 230,300
pounds of ashes were imported into Pittsburgh, and in 1848 the
amount jumped to 2,049,053 pounds. In the freak trade year of 1849

---

[59] In comparison with the Erie Canal, however, the Pennsylvania System carried a greater
variety of commodities. U. S. *House Executive Documents*, 50 Cong., 1 Sess., no. 6,
pt. 2, 211.
[60] It is questionable as to whether or not oil should be included in this class. There is
no indication in the *Reports* as to the type of oil, and it is included here because of
its present day status.
[61] In 1835 Pittsburgh imported 9,774 barrels of fish (exported 352 barrels). In 1847
the classification changed from barrels to pounds. Pittsburgh imported 5,977,891
pounds that year, and dropped to 21,566 in 1850.
[62] See Appendix III compiled from the *Annual Reports* of the Canal Commissioners, 1835-
1851.

no listing is recorded,[63] while in 1850 the amount shipped to the East dropped drastically and the imports reached 6,665,500 pounds.

From these figures, the Pennsylvania System evidently was not very important in the earlier years as a carrier of raw materials to the Pittsburgh glass manufacturers. Ashes for the making of glass were supplied from the lower Ohio Valley and from the northwest area of Pennsylvania, and while the supply was adequate for Pittsburgh, there was not much of a surplus for re-export. However, by 1845 glass manufacturing had so expanded that it needed more raw material than could be supplied locally and thus the increased shipments of ashes from the East. The shipments of boards were irregular and no definite trend can be noted; nor is it possible to indicate which route had the larger trade. At first, the exports from Pittsburgh were heavier than the imports, but in the later years of the period the reverse is true. Pittsburgh's "inexhaustible" supply had either decreased, was needed at home, or had found a better outlet. Nor was the Pennsylvania System a coal outlet for western Pennsylvania, for the amounts carried upon the State System were unbelievably small. Bituminous coal did not affect the traffic in the least, for it was not needed in the East, and by 1835, when the State System was opened, western Pennsylvania coal had already found a satisfactory market in the Ohio and Mississippi valleys.

The only items of the extractive class shipped exclusively to the East from the Pittsburgh area were furs and peltry. In 1845 the classification of deer and buffalo skins appeared separately in the reports; and if these items are included in the total amounts of furs and peltry, this trade may be said to have increased decidedly, but if they are not included, the trade was a decreasing one.[64] In 1835 furs and peltry shipped amounted to 277,070 pounds, while in 1850 the amount had dropped to 183,137 pounds. Deer and buffalo skins shipped in the same year amounted to 1,072,561 pounds, or a combined trade of 1,255,698 pounds. Pittsburgh was one of the outlets for the furs of the new West, although the actual business, so far as the trapping was concerned, was far removed from the Pittsburgh area. Thus the fur trade was significant only as a toll item passing through Pittsburgh because the Pennsylvania System was a satisfactory route, and because Pittsburgh had products which the new West needed.

The extractive articles shipped exclusively to Pittsburgh were salt, potash, gypsum, mahogany, slate, stone, wood (and bark), timber, marble, posts and rails.[65] Salt was the most important of these items;

---

[63] In 1849 the Ohio River was extremely low and conditions were further aggravated by a cholera epidemic in the entire Mississippi Valley.
[64] See Appendix III.
[65] See Appendix III compiled from the *Annual Reports.* In the chart iron ore is listed, but it is unimportant and, as it was shipped only on two isolated occasions, it is not mentioned here; Pittsburgh used pigs and blooms, see Appendix III.

and in 1835 the salt shipped to Pittsburgh amounted to 215,352 bushels, while the amounts for 1850 dropped to 128,225 bushels. This trade fluctuated from year to year; and although 1850 showed a decrease, 1849 was the peak year in the salt trade, the amount shipped being 495,324 bushels. The salt industry evidently was not solely dependent on Pittsburgh, and the amount sent there was for home consumption; the eastern markets were supplied directly from the salt works. Marble was imported into Pittsburgh in large quantities; and the trade, while it shows decided decreases in depression years, had a steady growth reaching 1,147,200 pounds by 1850.[66] Gypsum was shipped to Pittsburgh in varying small quantities until 1848, at which time it changed routes or may have been included under the heading of "sundries."[67] Stone, potash and mahogany do not appear in the *Annual Reports* until 1844, at least, not as separate items, and only then as articles of minor importance. An interesting sidelight concerns the item of mahogany. Pittsburgh by 1844 had evidently reached the stage in production where fine products were manufactured and marketable. In 1844 there were 74,693 pounds imported, but, from that time on, the decrease was appreciable.[68] Timber was not imporant as an article of trade from the East and the shipments were irregular and small; the Pittsburgh market did not rely on the Canal for its supply. Slate, however, showed a definite increase, for in 1838 the amount shipped to Pittsburgh was 3,500 bushels, while in 1850 the amount reached 770,200 bushels. The peak year was 1846, because Pittsburgh was a good market for building products that year, as well as in 1845, due to the great fire which necessitated extensive rebuilding. During those years slate imports tripled. Wood, bark, posts, and rails were articles of minor importance.

Thus, it may be concluded that extractive articles were not the mainstay of the Pennsylvania System's tonnage. In fact, this class which should have been valuable, especially as far as the eastward trade was concerned, was not even paying its way. Pittsburgh by 1835 had ceased to be a frontier settlement, but with her extensive trade ramifications and decidedly improved feeders as well as improved main avenues of trade, she might have been expected to make a better showing. The only explanation is that the Pennsylvania State System was not the *best route*, nor Philadelphia the best market, for these out-of-state products. On the other hand, it may be concluded that Pittsburgh, in her own right, was a growing market for raw materials for her own manufactures, and instead of sending the surplus east-

---

[66] See Appendix III compiled from the *Annual Reports*.
[67] The items included in the *Annual Reports* vary from year to year and it is difficult to say definitely whether minor articles ceased to be carried or merely lost their identity in reclassification.
[68] Except for 1846 at which time 50,532 pounds were imported, otherwise, the drop was definite.

ward, much of it was converted into a finished product to be marketed in a more profitable form.

The Pennsylvania System was an important carrier of agricultural products and provisions. While the majority of toll squabbles arose over the rates charged on this class of freight, agricultural products were absolutely necessary for the State System, as well as any other east-to-west route. Agricultural products, as well as provisions, were handicapped considerably by their very nature, being bulky and comparatively cheap, and unable to support a large tax in the form of carrying charges. But they were important if trade was to be maintained between the industrial sections and the frontier. The Pennsylvania System was not buit in time to help Pittsburgh through her agricultural stage but the improvement did help to develop Pittsburgh as a commercial center for the new West. Furthermore, the more mature southwest found the Philadelphia and Baltimore markets more desirable and steady than the unreliable New Orleans market, which had helped to make and, at the same time, to ruin so many Pittsburgh merchants. While the Pennsylvania System never carried as much agricultural products as its more successful rival, the Erie Canal, it did manage to command a certain amount of trade, principally because of its location, because it was a safer route than the Ohio River, and above all, because New Orleans was no longer a satisfactory market for agricultural products and provisions, especially if any eastern alternative were available.

Thirteen specific items and two general classifications make up the tonnage of the agricultural products and provisions.[69] Of these items, clover (and other grass and seeds), corn,[70] cotton, hemp, potatoes, and wheat were two-way trade articles, but all had a decidedly larger eastern trade with the exception of hemp and potatoes. Hemp was imported in large amounts up to 1838, and although it was also exported, a balance was never struck. In 1842, however, the tables were turned, and the amounts shipped from Pittsburgh far exceeded the amount imported, the peak year being 1847 when 3,204,110 pounds were shipped to the East.[71] Potatoes were only of minor importance in the System's traffic, being an imported article, and never exceeded the 1837 tonnage of 5,323 bushels. City life by 1850 had not yet developed to the extent that it was impossible to supply the table needs from one's own garden, or from the surrounding farms. Food products were still largely supplied by each local unit and had not yet begun to form a long-distance item of commerce. Grains, however, could not be grown in sufficient amounts in all areas and did

---

[69] See Appendix III compiled from the *Annual Reports*.
[70] Used in the English sense, and including all other grains, except wheat.
[71] Hemp exported:

1835	4,443 pounds	1845	865,444 pounds
1840	22,859 pounds	1850	809,528 pounds

form a trade item. Corn, up to 1848, was exported in increasing quantities, while the amounts imported by Pittsburgh never reached large proportions.[72]

Wheat, although the amount exported in 1836 reached the high total of 1,427,247 bushels, varied greatly in amounts, and, except for a few scattered years, never really formed a reliable trade item. The grain trade of the new West found the Erie Canal and New York more favorable than the Pennsylvania System and Philadelphia; this proved to be a sad disappointment to the advocates of the Pennsylvania System and also contributed to its undoing. The same is true of the flour trade, as will be shown later. The two items are under different classifications but they are complementary and their development was similar. In this connection it is necessary to note that in 1844, when the classification of tonnage was rearranged, other grains may have been included under the heading of "agricultural products" even though corn and wheat continued to be carried separately. Clover and other grain seeds were irregular and not significant as articles of trade. Cotton, however, which was both regular and valuable, was one of the products which found the State System a satisfactory outlet. Although not a product of the Pittsburgh area, cotton continued to be carried over that route in large quantities.[73] The more northern cotton areas found the eastern market more advantageous than New Orleans, and the increased cost of transportation was off-set by the higher prices offered in the East. The cotton trade, however, was affected by river conditions and in 1839 when the Ohio was exceptionally low, the the amount shipped eastward was only three hundred pounds while the imports reached 5,689 pounds; again in 1849, when the river was low and conditions were further aggravated by cholera, the trade dropped from its 1848 level of 1,679,428 pounds to 589,513 pounds. In the 15-year period under consideration the cotton trade grew from a mere 16,626 pounds in 1835 to 1,084,600 pounds in 1850.[74] The cotton imported into Pittsburgh by way of the Pennsylvania System was insignificant.

Thus in reality this two-way trade, with the exception of hemp, may almost be considered as one-way so far as volume is concerned. The reason for classifying it as two-way is to secure technically accurate statistics and to indicate that Pittsburgh was a depot for western products. Pittsburgh was not an importer of agricultural products by way of the Pennsylvania Canal but rather a distributor of products gathered from other agricultural areas.

---

[72] See Appendix III. The amounts imported into Pittsburgh in the years 1838, 1840, 1849, and 1850 exceeded the exports.
[73] The State System never offered serious competition to New Orleans for the cotton culture was expanding, the demand was general, and there were sufficient amounts for many outlets.
[74] See Appendix III, for intervening years.

The articles shipped almost exclusively from Pittsburgh were bacon, butter and cheese, feathers, lard and tallow, salted beef and pork, and wool. These items were large in volume and formed a regular and reliable trade.[75] Bacon formed the largest single item in this classification; the amounts shipped increased yearly, during good and bad trade seasons alike and seemingly were undisturbed by local conditions. In 1835 a total of 5,249,639 pounds of bacon was shipped eastward; in 1840 the total amount exported increased to 7,203,177 pounds; in 1845 the tonnage reached 15,155,344 pounds; in 1850 the sum was 38,956,065 pounds.[76] Lard and tallow, while never so large as the bacon shipments, were not items to be overlooked for they increased rapidly until 1850.[77] Thus, it may be concluded that the East, and Baltimore in particular, was a favorable market for provisions, and that Pittsburgh had extensive trade connections with Cincinnati, the "porkopolis" of the West.[78] Salted beef and pork, as trade items, never reached the high levels of bacon exports; nor can the growth be noted with regularity. The trade was spasmodic and variable, and the Pennsylvania System did nothing more than scratch the surface of this traffic. Up to 1846 the *Annual Reports* carried the heading of "Provisions not specified" on articles not enumerated, and the volume was significant and growing and should not be overlooked in an analysis of this trade, for the real increase of provisions would not be complete without its total.

Butter and cheese complete the provisions shipped to the East and the amounts were large. A study of Pittsburgh's western trade connections reveals that Pittsburgh drew these items from the old northwest region, as well as from the areas West and South.[79]

Feathers were shipped to the East regularly and in varying quantities. The amounts exported were never so large as the provisions, but this trade may be described as regular and expanding slowly. When compared with the importation of wool, however, the above article is not so important as a trade item. Wool had its local origin in Washington County especially, as well as being an important article which merely passed through Pittsburgh. The volume exported increased from 988,205 pounds in 1835 to 4,586,432 pounds in 1850.[80]

Agricultural products and provisions were basically exported articles on the Pennsylvania State System. It is significant to note the variety and volume of the articles drawn to Pittsburgh by virtue of its being the western terminus of the canal, for every pound of

---

[75] See Appendix III, compiled from the *Annual Reports*.
[76] See Appendix III, for intervening years.
[77] Lard and tallow amounted to 408,576 pounds in 1835 and reached the highest level in 1849, when 5,382,854 pounds were shipped eastward. In 1850 the total dropped to 580,622 pounds.
[78] From a study of the Ohio River trade this fact is definitely established. See Chapter III.
[79] Butter and cheese shipped eastward. See Appendix III.

1835	30,452 pounds	1845	1,126,750 pounds
1840	393,336 pounds	1850	2,674,185 pounds

[80] See Appendix III, for intervening years.

bacon and every bale of cotton helped to develop Pittsburgh as a commercial center. If raw materials were shipped from a particular area, *something* undoubtedly was returned in comparable amounts. That *something* may have been the product of Pittsburgh, or an article imported, but in either case, Pittsburgh received the commercial benefit. Agricultural products, as a class, were the bulwark of the western trade; and although the agitation of western interests for toll reductions was loud and chorus-like, the West profited greatly by its creation, whether or not they liked the rates.

The true picture of the commerce of the Pennsylvania System is seen only when the manufactured articles are studied. The Pennsylvania route may have been built to carry the western goods to the East, but eastern merchants, particularly those of Philadelphia, might well be said to have built the System for the transportation of eastern merchandise to the West. By 1846 the Pennsylvania Improvement supplied the Ohio basin with more manufactured goods than the Mississippi River.[81] Western editors might rant and scold for the lack of appreciation of home manufactures, but nevertheless, the amounts imported increased yearly. A hasty glance at Appendix III will show that the trade was largely a two-way trade, but that the volume of the exports was ridiculously small in most cases. Twenty-eight individual items and two general headings appeared under the class of manufactured articles,[82] none of which was shipped eastward exclusively, although flour and window glass might be considered as one-way trade because the imports of these were almost negligible.[83]

The quantity of flour shipped to the East *via* the Pennsylvania System was large, and the trade increased by leaps and bounds except in years of depression. In these periods of business upset, the flour trade, like all the other items of trade,[84] was affected, but the comeback was immediate and the increase in the following year covered the losses of the preceding one.[85] In 1847 the huge increase was due to the famines in Europe and the gains were only temporary. The American flour market boomed that year, for grain of all kinds was at a

---

[81] U. S. *House Ex. Docs.*, 50 Cong., 1 Sess., no. 6, pt. 2, 211.
[82] See Appendix III, compiled from the *Annual Reports*.
[83] After 1844 "bagging" was listed and shipped exclusively to the East—but it was only a minor trade article.
[84] Except for the panic year of 1837; in that year the flour trade actually increased by 25,949 barrels; and although the prices received for flour dropped considerably, the additional shipment tended to offset the losses.
[85] Barrels of flour shipped to and from Pittsburgh, 1835-1850:

	To	From		To	From
1835	7	37,515	1843		130,858
1836		45,587	1844		100,454
1837		71,536	1845	139	82,092
1838		101,725	1846	316	156,412
1839		55,229	1847	1,279	297,944
1840	47	139,637	1848	396	182,527
1841		109,878	1849		139,203
1842		114,103½	1850	4,295	121,319

premium and speculation resulted with the inevitable repercussions. The Pennsylvania System in 1847 was sorely taxed to transport the supply to the East, because transportation facilities of the day were not elastic enough to meet the unexpected sudden increase in demand. The State System supplanted the Ohio River as the favorite flour outlet for the Pittsburgh area, because the flour was less likely to spoil and the barrels were in better condition at the end of the route. Furthermore, the eastern terminus was superseding New Orleans as a flour port because of its nearness to the European market, better warehousing and credit facilities, and a better climate.[86] Trade was beginning to take on a specializing aspect. Conditions in transportation had improved also to the extent that the exporter had something of a choice in selecting markets, and he was not forced by necessity to accept one route or one market. In addition, the paternalistic policy of the Canal Commissioners favored flour, and a system of drawbacks went into effect in 1840 which aided the trade considerably.[87] Despite this concession, the Pennsylvania Canal was not the principal flour outlet of the West.[88] The Erie Canal claimed this honor because it commanded the larger part of the lake traffic and the surrounding flour exporting region, and also because New York, in comparison to Philadelphia, was the better flour port. But, nevertheless, the Pennsylvania Canal did carry her share.

Window glass as an export product was never exceptionally large, but the mere fact that glass was exported is significant, for it shows that Pittsburgh manufacturers were competing in the eastern markets and that Pittsburgh had a surplus to send to the East after supplying her western markets.[89] The shipments of window glass increased until 1844, at which time a decided decrease set in, and after 1848 the item was no longer listed separately.[90]

Of the two-way trade, dry goods, groceries, coffee, furniture, hardware, shoes and hats, which were included in the eastern merchandise, were by far the heaviest and most valuable articles of commerce. This class of tonnage paid the largest tolls, and while it was technically a two-way trade, the balance was always in favor of the East. From 1835 to 1844 the separate listings in the *Annual Reports* included only furniture, groceries, and merchandise, but in 1844 separate items appeared for coffee, hardware, glassware, earthenware, muslin, and dry goods, and in 1846 hats and shoes were grouped separately. No

[86] *Pittsburgh Gazette,* January 28, 1825.
[87] Pennsylvania *House Journal,* III, 1841; The *Annual Report* of the Canal Commissioners for the year ending October 31, 1840, 8. A drawback of 20 cents per barrel was allowed on flour shipped from Pittsburgh and carried the entire distance on the Improvement to Philadelphia.
[88] U. S. *House Ex. Docs.,* 50 Cong., 1 Sess., no. 6, pt. 2, 211.
[89] *Pittsburgh Gazette,* December 11, 1833, two merchants alone imported 3,300 boxes of glass from Pittsburgh for the Detroit and Buffalo markets.
[90] It is probable that window glass may have been included under the heading "glassware."

explanation is given as to what was included in the general term merchandise, but it appears from the later classification that *merchandise* before 1845 meant dry goods, hats, shoes, earthenware, hardware and possibly glassware. In 1844 the term was dropped from the *Reports* and only the individual items were listed; this was probably due to the fact that the amounts had increased sufficiently to be considered individually significant. For purpose of comparison the totals of these articles will be given the general name of merchandise, but it will be necessary to keep in mind that there was a change in the official classification in 1844, and that there is no absolute proof as to what the term merchandise previous to 1844 really did include.[91]

Merchandise shipped to Pittsburgh in 1835 was the largest item in any class carried over the State System, amounting to 30,280,506 pounds. In 1840 the amount dropped to 15,638,200 pounds. During the next five years the recovery was rapid and in 1845 the total amount imported reached 38,498,926 pounds. In 1850 the amount imported jumped to 48,460,228 pounds.[92] Business cycles were accurately reflected in this traffic. The West was a powerful and potential market, but due to the fact that cash was needed to pay the balance to the East, the numerous financial upheavals of the period were hard on such luxury trade articles. The eastern trade articles might be compared with the status of fine imported woolens or linens of today, and the struggling manufacturers of the frontier, or the one-step-removed frontier, were none too happy to find their people so addicted to these ruinous luxuries. Although Pittsburgh editors lamented the disastrous effects of the import trade and urged their readers to patronize local manufacturers, the trade continued to increase. Not all merchandise, however, was intended for Pittsburgh, but the huge pile of boxes and crates being exported to the West constantly irritated Pittsburgh

[91] A writer in the *Pittsburgh Gazette*, February 2, 1846, compared dry goods of the later classifications with the entire total of merchandise, but it appears that "Eastern merchandise" included all eastern manufactures and newspaper editors spoke of eastern merchandise and Pittsburgh manufactured articles in the same breath.

[92] Chart showing merchandise (pounds) shipped to Pittsburgh, 1835-1850:

	Dry Goods & Muslin	Earthenware Chinaware	Glassware	Hardware	Hats & Shoes	Merchandise
1835						30,280,506
1836						20,394,638
1837						14,932,410
1838						30,821,331
1839						15,638,200
1840						
1841		2,678,165		4,505,555		18,547,603*
1842		1,080,175		2,324,519		14,540,412*
1843						28,368,868
1844	29,758,319	4,565,005	57,988	8,417,359		42,798,671**
1845	23,173,694	4,648,235	95,598	10,581,399		38,498,926
1846	16,621,052	4,957,454	121,951	10,522,463	2,049,540***	34,272,460
1847	23,201,074	8,400	69,533	14,501,693	2,690,881	40,471,581
1848	25,299,444	7,800	17,400	11,530,579	3,338,191	40,243,414
1849	25,166,708		18,600	10,307,464	3,378,584	38,871,356
1850	29,516,843		41,700	14,681,335	4,220,350	48,460,228

* Totals did not include earthenware and hardware.
** Totals from 1844 to 1850 arrived at by adding single items.
*** Classed with dry goods before 1846.

merchants and manufacturers and forcibly reminded them that it might have been their products. For, as Wheeling said, Pittsburgh liked to have her finger in every and any pie! It is true that Pittsburgh exported a small amount of merchandise, but the balance was against her.

The amount of furniture imported was large and increasing. As the frontier dropped its homespun, a demand arose for better home furnishings, and as civilization became more complex the simple wants disappeared, and people were no longer satisfied with bare subsistence. Furniture imported into the Pittsburgh area rose from 258,202 pounds in 1835 to its highest level in 1847 of 1,390,767 pounds. In 1850 the drop was drastic, and only 680,400 pounds were listed.[93]

The grocery tonnage exceeded the furniture volume of traffic, and, likewise, the amount of groceries shipped from the East was greater than the amount sent from the West. But the puzzling angle is that the total grocery tonnage exported from Pittsburgh was by no means insignificant. The only explanation is that "Groceries-East" did not mean the same thing as "Groceries-West." The imported and fine staples were shipped to Pittsburgh, and coffee, dried fruits of all kinds, dried beans and peas, cereals, and sugar were the types of groceries shipped to the East.[94] After 1844 coffee was listed separately and it was shipped both ways over the System, the imports, however, being larger.[95]

The Pennsylvania System might well have been built for the transportation of eastern merchandise, but the iron interests anticipated, and later found it to be, a virtual life saver.[96] A local improvement would have been adequate to bring the needed supplies to Pittsburgh, but the undertaking was too costly for the iron interests to carry, and so they were forced to use the old expensive channels. Much of the iron was transported from forges east of Johnstown to Pittsburgh, but the articles exported directly from the forges to the East found a growing market, and the iron trade increased rapidly. The iron trade was one

[93] Pittsburgh exported in 1850, 352,505 pounds of furniture. This was not the largest amount shipped eastward however, for in the peak year of 1842 furniture exports reached 446,820 pounds.

[94] Groceries shipped from Pittsburgh and to Pittsburgh in pounds, 1835-1850:

	From	To		From	To
1835....	696,917	4,877,686	1843.....	1,357,836	4,445,705
1836....	158,540	Not listed	1844.....	1,379,780	5,108,266
1837....	403,972	6,512,188	1845.....	1,063,472	5,118,460
1838....	315,680	7,456,634	1846.....	1,571,889	6,933,856
1839....	525,524	10,813,116	1847.....	1,978,822	7,833,925
1840....	678,612	9,345,638	1848.....	4,109,086	8,506,898
1841....	954,777	11,104,818	1849.....	3,471,385	9,180,396
1842....	1,263,006	4,952,577	1850.....	2,757,817	10,752,036

[95] Pittsburgh Gazette, August 6, 1847. The editor questioned the correctness of the amount of coffee shipped to Pittsburgh. He complained that nearly one tenth of all coffee imported into the United States in 1846 must have been shipped along the Pennsylvania Canal "or other goods were shipped as coffee."

[96] Ibid., March 11, 1825. The Gazette reported in 1825 that transportation charges on iron to Pittsburgh ranged from $16 to $20 per ton. If a canal were built, iron could be transported from the Juniata at $3.00 per ton.

phase of Canal commerce which exceeded the eastern shipments and the amounts shipped each way are not comparable. Pittsburgh's rate of development as an iron manufacturer may be seen by glancing at the amount of iron sent to and from Pittsburgh:[97]

	PIGS AND CASTINGS		IRON, BLOOMS AND SHEET	
	FROM	To	FROM	To
1835	1,070,733	1,079,132	2,997,478	22,428,098
1836	337,683	Not listed	176,557	Not listed
1837	366,715	1,132,738	816,441	25,425,868
1838	409,814	1,193,312	1,880,357	15,172,607
1839	449,127	872,786	585,237	32,958,817
1840	709,127	601,091	1,658,261	20,953,244
1841	Not listed	Not listed	Not listed	22,468,706
1842	Not listed	Not listed	Not listed	14,106,698
1843	1,447,090	2,473,505	2,426,047	22,793,704
1844	2,646,167	5,094,724	778,840	18,824,166
1845	3,956,728	7,374,738	Not listed	15,332,782
1846	2,675,341	15,410,966	319,736	13,890,707
1847	316,447	22,104,015	563,252	19,339,658
1848	3,479,703	26,159,481	544,782	18,191,782
1849	187,240	21,957,567	242,349	14,466,504
1850	4,104,542	23,879,968	5,458,000	15,862,482

Iron and nails were listed separately after 1844, and steel was first listed in 1846.[98]

Tobacco formed a two-way trade on the State System but, like iron, was predominantly an export product. It is questionable whether tobacco should be included under the heading of manufactured articles, for the largest part of the trade was in leaf tobacco. The shipments eastward were largely leaf, while those shipped westward were of a manufactured type; but for convenience, and because the *Annual Reports* make no distinction until 1844, all tobacco has been grouped together. Tobacco, like cotton, found the eastern market more advantageous; and consequently, the Pennsylvania Improvement and Pittsburgh were benefited by its custom.[99]

Leather and raw hides were imported into Pittsburgh in larger amounts than were exported and the trade increased substantially. From the nature of things one would expect the reverse to be true, but instead of exporting leather the Pittsburgh area relied on the Canal instead of furnishing a surplus.[100] Drugs and dyestuffs, which included paint, were two-way products, but were imported in larger amounts.

[97] Compiled from the *Annual Reports*.

[98]
Steel		From Pittsburgh	To Pittsburgh
1846		13,369	197,171
1847		10,870	169,500
1848		Not listed	138,900
1849		Not listed	42,400
1850		6,156	94,000

[99] U. S. *House Ex. Docs.*, 50 Cong., 1 Sess., no. 6, pt. 2, 211.
[100] See Appendix III, compiled from the *Annual Reports*.

Rags which, in earlier days, had been so urgently needed, were exported, although a few irregular entries from the East appear in the *Annual Reports*. Whiskey and domestic spirits were shipped to the East, and foreign liquors were imported *via* the State System, both in large amounts. In 1835 whiskey exports amounted to 45,937 gallons; in 1840 the amount was 66,666 gallons; in 1845 the export total reached 112,841 gallons; and in 1850 the total was 457,217 gallons. The imports of foreign liquors never reached the high level of the exports.[101] The Pennsylvania Canal was not the only outlet for Pittsburgh whiskey but it did lay claim to a significant part. Copper, tin, and lead were regular import items, and while the amounts carried were never very large, they must be mentioned as trade items. Tar, pitch, rosin, shingles, and staves were also trade items, both imported and exported, but they were items which never played a decisive role one way or the other. Under the heading of sundries, a large amount of freight was shipped both East and West, but these articles had no importance at this time, except as toll items.[102]

Thus, it would appear that the Pennsylvania State System carried a great amount of traffic and that the enterprise was a success. But the company ledgers record the contrary and the difference becomes apparent when one considers the upkeep and the expense. The Pennsylvania System made money, but more money was spent on enlargements, branch canals, and upkeep than should have been spent to make the System a financial success. However, no one factor alone was responsible for its failure, but rather it was due to a combination of factors which worked unconsciously, and yet steadily, to ruin the System. The underlying cause appears to be the fact that the physical character of the State Works prevented it from being efficient and cheap. The complicated system of railroads and canals necessitated too many transfers and involved too much stock and equipment. Both time and money were wasted, and yet no one person could be blamed, nor was it possible to do much to alter the situation.[103] The cost of repairs was a constant problem to the Canal Commissioners.[104] Floods would tear out the canal banks, overflow the towpath, and wash debris into the canal bed. Frost spread the rails and tore loose the sleepers. The ropes on the incline planes had to be replaced frequently, and the stationary engines and locomotives broke down. Every year brought

---

[101] See Appendix III, compiled from the *Annual Reports*.
[102] See Appendix III, compiled from the *Annual Reports*.
[103] The portable boat system came closer to removing the difficulty than any other remedy, but the mountains still remained an expensive obstacle.
[104] The Canal Commissioners listed two types of repairs: (1) ordinary repairs which rose from the natural dilapidation or decay of the materials used in construction, (2) extraordinary repairs resulting from "peculiar and unexpected combinations of the natural elements." The Pennsylvania *Senate Journal*, 1836-37, Appendix to Volume II; The *Annual Report* of Canal Commissioners for the year ending October 31, 1836, 9-10. The *Annual Reports* record that one or the other, or both usually constituted a large item.

new expenditures along with the old ones. For example, in 1836 the
cost of repairs to the Portage-Allegheny Railroad alone amounted to
$23,923.24. This report has been picked at random, but it does
not differ radically from any other report. The superintendent
explained:[105]

As the sum which has been required to keep the road in repair this season is
somewhat greater than had been previously estimated, I beg leave here to make
a few remarks touching this matter. . . . From the very commencement of the
spring business I had many difficulties to contend with, and it sometimes appeared almost impossible to prevent a temporary suspension of business upon
the road. In order to put the road in a condition to accommodate the opening
spring trade, I was compelled to have the snow and ice removed from those parts
of the road which lay on the northern side of the hills which left no time for
repairing the road, in many places, until a brisk business had commenced. The
frost during the last winter, having penetrated to an unusual depth and many
of the through cuts and side cuts . . . having been left with steep banks. When
the ground thawed in the spring immense quantities of earth were detached
from the bank and fell into the bed of the road. The ditches or side drains,
too, were nearly all filled, which caused the road to be flooded, and saturated
with water during every fall of rain, and consequently, to be much injured. At
this time an extensive business had commenced and the road began to spread in
many places, until the cars would fall in between the tracks. The great demand
for labor this season, and the scarcity of hands, not only compelled me to increase the wages, but also to employ nearly every description of hands that
offered, and still was unable to procure a sufficient force, in the early part of the
season, to do the amount of work the public interest required.

Furthermore, the State suffered because individuals usually charged
top prices for State purchases. Individuals evidently assumed that the
State had plenty of money and could afford to pay. The various
superintendents reported time and time again that the charges were
extravagant, but, nevertheless, the practice continued.[106] Another item
of expense resulted because the railroads were in the experimental stage
and not well understood. Changes and improvements were being added
regularly, but the trial and error method was costly.

Short seasons of navigation also reduced the expected revenue, for
the Pennsylvania State System rarely was able to open when the Canal
Commissioners predicted. Long winters delayed the spring opening;
a mild winter and an early opening was occasional rather than cus-

---

[105] Pennsylvania *Senate Journal*, 1836-37, Appendix to Volume II; the *Annual Report*
of Canal Commissioners for year ending October 31, 1836, 70.
[106] *Annual Reports* of the Canal Commissioners, 1846-48, 6. "The repairs upon the
road (Philadelphia and Columbia) have been more than ordinarily expensive during
the past season, owing to the rapid wear of the rails, and the heavy burdens carried
over it. It has been found necessary to insert forty tons of new rail, which cost,
at the works at Danville eighty dollars per ton. When it was ascertained by the
Board that this price was demanded for the new rails, they would have deferred
ordering them at the time, indulging the hope that they might be subsequently obtained at a lower rate; but the condition of the road, and the absolute necessity of
immediately supplying the place of old rails with new ones, on many parts of it, to
maintain it in order for transporting freight and passengers safely, left the Board
no alternative but to direct the superintendent to make the purchase at what they
considered an extravagant price."

tomary.[107] Furthermore, the various sections opened at different times; and even if one section did have an early opening, East and West traffic could not pass until the entire route was open. The goods were jammed and delayed along the way. Seasons were frequently interrupted by drought and by floods, both of which disrupted trade. In 1838 sufficient water levels could not be maintained in the Western Division to pass freight boats and goods were detained at Johnstown.[108] In 1841 low water on the upper Ohio River also diverted trade from the Pennsylvania System.[109] Certain years were especially bad, but even in the normal year of 1837 navigation was suspended for 132 days for various reasons.[110]

Another reason which goes a long way to explain why the system failed was because of the fact that the Pennsylvania Improvement gradually developed into a political issue. Branch canals were built to satisfy dissenting constituents, and they hung like leeches upon the Main Line. The Pennsylvania System would probably have made expenses had it not been forced to carry the expense of these feeders. As early as 1836 the Canal Commissioners partially realized this fact for they pointed out that the revenue derived from the Main Line:[111]

. . . will be found almost adequate to the payment of the interest on the cost of construction, the repairs and supervision. The branch canals, in which is involved a large expenditure, are comparatively unproductive; and must, in their interest, repairs and supervision, remain a charge upon the main line, until the original design in their projection is carried out.

But the Canal Commissioners were confirmed optimists and they always hoped for the best, which in many instances would have required a miracle. Branch canals continued to be authorized and built.

Politics also entered into other aspects of the System. The original costs were exorbitant and it has been said, "that no possible chance

---

[107] Chart compiled from the *Annual Reports* for the date of the opening of Western Division :

1834—March	8	1843—May	7
1835—March	15	1844—March	14
1836—April	1	1845—March	10
1837—March	20	1846—March	23
1838—March	27	1847—March	15
1839—March	26	1848—March	20
1840—March	16	1849—March	25
1841—March	27	1850—March	20
1842—March	7		

[108] Pennsylvania *House Journal*, 1838, III ; The *Annual Report* of the Canal Commissioners for the year ending October 31, 1838, 11.
[109] Pennsylvania *Senate Journal*, 1842 ; The *Annual Report* of the Canal Commissioners for the year ending October 31, 1842, 40. After 1842, however, this situation was remedied by the new light draught steamers, which had a capacity of forty or fifty tons and which were used extensively for freight. Pennsylvania *House Journal*, 1843, II ; The *Annual Report* of the Canal Commissioners for the year ending November 30, 1843, 112.
[110] Pennsylvania *House Journal*, 1837 ; The *Annual Report* of the Canal Commissioners for the year ending October 31, 1837, 26.
     December 3—March—106 Days ice ; June 16-20, 4 Days Breach
     April 5-6, 1 Day Breach ; July 1-7, 6 Days High Water
     May 16-17, ¾ Day Breach ; September 18-22, 4 Days Breach
[111] Pennsylvania *Senate Journal*, 1836-37, Appendix to Volume II ; The *Annual Report* of Canal Commissioners for year ending October 31, 1836, 5.

to defraud the public seems to have been overlooked."[112] Appointments to positions were filled with an eye to party loyalty.[113]

Not only were the politicians finding the spoils easy, but the people themselves made exorbitant claims for damages and relief. The *Journals* of the Canal Commissioners are filled with page after page of petitions,[114] and after reading them one is apt to think that the State System was a thing of corruption and evil.

Nevertheless, despite these handicaps, the Pennsylvania State System was a step in the development of transportation; expensive and intricate, it is true, but still a positive benefit to Western Pennsylvania. Towns and industries alike were stimulated; and even if the ledgers do not balance, the indirect results were permanent and rewarding. Pittsburgh's trade area was extended considerably and her commercial status was strengthened as her trade arteries were improved. The Pennsylvania State System was a strong spoke in Pittsburgh's giant wheel.

[112] Bishop Avard L. "Corrupt Practices Connected with the Building and Operation of the State Works of Pennsylvania," from the *Yale Review,* Vol. 15, (February, 1907), 407.
[113] Manuscripts in Public Records Division, Pennsylvania Historical and Museum Commission. For example, one letter to Governor Porter stated:
"We the undersigned Democratic citizens of the city and county of Philadelphia being firmly in person with the belief that the Eastern part of the State should be ably represented in the Board of Canal Commissioners. Take great pleasure in recommending to your Excellency's notice our worthy and esteemed friend and citizen Dr. John Weintselman. As a tried and consistent Democrat and a warm and active friend of the late Democratic contest. And a devoted friend of the General Administration. His acquirements and experience being general will fit him peculiarly for the Situation we solicit for him and will meet with the general approbation of your democratic friends."
[114] Pennsylvania *Senate Journal,* 1835; The *Annual Report* for the Canal Commissioners for the year ending October 31, 1835, III. A single example is included:
"Resolved unanimously, That the claim of George Fisher ought not to be allowed; because, in the opinion of the Board, the advantages derived by him from the canal are a sufficient compensation for any injury he may have sustained. He is the owner of several valuable estates on and contiguous to the canal, which have been made more valuable by the improvements; and the sum of $2,030 has already been paid to him for the injury to his property in Dauphin County by the construction of the Canal."

VII

Subsidiary Trade and Commercial Arteries

WHILE PITTSBURGH merchants were concentrating money and energy on the improvement of their eastern arteries of trade, Ohio merchants were also struggling to improve their eastern connections—and Pittsburgh lay in that line of vision. Neither one was able to capitalize on this fortunate location until Pittsburgh began to manufacture her own products, because all towns west of the mountains had too many local economic difficulties to be mutually helpful. Pittsburgh, like Ohio, sought a favorable balance of trade; she needed either purchasers with available specie, or producers who could cheaply supply the much needed manufactured products. Pittsburgh's western trade, aside from the Ohio River commerce, developed gradually and elicited no particular concern from anyone in Pittsburgh. Merchants did not willfully neglect their western neighbors; they merely overlooked them for more important trade. Furthermore, much of the Pittsburgh commerce that was destined for Ohio, Indiana, and Illinois lost its identity in the larger Ohio River traffic. Towns of northern Ohio on Lake Erie, such as Cleveland, Sandusky, and Toledo, as well as Detroit and smaller ports of Michigan, had a comparatively easy approach by way of the lake to New York as their market, therefore, they were not interested in Pittsburgh.[1] Ohio merchants were as interested in their own welfare as were Pittsburgh merchants, and until Pittsburgh had something definite to offer, Ohio merchants used other markets or did without the product entirely. Merchants from Steubenville, Zanesville and other towns of the northwest had frequently traveled through Pittsburgh on their way to the East; occasionally they stopped in Pittsburgh, disposed of their goods and bought supplies. Gradually, Pittsburgh merchants began to see them as desirable customers, but the difficulty lay in the fact that their trade had to be carried overland.

The few roads that did exist between Pittsburgh and Ohio were no better than the roads to the East.[2] Freight rates to Ohio were high and just as prohibitive. But, despite the handicaps, the Ohioans' needs for manufactured articles were greater, and as one-way freight never paid dividends, Ohio products had to be taken in exchange in Pittsburgh. Advertisements in the *Cleveland Herald* indicated that Pitts-

---

[1] Kohlmeier, *The Old Northwest*, 8.
[2] Even as late as 1821 the *Cleveland Herald*, February 27, 1821, was issued on a smaller sheet of paper "in consequence of the badness of the roads preventing the arrival of paper."

burgh was supplying Cleveland merchants with tools, agricultural implements, glassware, paper, tinware, and utensils. One advertisement
raised a doubt as to the amount of stock for it read:[3] "Nathan Perry
has just received one small box of tinware from Pittsburgh assorted,
which makes his assortment *more* complete than any others within
one hundred miles of this place."

After the feeble Pittsburgh and Ohio trade had begun, the building
of the Erie Canal almost obliterated it completely. Pittsburgh could
not compete with New York City and the seaboard in general, nor
could even Philadelphia compete against the reduced rates offered by
New York.[4] In Ohio the price of salt, glassware, and iron fell off 50
per cent.[5] The Erie Canal had made possible cheaper rates and as
was pointed out:[6]

It is true that our iron and glass do not come to us by way of the *Grand Canal
entirely,* but there is now opened, between the South and the North, a competition in these articles and prices have consequently fallen. Foreign goods
generally, can be brought to this county as low, if not lower, than any county
in Western Pennsylvania.

To complicate matters still further for Pittsburgh, the state of Ohio
began a canal building program to connect the Erie Canal. In February, 1825, the Ohio legislature passed a bill for the building of the
Ohio and Erie Canal which extended from Portsmouth on the Ohio
River to Lake Erie. The Canal traversed the entire State and drew
trade from a large, as well as an important area.[7] Pittsburgh merchants became apprehensive because canals were considered as better
avenues of trade and preferred to roads. Pittsburgh now began to
take an interest in the trade and under the leadership of Neville Craig,
editor of the *Gazette,* began a campaign to recover the trade which was
slipping away from them.[8] Sadly Pittsburgh viewed the impending
danger:[9]

Before the Ohio Canal was made, when produce from that part of Ohio was
sent to market by common roads, Pittsburgh, Philadelphia, and Baltimore were
the usual destination of all the surplus productions of this part of the country.
The completion of the Ohio Canal has produced an entire change in this respect.

Thus, despite the slow, unostentatious development of the early
western trade, Pittsburghers and Pennsylvanians generally began to
show considerable interest, especially when the danger of New York's
expansion became more apparent. New York was accused of boldly

[3] *Cleveland Herald,* February 6, 1821.
[4] The *Ohio State Journal,* published at Columbus, reported that goods could be brought
from New York City in 20 days at $2.50 per cwt., while goods from Philadelphia
required 30 days and cost $5.00 per cwt. *Niles' Weekly Register,* September 16, 1826,
Vol. 31, 38.
[5] *Pittsburgh Gazette,* May 27, 1825.
[6] *Ibid.,* May 27, 1825. An advertisement from a New York paper even offered to transport goods to Albany and "the region west and north of that place including Pittsburgh in Pennsylvania and the several intermediate settlements south of Lake Erie."
Pittsburgh Gazette, March 18, 1825.
[7] Harlow, *Old Towpaths,* 244.
[8] Andrew, J. Cutler, *Pittsburgh's Post Gazette,* (Boston, 1936), 95-96.
[9] *Pittsburgh Gazette,* December 30, 1831.

scheming to monopolize the entire trade of the West.[10]   The growing
success of the Erie Canal roused competitors and made western trade
a fighting issue by 1830.   Pennsylvania, to the last merchant, saw
New York's business and transportation expansion program threatening ruin to themselves and to the State in general.   The whole seaboard suddenly appeared to find the western trade extremely valuable and indispensable.   In an effort to combat New York's influence,
Pennsylvania began work on a state-wide internal improvement plan
of her own.[11]   Lateral feeders were attached to the Main Line of
the Pennsylvania State System even before the original work was
completed.   Survey after survey was made in all parts of the State
with each section fighting desperately for its share.   Internally, Pennsylvania was quarreling vigorously, but on one point all factions
agreed: Pennsylvania must be covered with a network of good trade
avenues, and as canals were considered the best type, canal building
expanded with a startling rapidity.   New York was the nemesis, but
political cupidity exaggerated its strength.

Pittsburgh, after being assured of the Main Line terminus, began
agitation for further extensions westward.   Before the main work was
completed, numerous editorials appeared urging a tie-up with the
Ohio State improvements.   The editor of the *Gazette* argued that:[12]

To compete successfully with New York for the Western trade, we must have
a connection with the Ohio Canal, and improve the Ohio River, from Pittsburgh
to the mouth of Scioto, so that steam boats may run at all times.   This latter
improvement would be almost as injurious to New York as it would be useful
to Pennsylvania.

Faced by the prospects of losing trade, Pittsburgh merchants suddenly realized that they, too, needed the western business.   The value
of the western trade was also heightened by the fact that Pittsburgh's
manufacturing interests were producing goods in larger quantities
and markets had to be extended to absorb the surplus.   In the decade
prior to the panic of 1837, Pittsburgh concentrated on market expansion and the development of home industries.   At this time, when the
drive was strongest and the need the greatest, the fear of losses made
the contest for the western trade more active.

Merchants began to estimate the amounts of trade to show how
important it was to them; newspapers were no longer silent on the
subject of western trade; and all put on a concerted drive to retain
the business.   One of the earliest estimates of the volume of business
was given in a letter from Warren, Ohio, showing the accounts of two
local merchants.   One of the houses had purchased in Pittsburgh
"14 hundred boxes window glass, which were transported by land to

---

[10] *Pittsburgh Gazette,* October 8, 1833.
[11] See page 86.
[12] *Pittsburgh Daily Gazette,* October 8, 1833.

the Lake and from thence shipped to Detroit and Buffalo."[13]　This same merchant had sent to Pittsburgh, during the same year, from 70 to 80 tons of pearl ashes, 80 tons of cheese, 400 to 500 barrels of whiskey and "considerable quantities" of rags, pork, beeswax, deer skins, etc.　The letter continued:[14]

The operations of this house, in the Pittsburgh market, in glass and pearl ashes, for the last 5 years will not fall short of the above amount each year, and some of them will far exceed it. William A. Otis, of Bloomfield Township, situated upon the north line of the county, the most accessible to the Lake, and it may be added, one of the most remote from your city, purchased, the last year, in Pittsburgh, 19 hundred boxes of glass, destined for Detroit and Buffalo markets, and sent to your place more than 80 tons of pearl ashes, besides other commodities. Many years within the last six, his dealings in those articles with Pittsburgh have exceeded those of the year past, and in others he has sent still greater quantities of pearl ashes to Montreal and New York than to your market.

The first total estimate of the Ohio trade was given by Harris in his *Directory for 1837*.　Harris estimated that about 20 wagons arrived in Pittsburgh daily from Ohio and points west.[15]　Each wagon was estimated to carry an average load of three thousand pounds, and that on the return trip, each wagon carried two-thirds of that amount. The total yearly arrivals from all parts of Ohio, Western Pennsylvania, and Virginia were reported to have been about six thousand wagons.　The products sent to Pittsburgh were flour, grain, cheese, beef, pork, bacon, lard, tallow, wool, clover, timothy, flax seed, scorchings, pot and pearl ashes.　Pittsburgh sent back manufactured goods, which consisted chiefly of window glass, nails, iron, groceries, foreign and domestic goods.[16]

Pittsburghers not only tried to arouse their own merchants to action, but they also started an active campaign to sell Pittsburgh goods to the Ohioans by pointing out the advantages of trading with Pittsburgh and Philadelphia as compared to the disadvantages of buying from New York.　Quite a "featured" article appeared in the *Gazette* comparing the trade advantages.　The article was in the form of a letter from an Ohio merchant, giving the case histories of trade between Warren and the East.　The letter stated:[17]

Mr. Gilbert, a merchant of this place made his purchases this season, partly in Philadelphia and partly in New York. His goods left Philadelphia *via* Pittsburgh the 2nd of October, were received at Warren about 21st of the same month. Those purchased in New York left that city *via* Albany on the 8th of October, and have not yet arrived here. They were landed at one of the ports on the shore of Lake Erie, a few days since. Mr. Lewis, another merchant in

[13] *Pittsburgh Gazette*, December 11, 1833.
[14] *Ibid.*, December 11, 1833.
[15] Harris, *Directory*, 1837, 183.
[16] *Ibid.*, 173.
[17] *Pittsburgh Gazette*, December 11, 1833. Numerous other articles stressed the dangers of Lake navigation, and Pittsburgh took a keen delight in the fact that spring navigation was usually delayed due to lateness of the winter season.

this town, shipped his goods from New York by the same route, on the 22nd of October, and has not yet received any information from most of them since they left Buffalo—two other merchants of this place, whose goods were shipped at New York, about the 20th of October have, within 2 or 3 days, received information that portions of them have been landed at different ports from that to which they were consigned. A letter, under date of November 22nd, from the forwarding house in Buffalo, in reply to inquiries respecting the detention of the goods last mentioned, says 'We have shipped all your goods for Grand River. They left here day before yesterday, with the fleet, the first sail that has left this port in 2 weeks.'

Another letter from the same place, under date of November 18, 1833, states, 'snow is from a foot to 18 inches deep, and has added much to our apprehension of an early close of navigation on the canals. We hope your goods have got up, tho' for a time, we thought there was little prospect of it. We have a fleet of some sixty sails in port now, and not a vessel has left for the last 10 days.' Another letter, dated Buffalo, September 28, 1833, to a merchant in Warren, says, 'you wrote us some days since, on the subject of the delays of your goods; I think this will convince you that we are not to blame, your goods were shipped immediately on their arrival at Buffalo, but the vessel that had them was driven by Ashtabula in a gale, and brought up at the upper end of the Lake. She returned with the goods as soon as the weather permitted. Other vessels were driven by in the same gale.

Nor were the Pittsburghers contented with the idle talk. In addition to exposing the uncertainty and risks involved in the Lake route, Pittsburgh began a movement to improve her own western avenues of trade. Cleveland merchants wholeheartedly supported the idea and agreed that:[18]

The only way to build up a commercial town is to *bring business* to it, by improving roads and other facilities for approaching and communication with it— to supply such articles of commerce as are wanting—to purchase such as are for sale at fair prices, and to adapt and practice a liberal and honest method of dealing.

Pittsburgh realized that the hazards and ice of the Lakes were not much worse than the difficulties of her overland connections. Merchants believed that if a canal existed their worries would vanish. Agitation in both Pennsylvania and Ohio for an interstate canal started almost simultaneously with the plans for major canals. Ohio had chartered the Ohio and Erie Canal and work had been commenced by 1827. Pennsylvania, too, had broken ground on her Philadelphia to Pittsburgh Canal in 1826. By connecting these canals already provided, Pittsburghers saw their opportunity to retrieve their lost trade, while Ohioans visioned an alternative route to Pittsburgh and the seaboard as a way to reduce their transportation charges. Philadelphia merchants also hoped to enlarge their market and they, too, endorsed the plan for an extension of the Pennsylvania System to the Ohio border.

---

[18] *Cleveland Herald,* August 19, 1825.

The first step in the direction of tying up Pennsylvania and Ohio canals was taken when the General Assembly of Ohio on April 14, 1827, named a group of citizens to act as corporators in opening books for the subscription of stock and in organizing the Pennsylvania and Ohio Canal Company.[19] That same year, the Pennsylvania Assembly concurred and confirmed the act. The cost of the canal was estimated at one million dollars; Pennsylvania decided that the portion of the canal lying within her territorial limits should be constructed at her own expense and should be considered as an extension of her Main Line.[20] Work was delayed by the feverish rush to complete other State projects. Every road in the West seemed to require enlargement or improvement at the same time. Neither capital nor human capacity were adequate to meet the sudden expansion program. But during the summer of 1835 the Pennsylvania and Ohio Canal was finally located and the Mahoning Valley route to Akron was chosen. The Pennsylvania Canal Commissioners decided on Beaver as the eastern terminus.[21] Stock had been sold to the amount of $900,000 and contracts were let for the entire distance, a total of 83 miles. The directors of the company had expected that the work would be finished within the succeeding two years. But, in this they were disappointed because:[22]

... great changes ... soon took place in the price of the labor and provisions, and the extreme difficulties in making collections of money, retarded the work and compelled many of the contractors to abandon their jobs, this procrastination, and the increased prices at which new contracts must be made, necessarily enhanced the aggregate expense of the work beyond the amount of subscriptions, and serious apprehensions were entertained that it would have to be abandoned.

The company was saved from the worst consequences by the governor of Ohio, who, in response to a plea from the directors on May 11, 1837, subscribed to $450,000 worth of stock on behalf of the State of Ohio.[23] But the aid was still not sufficient to complete the work. The reasons for the delay, it was said, were due to the embarrassed condition of the country in general and also due to loss of confidence in the project by the stockholders in Philadelphia. The capitalists of Philadelphia were denounced because:[24]

---

[19] Pennsylvania and Ohio Canal Company, *Third Annual Report,* (1839), 8-9.
[20] *Ibid.,* 9. Pennsylvania met this obligation in a peculiar fashion: the Legislature passed an act, which increased the capital and extended the charter of the Mechanics Bank of Philadelphia and which exempted the said bank from taxation for 20 years, on the condition that it subscribe one thousand shares of stock ($100,000) to the Pennsylvania and Ohio Company and that it should transfer the stock to the State after five years.
[21] Pennsylvania *House Executive Documents,* 1835, The *Annual Report* of Canal Commissioners for the year ending October 31, 1834, 144.
[22] Pennsylvania and Ohio Canal Company, *Third Annual Report,* (1839), 9.
[23] Pennsylvania and Ohio Canal Company, *First Annual Report,* (1837), 3. The State of Ohio required that previous to the payment of each instalment by the State, collections should be made from stockholders other than the State, to an amount equal to 25 per cent on the estimated expense of the work.
[24] *Niles' Weekly Register,* October 6, 1838, Vol. 55, 83. The article was a letter from the Honorable Elisha Whittlesey, member of Congress from Ohio "to a gentleman in this city" (Philadelphia).

They have either inherited their property from money-making and money saving
ancestors, who instructed their children to practice the good old adage that a
'penny saved is worth two pence earned,' or they have earned their fortune
themselves and duly estimate them. Philadelphia contains very few speculators
who are rich one day and poor the next. It was reasonable that the stockholders should distrust a work they had not seen, when so many projects were
found to be visionary and useless. If they had sent a deputation here, when
their confidence began to yield to fear, I am satisfied they would have promptly
paid up their instalments. . . .

Whether the published letter made the Philadelphians change
their minds is not known, but they did come forth with aid. The
Mechanic's Bank advanced the whole amount of its subscriptions, and
private stockholders in the same city contributed sufficiently to cancel
the company's debts and to make it possible to continue work.[25] On
May 23, 1839, that portion of the canal between Beaver and Warren
(Ohio) was ready for navigation, and a canal boat loaded with
"respectable citizens" started from Beaver, traveled through the Beaver
Division of the Pennsylvania Canal into the Pennsylvania and Ohio
Canal and to Warren, "where it was greeted with every demonstra-
tion of joy such an event was calculated to inspire."[26] Early in June
a daily line of boats was established between Pittsburgh and Warren,
and work on the Western Division was pushed to completion in time
for the opening of navigation in April, 1840.[27]

Pittsburgh was informed of the completion of the Pennsylvania and
Ohio Canal, generally referred to as the Cross Cut Canal, by a letter
from Leicester King, President of the Canal Company, to the editor
of the *Gazette*. The letter reported that the packet boat *Mohawk* of
Beaver was the first boat to pass through the entire line of the Pennsylvania and Ohio Canal and that great celebrations were held
en route. On April 7 a second boat of the Clark and Company's Pittsburgh to Cleveland Line arrived carrying goods destined for Detroit
and Cleveland. A notice appeared in the *Cleveland Herald and
Gazette* on April 15, 1840:[28]

For Pittsburgh: By handbills in the street we see that a Canal Boat will leave
Cleveland for Pittsburgh tomorrow, April 16. Cleveland to Pittsburgh by Canal!
New route this, but we opine that [it] will be much used in coming years, while
Buffalo is ice bound and the Erie Canal is waiting on Brandeths' pills.

Pittsburghers were delighted with the prospects, and shortly thereafter the opening heavy shipments of iron and merchandise were sent to
various points in Ohio.[29] George Hutton, agent for the Pittsburgh and
Beaver Line, estimated that about one hundred tons of iron, nails,

---

[25] Pennsylvania and Ohio Canal Company, *Third Annual Report*, (1839), 10.
[26] *Ibid.*, 5.
[27] *Cleveland Herald and Gazette*, April 13, 1840.
[28] *Ibid.*, April 15, 1840.
[29] *Pittsburgh Daily Gazette*, April 22, 1840. The editor received a barrel of flour by the
Mohawk on its return trip because he had always been a friend to the Cross Cut
Canal. *Ibid.*, April 15, 1840.

glass, white lead, tobacco, and Pittsburgh manufactured articles passed
weekly to Cleveland throughout the summer of 1840; large orders
were also shipped to Detroit and other ports on the Lakes.[30]   The
amount of business for the season can be seen from the report of the
collector at Akron, who listed the arrival of the following items:[31]

38,137 barrels flour	86,427 pounds merchandise
611,875 pounds iron ore	27,514 pounds iron, nails, glass
99,021 bushels mineral coal	20,406 pounds dried fruit
25,222 pounds furniture	29,404 pounds machinery
42,199 pounds stone ware	30,141 bushels wheat
11,122 pounds extra baggage	82,520 pounds pig iron
15,829 pounds paper	5,347 staves
59,323 pounds butter	57,913 feet lumber
15,636 pounds cheese	1,199 passenger conveyed
2,000 pounds pot ash	57,188 miles

Unfortunately it is impossible to state the origin of this trade.   Pittsburgh probably sent coal, paper, merchandise, iron, nails, glass, machinery and pig iron.   The remaining products were more common to
Ohio and were probably local trade intended for reshipment at the
Lake.

The directors of the canal were satisfied with the results of the
season's business.   They estimated that the Cross Cut Canal had
brought about four million pounds of new business to the Ohio and
Erie Canal, and that the new trade constituted nearly one-half of the
quantity of merchandise cleared at Cleveland.[32]

The amount of clearances from Akron for the first year of operation
were greater than the amount of arrivals.   Ohio merchants and farmers
were quick to take advantage of the lower toll rates, as well as the
certainty of early opening of the route.   The following goods were
cleared from Akron in 1840:[33]

507,679 pounds merchandise	24,054 pounds castings
577,139 pounds gypsum	113,769 pounds pot and pearl ashes
27,172 bushels wheat	4,644 pounds agricultural imple-
611 barrels lake fish	ments
7,703 do salt	5,873 pounds tools
226 do whiskey	57,013 pounds patent ware
43,072 pounds extra baggage	194,000 shingles
47,443 pounds furniture	1,395 pounds machinery
19,702 pounds iron and nails	145,447 pounds pig iron

The *Annual Reports* do not include the total volume of goods
carried, nor are the lists complete, but the individual items are, in
most cases, substantial amounts.   There was no apparent indication
that New York was alarmed by this competition.   The New York *Star*
wrote:[34]

---

[30] *Ibid.*, August 29, 1840.
[31] Pennsylvania and Ohio Canal, *Fourth Annual Report*, (1841), 4.
[32] *Ibid.*, 4.
[33] *Ibid.*, 4.
[34] *Niles' Weekly Register*, July 18, 1840, Vol. 58, 309.

The *Cross Cut Canal* . . . which Pennsylvanians believe would divert a large portion of the lake trade to them is now completed and in full operation, and has in effect directly the reverse; so that even the northeastern counties in Ohio, on the river between Pittsburgh and Portsmouth, are actually sending their produce and flour up the canal to Lake Erie, and thence to Buffalo and New York. . . .

In an effort to encourage more traffic on the Canal the board of directors reduced the tolls in 1841 on many articles and on others they allowed a drawback equal to one-third the amount of tolls.[35] As a result of these reductions, the amount of business (and of tolls) for 1841 increased more than one hundred per cent.[36] Coal, merchandise, and wheat were items which showed the greatest amount of increase. In fact, the amount of trade had so increased during 1841 that it was nearly equal to two-thirds of the tonnage which was cleared at Cleveland for the same period.[37] The Canal Commissioners anticipated even greater increases "when the Wabash and Erie, and Miami Canal shall have opened new markets to the enterprising manufacturers of Western Pennsylvania. . . ."[38]

Nor did the "enterprising manufacturers of Western Pennsylvania" disappoint the Canal Commissioners. Throughout the 1840's Pittsburgh kept a watchful eye on the western trade. Numerous newspaper accounts brought news of market reports and business trends to the Pittsburgh merchants. Cleveland's trade conditions were as frequently mentioned as the eastern markets, and the western trade was no longer shrouded in obscurity. Western merchants were now courted by Pittsburgh manufacturers and they were invited to come to Pittsburgh to make their spring and fall trade purchases. Pittsburgh market reports noted the presence or absence of the western merchants, and their numbers usually helped to determine whether business was described as "dull and inactive" or "lively."

Pittsburgh succeeded in selling her products to the western markets, and the Cross Cut Canal was one of the most reliable channels which carried the freight for distribution to the growing northwest markets.

---

[35] Pennsylvania and Ohio Canal Company, *Fifth Annual Report*, (1842), 4.

[36] *Ibid.*, 4. The following chart shows the principal items of business which paid tolls during the season to November 1, 1841:

Merchandize [sic], including iron, nails, and glass..	10,620,247	lbs.
Butter and cheese	1,516,977	do
Pot and pearl ashes	1,222,987	do
Pig iron	1,016,000	do
Iron ore	2,346,000	do
Extra baggage and furniture	301,000	do
Flour	36,500	bbl.
Salt	12,486	do
Fish, whiskey, beef, & pork	1,610	do
Wheat	147,124	bu.
Mineral coal	377,000	do
Tolls 1840	$13,257	
Tolls 1841	$26,000	

[37] The Canal Commissioners used Cleveland tonnage as a sort of barometer to judge trade on the Pennsylvania and Ohio. In 1840 the tonnage had equalled about one-half of that of Cleveland's; in 1841 the increase had made it two-thirds.

[38] Pennsylvania and Ohio Canal Company, *Fifth Annual Report*, (1842), 6.

The iron trade, which was definitely Pittsburgh's, increased appreciably. The Cross Cut Canal was directly responsible for the opening of this trade between Pittsburgh and Cleveland. The extent and development of the iron trade with Cleveland can be seen from the following figures:[39]

1841— 3,842,420 lbs. (1,921 tons)   1844— 5,211,054 lbs. (2,605 tons)
1842— 3,157,576 lbs. (1,578 tons)   1845— 8,303,052 lbs. (4,151 tons)
1843— 7,008,150 lbs. (3,504 tons)   1846—11,526,908 lbs. (5,763 tons)

Other articles probably could be traced in the same manner, but comparisons are impossible because of frequent changes in reclassification of the tonnage reports. The reports usually list collections made at each of the three offices (Warren, Youngstown, and Akron) separately and no attempt was made to give a total report.[40]

By 1840 Pittsburgh had so enlarged her vision and extended her markets that she began to look to new horizons. The frontier had been projected to the Far West and by 1840 Pittsburgh became interested in the famous Santa Fe trade. Newspapers proudly pointed out the fact that Pittsburgh products had penetrated that market. The Santa Fe trade was no longer an infant enterprise by the time Pittsburgh entered the field, but that did not matter for Pittsburgh merchants felt exuberant that they could at last compete with the East on equal terms. The Santa Fe trade also possessed a magical and romantic note which appealed to the settled and urbanized world, not to mention the fact that the traders also brought with them huge amounts of specie.[41] In 1842 three Santa Fe traders, Otero, Armego and Perea, purchased a large amount of merchandise in Pittsburgh.[42] The editor of the *Morning Chronicle* reported that he saw 40 packages containing harnesses for 172 mules at R. H. Hartley's shop on Wood Street; that Cyrus Townsend and Company had also sold 26 large wagons to the traders; and that the goods were all paid for in gold. The editor said that the cost of the articles had amounted to five thousand dollars which was "no inconsiderable item in these hard times."[43] The editor interviewed the "Spanish gentlemen" and gave to Pittsburghers an account of the Sante Fe trade. He concluded by saying

[39] *Pittsburgh Gazette,* August 13, 1847.
[40] Difficulty in organization of tonnage reports can be seen from the ways in which the reports were made: in 1840 total items arrived and total items cleared were recorded; in 1841 one single list of items from all offices was given; in 1842 Akron failed to make returns, and, only Warren and Youngstown's principal items are included; from 1843 to 1848 total items which arrived and which were cleared at each of the three offices are recorded; in 1849 and 1850 only total items cleared at each of the three offices were listed. Consequently, the only classification that can be made is by offices rather than by total trade.
[41] An editorial in the *Cleveland Herald,* December 5, 1822, wrote of the Santa Fe trade, "This is no doubt the commencement of a great deal of business, and that profitable, too, on the part of our people. Mexico is the land of precious metals—articles to which the Americans are much attached, and which we shall be glad to see flow in upon us, as they most assuredly will. . . ."
[42] *Pittsburgh Morning Chronicle,* March 5, 1842.
[43] *Ibid.,* March 5, 1842.

that the "Iron City can be proud!" Nor was he mistaken—The "Iron City" was proud, and much newspaper space was devoted to the Santa Fe trade. The merchants sold the traders goods and the editors scanned the western exchanges for news of the traders as they carried their goods westward.

In June, 1843, the Santa Fe traders arrived in the East with $270,000 in specie to purchase goods. Pittsburgh merchants received $20,000 of this sum, and among the goods purchased were 50 new wagons which had been made by Mr. Townsend; "full sets of gear" for about 700 mules, made by R. H. Hartley; five hundred dollars worth of tin-ware sold by Mr. Dunlap, and seven hundred dollars worth of glass sold by Bakewell and Company.[44] No wonder Pittsburgh was proud— glass being transported 3003 miles overland! *The Morning Chronicle* on September 6, 1843 reported that the caravan had started on its journey and that it was the largest one ever to have gone.[45]

The developments in the Far West occupied Pittsburgh's attention throughout the period of the Mexican War, but gradually the Santa Fe trade was eclipsed by newer events and local interests. By 1850 the western trade was being revolutionized by new methods in transportation. The trade which had been so unostentatious and so obscure was now appreciated; Pittsburgh had become easternized and established, and like the seaboard, depended on the West as a market for her manufactured goods. In this she was assured because a definite alignment had taken place between the East and the West, and trade began to follow a more logical pattern. As the *Cleveland Herald* had observed in 1822: "Every year the growth of the Union produces ir-resistible evidence of the importance of the West."[46] Pittsburgh agreed with this principle and by 1850 was ready to meet the West's demands for goods.

---

[44] *Pittsburgh Mercury and Manufacturer,* June 10, 1843; July 22, 1843.
[45] *Pittsburgh Morning Chronicle,* September 6, 1843, quoting the *St. Louis Republican,* July 28, 1843.
[46] *Cleveland Herald,* December 5, 1822.

VIII

Local Merchants and Merchandising, 1800-1850

THE PEOPLE of the little triangular town, located at the forks of the rivers, had small choice in the matter of occupation. Nature and man had designated Pittsburgh, so to speak, for a commercial center. Along the banks of the Monongahela were deposited increasingly large amounts of products for shipment down the Ohio Valley and, after the invention of the steamboat, more and more products were sent up the same route for sale or re-export to the East. On the north side of the town, products of the Allegheny Valley and, after 1834, products of the Pennsylvania State System, were received. Heavily ladened wagons from the East and from the West congregated on Liberty Street and made that district famous for the wagon trade. From all angles, roads led into Pittsburgh, and goods of many regions changed hands. The entire area of Western Pennsylvania depended upon Pittsburgh for commercial facilities and trade goods. Nor were the early Pittsburghers slow to grasp their natural opportunities; succeeding generations not only retained their economic heritage, but sought means for further expansion. Surrounded by favorable circumstances, the industrious and enterprising citizens built personal fortunes for themselves and made Pittsburgh an industrial and commercial center of enviable reputation.

Merchandising in Pittsburgh in 1800 was a decidedly different process from business methods of today. Strangely enough, the general retailing procedure did not change radically before 1850. The volume of business grew, but methods did not change until large scale production and improved transportation made business a national instead of a local concern. Big deals were accomplished prior to 1850 it is true; markets were cornered, and goods were bought and sold, but the speed, efficiency and size that characterize the business world today were unknown. Business was small, restricted, intimate, hampered, and encumbered by numerous handicaps, but these were accepted as ordinary routine.

One of the cardinal principles of merchandising was to buy only the necessities of life. Both merchants and individuals were governed by this philosophy, because money and products alike were relatively scarce. Even if one possessed the means to purchase, the market was comparatively limited for manufactures were confined largely to the production of essentials. Pittsburgh, as yet, was a young community and deeply concerned with building a solid structure. Luxuries and the variety of nonessentials which today form such a great item of trade did not exist to tempt buyers in the days prior to large scale production. Fashions and styles were minor worries to merchants or consumers; clothes were usually used until they were worn out. If a lady needed muslin or broadcloth or silk for a dress, it was because she needed a dress, and not because a new style had come into being; likewise, if a lady needed a shawl she needed it for warmth. With the clothing business relegated to the proportion of need only, one of today's largest markets was considerably curbed. Household items were also bought on the basis of need, and were replaced only when the articles wore out.

The business methods reflected the tempo of the times, and the period was highly personalized and local in outlook. Friendship, or at least acquaintance, was an important element in business, because merchants were primarily citizens of a community, and customers were individuals, not mere sales slips. Wholesalers and retailers alike personally ordered their goods, and the larger Pittsburgh merchants usually made spring and fall visits to the eastern markets, although after 1830 the "Western" merchants were urged to come to Pittsburgh instead of going to the East to select their stock. Manufacturers as yet could not offer the modern facilities of traveling salesmen, samples, and mail orders, because business was not standardized; nor had mass production or mass consumption, for that matter, made possible buying on a large scale. Buying done on a small scale, therefore, made it something more important than daily routine; and a shopping trip was a special occasion for both merchants and individuals. Furthermore, the character and integrity of the merchant was considered of prime importance because trademarks were unknown.[1] In the absence of standards, goods had to be personally examined, or at least, vouched for by a "friend." Every grade of products was marketed and the quality varied from one extreme to the other. Flour was branded *fine*, *super*, *extra*, and then it was still a gamble which grade one would get.[2] An attempt was made in Pittsburgh to have flour inspection, but the standard was different from that in Philadelphia, and inspection was not required by law. Some prices were set, therefore, subject to a certain inspection,[3] but the local market was usually open to violation. Pork was branded *bulk*, *mess*, *prime*, and *cargo*, while the quality and grade of salt also varied. Both pork and salt were inspected, as well as whiskey, tobacco, molasses, and various liquids.

---

[1] See *Craig Papers*, Isaac Craig to Colonel Isaac Meason, Pittsburgh, May 8, 1801.
[2] Newspapers contain numerous references to the need for flour inspections because of the short weight of the flour barrels. See *Pittsburgh Gazette*, September 24, 1840; January 22, 1845; May 24, 1847; also *Pittsburgh Evening Visitor*, December 2, 1837; *Pittsburgh Commonwealth*, August 20, 1816.
[3] *Pittsburgh Gazette*, March 4, 1840.

Inspection was not completely successful in raising standards, because it was optional, and for the most part, one had to rely on eyes and nose and a sound judgment. Weights and measures were equally as varied as grades and shops. Every conceivable container was utilized, and the size and weight depended on the fancy of the producer.

Business, for the most part, was restricted to a small area, and that which was not, moved at the speed which was possible at that time. Haste was physically impossible; nothing faster than the speed of a horse was known at the beginning of the century, and even the horse was restricted by the lack of good roads. Business was tuned to meet the needs of a slow-moving world, and its methods, as compared to those of the present, were dilatory and wasteful. Efficiency experts and time-saving devices were unnecessary where time was plentiful and clock punching was unknown. Eight-hour working days and five-day weeks were impossible, for time meant nothing; business was a twenty-four hour job with time out for numerous short naps. Keyed to a slower tempo, business demanded long hours and one's work was never done.

The entire process of buying and selling was not only extremely personal in the days before the telephone and the telegraph, but was so closely interwoven with production that the two operations were inseparable. A large part of Pittsburgh's independent retailing originated in the small "manufacturies" where the producer made, and also sold the article directly to the consumer. Business had not as yet become standardized, and goods were made to suit the taste of the consumer. Such commodities as boats, shoes, hats, men's suits, and furniture were made largely to order. Pittsburgh in 1802 boasted of 46 different classes of master tradesmen.[4] These master-craftsmen, totaling 163, offered to their customers a variety of products, such as shoes and boats, trunks, brushes, cabinets, chairs, candles, clocks and watches, cloth, guns, hats, pottery, glass, nails, pumps, saddles, wagons, coaches, scythes, sickles, and other tools. In addition to these small factories and shops, Pittsburgh had 30 mercantile stores, 27 taverns, two printing offices, and one book and stationery store. No information is given as to what these "mercantile stores" sold, but the newspaper advertisements give the impression that these stores handled primarily the products of eastern manufacturers. James McDowell announced to the public that he had just received a "fresh assortment of Dry Goods, Groceries, Queensware, Glass and Hardware" which he would sell for cash or country produce;[5] John A. Tarascon advertised "Woollens [sic] Linnens [sic] and Cotton Goods."[6] Joseph McClurg offered his store goods from Baltimore and Philadelphia either "whole-

4 Cramer, *Almanack*, 1802; see page 11 for complete list.
5 *Pittsburgh Commonwealth*, December 11, 1805.
6 *Ibid.*, November 20, 1805.

sale or retail for cash or approved produce."[7] Other retail establishments were also frequently described as selling "general merchandise" and, although the proprietors were local merchants, they did not sell local products exclusively. Thus, Pittsburgh merchants might be divided into two distinct classes: first, those who were retailers, or shop keepers, dealing primarily in eastern merchandise; second, the small merchant-manufacturer who made a certain type of product and sold it directly. Both classes were important factors in Pittsburgh's commercial history; both contributed to make Pittsburgh the great commercial center, but the merchant-manufacturer was the basic foundation for Pittsburgh's commercial progress.

The importance and magnitude of commerce in Pittsburgh can be illustrated from a study of James M. Riddle's Directory for 1815,[8] and Pittsburgh might well be called a city of tradesmen for nearly every family was concerned either in trade or manufacturing. A total of 1,314 names appeared in the Directory, and although Pittsburgh's total population in 1810 was 4,768, the Directory contained only the names of the heads of families, or the wage earners who made a living in Pittsburgh. Out of the total listings only 18 names appeared without an occupation and 16 others were listed as "Gentlemen."[9] Many of the "gentlemen" were men who had been engaged in trade and who by 1815 had retired or had relinquished their business to their sons. Professional men numbered 82,[10] and the remainder of Pittsburgh inhabitants were engaged in either commerce or a combination of manufacturing and commerce. Riddle listed 93 merchants, 20 commission merchants, 21 store keepers and two "traders" as doing business in Pittsburgh proper. The nature of their enterprise was not disclosed, but apparently they were "general stores" which sold both retail and wholesale. Specialty shops were not as numerous as the general stores; the largest number of this group were the grocery and liquor stores, which totalled 20 in Pittsburgh in 1815. Groceries and liquors were usually combined and only four shops specialized in liquor alone, of which one was an "imported liquor store, E. side of the Diamond,"[11] owned by James Laubie. Another type of specialty store was the baker and confectionery shops of which there were nine in 1815; two additional shops sold confectionery only. Special commodities were sold

[7] Ibid., September 18, 1805.
[8] James M. Riddle, compiler and publisher of the Pittsburgh Directory for 1815, containing the Names, Professions and Residence of the Heads of and Persons in Business, in the Borough of Pittsburgh, etc., (Pittsburgh, 1815), was the first complete list. John Taylor's The Honest Man's Extra Almanac published in 1813, listed 141 names of merchants, manufacturers, and professional men, and although earlier, is not as complete as Riddle.
[9] The "Gentlemen" consisted of the following: James Adams, Abner Barker, Joseph Barker, James R. Butler, Thomas Cromwell, William Graham, Alexander Hill, Nathaniel Irish, John Irwin, Joseph McClurg, Robert Simpson, Robert Spencer, Samuel Stirling, Adamson Tannehill, Samuel Thompson, William Wusthoff; one "gentlewoman" was also listed—"Catherine Wilkins, widow."
[10] Professional men included: 12 lawyers, 8 physicians, 37 government employees, 20 teachers and ministers, 4 bankers, and 1 architect.
[11] Riddle, Directory, 1815, 46.

also by six lumber merchants, 21 butchers, three shoe merchants, four milliners, and three druggists. Probably the unique commercial enterprise at this period was that of selling water. Riddle listed five water carters in 1815, and evidently the business, unlike many others, was a full-time job.[12] The total number of Pittsburgh residents who made their livelihood exclusively by selling products was 255, and the list included all grades of business enterprise from Anshutz, Rahm & Co., Commission Merchants, to Richard Freeman, "water carter."

Riddle listed 706 individuals as having been engaged in some phase of manufacturing or crafts. The largest group was the blacksmiths which totalled 35; boot and shoe makers comprised the second largest group.[13] The number of weavers listed in 1815 totalled 23, of which one specialized within the field and was described as a "shawl weaver." Twenty-one "nailors" were listed although the majority of these were probably employed by J. Whiting and Company or their rival, M'Donnell, Brown and Company, instead of being in business for themselves. Pittsburgh also was well supplied with tailors and dressmakers. Riddle listed 27 tailors, of which six were described as "merchant taylors" [sic] 25 seamstresses and sewers; and 2 mantua makers. Three of the "Taylors" even had shops separated from their dwellings, which was unusual because tailoring was well adapted to home production.

Seemingly every one in Pittsburgh who could make something or perform a service hung out a shingle and looked for customers.[14] A shop in the yard or the front part of the house was adequate space for the majority of enterprises. Of the 32 blacksmiths in Pittsburgh in 1815 only four maintained shops not on the same premises as their dwellings; six of the 20 boot and shoe makers had separate establishments; three of the eight tanners; one of the nine bakeries; one of the three druggists; one of the two hair dressers. None of the storekeepers had separate establishments; only seven merchants out of the total list of 85 had separate houses of business; and three of the 17 commission merchants had business establishments.

Business had become separated to a greater extent, however, among the so-called heavy industries which needed a large amount of ma-

12 Several hundred names listed two occupations and the combinations were often so decidedly different that one wonders about the results. For example, John Baird "taylor [sic] and porter bottler"; Joseph Brittingham, "nailor and violin maker"; Samuel Crow, "tanner and grocer"; William Earl, "carpenter, bellows maker and chandler"; Oliver English, "machinery and blue dyer"; Thomas Carter, "merchant, and cordial distiller".
13 Boot and shoe makers totalled 23, and this group does not include the 21 names who were classified only as "shoe makers"—if the two were combined their numbers would exceed the blacksmiths.
14 A surprisingly large number of women were listed in the *Directory* as having occupations. Of the 64 widows listed, only one was listed as a "gentlewoman", and 21 were credited with some kind of occupation. Fifty-three single females were listed as having occupations. The majority were listed as seamstresses, or sewers, (25); washers (19); boarding house keepers (12); storekeepers (6); milliners (4); spinners and dyers (4); one woman was listed as a sausage-maker; another a glover; one a soap boiler, and Mrs. Mary Mercer, widow, was keeper of the jail. No record is made of a married woman being in business.

chinery. The iron mills, foundries, steam engine factories, and glass houses had already outgrown the confining space of the home.[15] Significant among these factories was the Pittsburgh Steam Engine Company, located on the "North side of Front Street below Ferry Street," which in addition to manufacturing and selling steam engines on the Oliver Evan's plan of construction, also made "castings of every description," anvils and anchors. The company included a brass foundry, too, "calculated for general castings, but more particularly for machinery and large bells which will be warranted of the first quality."[16] The company also manufactured "butt-hinges . . . on a scale sufficiently large to supply any demand"; lathes and turnings of iron, brass and wood, and screws of many descriptions.[17] Pittsburgh also had three foundries which were advanced to the extent that they boasted of being able to supply "castings of every description, from a cannon to a spider."[18] George Cochran maintained a separate textile establishment at the corner of Diamond Alley and Liberty Street; he offered his goods at Philadelphia prices and he "warrants the color and durability of his cloths equal to that imported from Great Britain."[19] A great variety of textiles were made at Cochran's factory, such as, superfine and common broadcloths, blankets, felting, kerseynettes, sattinettes, and hosiery of all kinds. But George Cochran, as well as other Pittsburgh manufacturers, had to face serious competition from eastern goods, and even though they offered goods reputedly equal to Philadelphia products at Philadelphia prices, they were constantly forced to appeal bluntly for patronage. Riddle included an appeal:[20]

G. C. having surmounted great difficulties in the establishment of a new manufactury, commenced nearly three years ago, when workers and machinery were difficult to procure, relies on the patronage of a patriotic and generous public, for the support of an establishment important to the interest of the western country.

The large majority of the less complicated "manufactures", however, continued to work in a part of the home and under the conditions best suited to them. By utilizing the front part of the house, or a shop in the rear of the house, the merchants during this period had a minimum of overhead expense. High rents for separate quarters were thus eliminated; the family usually comprised the sales force; and customers did not demand the many services which are so costly for present day merchants to supply. Consequently, many more people were in business for themselves. The triangle was filled with shops of all types and sizes. Signs informed the public where a particular

[15] See the Pittsburgh Council's Report on Manufacturing for 1815; *Pittsburgh Gazette,* January 1, 1820.
[16] Riddle, *Directory,* 1815, 137.
[17] *Ibid.,* 138.
[18] *Ibid.,* 139.
[19] *Ibid.,* 141.
[20] *Ibid.,* 142. Trotter and Company also manufactured pottery "similar to those of the Potteries in Philadelphia."

shop or factory was located, although the signs themselves were more picturesque than informative. Merchants who did not possess such an identification described their location in relation to a more prominent landmark. Advertisements declared shops "next door to" (or even two or three doors to) a well known merchant; "across the street" from the court house; or "on the corner" of a specified intersection. Strangers on their first trip to Pittsburgh must have been greatly confused, especially after the population had increased; but the situation remained the same until the 1830's when house numbers were introduced. No particular street had a monopoly of business houses, although the larger and earlier established merchants were located in close proximity to the Point. As the town expanded, business became more and more segregated and by 1835 Penn Street was considered the residential section, although residences were not by any means excluded from the triangle.[21] Throughout the period of 1800 to 1850 the small shop keepers flourished. The manufacturers were the first to grow full sized, and they gradually deserted the retailing field.

In addition to the little merchant-manufacturers and stores, Pittsburghers did a vast local business at the public market houses.[22] As early as 1800 Pittsburgh had three market houses—one located at the Diamond opposite the Courthouse; another at the corner of Market and Second Streets; and the third at the end of Market Street on the bank of the Monongahela River. Here the farmers of the surrounding countryside brought their products to sell in order that they might get cash to buy Pittsburgh store goods.[23] During the first decade of the 19th century the newspaper carried scattered accounts of the "Prices Current" at the Pittsburgh Market. An example of the prices and the types of articles sold in 1801 can be seen from the following report:[24]

	$	¢	$	¢		$	¢	$	¢
Beef per lb		3		5	Turnips		20		25
Pork		3		4	Apples		50		75
Mutton		4		6	Oats		20		25
Veal		4		6	Butter per lb.		10		13
Vennison [sic]		3		4	Hogs lard		5		7
Flour superfine per cwt. .				2	Eggs per doz.		7		12
Flour common	1	25	1	50	Turkeys, a piece		40		60
Flour buckwheat	1		1	10	Geese		25		33
Indian Meal per bu		33		44	Ducks		12		17
Potatoes		25		33	Fowls		7		10

---

[21] *Blythe Mss.*, Ellen Blythe to John C. Green, June 9, 1835.
[22] A newspaper account reported that two fairs would be held when Pittsburgh became a borough. The fairs were to last two days each, and were scheduled for June 4 and October 27. The public square was designated as the place and all kinds of merchandise and animals were to be sold. *Pittsburgh Gazette*, October 4, 1794. What was the outcome of this notice is uncertain because later newspapers made no further notice.
[23] Wednesday and Saturday were designated as the regular market days. Cramer, *Navigator*, 1821, 155. Cummings related that on one market day a merchant had sold goods amounting to $150 "ready money", and that on another such day "he had taken in $180 besides the credit business." Cummings, *Tour of the West*, 245.
[24] *Pittsburgh Gazette*, January 9, 1801.

The farmers, however, were not limited to these markets, and the majority of Pittsburgh merchants would take produce in exchange for their manufactured articles. Bartering was a common practice in Pittsburgh because money was scarce. Lacking an adequate medium of exchange, local merchants took products in place of cash. Denny and Foster's advertisement illustrated the common practice; they advertised that they had "Prime Soal [sic] leather, of clean, well-trimmed, Spanish Hides which they will exchange at the rate of 2s. per pound for Flax linen at 3s. per yard, tow linen at 2s. per yard and good twilled Bar at 7s.6p."[25] Not all trade was barter, however, and merchants even advertised for certain products offering cash for them. George Evans and Company advertised regularly for grains; on October 9, 1812, the company offered one dollar per bushel cash for wheat delivered to the Pittsburgh Steam Mill; 50 cents a bushel was offered for corn and rye, and 33 cents was quoted for buckwheat.[26] Hamilton and Brown, Brewers, advertised five shillings cash per bushel for barley.[27] William Masson, sail maker, at Water Street, offered "3s. cash will be given for 700 linen, whole bleached, half-bleached, or one-third bleached, delivered at Pittsburgh."[28] Mary Irwin, proprietor of the rope walk, advertised her products and offered seven cents a pound for "sound clean hemp."[29] John Linton, tailor, also offered 40 cents per yard for "700 Linnen" [sic] and ten cents for "good thread per cut."[30] Isaac Harris advertised for 20,000 pounds of ginseng and offered cash; and Gilland and Company offered "75¢ cash for good flaxseed."[31]

The Monongahela and Allegheny wharves were also busy markets, and goods were sold directly from the boats at a slightly lower price. Flour and salt were items frequently exchanged at this place and the prices quoted were about 25 cents lower than the wholesale prices current.[32] During the navigable season boats of all types and sizes were constantly loading or unloading. Goods were landed pell-mell on the banks and piled high waiting to be carted away; Pittsburgh goods were also waiting to be put aboard. Merchants argued with ship captains over freight rates and berated the captains for the postponed

---

[25] *Ibid.*, November 5, 1806.
[26] *Ibid.*, October 9, 1812.
[27] *Ibid.*, July 24, 1812. English coins were in common use in Pittsburgh; prices ceased to be quoted in shillings after 1815.
[28] *Ibid.*, November 15, 1808.
[29] *Ibid.*, July 10, 1812.
[30] *Ibid.*, September 30, 1815.
[31] *Ibid.*, November 25, 1815.
[32] *Ibid.*, April 7, 1836. In 1844 the *Gazette* reported that commission merchants in St. Louis were circulating a paper for signatures of persons who would agree not to patronize boats which brought merchandise to sell on the wharf. The Pittsburgh editor remarked that in Pittsburgh the same situation existed, especially in the salt trade, and he concluded that the practice should be stopped because "the legitimate business of all common carriers is indisputedly confined to the conveyance of freight and dealing in any article is clearly an aggression on the rights of merchants." *Ibid.*, October 6, 1844.

delay in pushing off.[33] Steamboat runners, keeping an eye on prospective customers, vied with one another for trade.[34] The wharf, like Pittsburgh's streets and alleys, was in dire need of paving and grading. The boats found landing satisfactory, but the drays and carts found the waterfront a difficult road. Traffic became entangled as business increased, and men, horses, and merchandise seemed hopelessly confused in the rush. During low water in 1818 thirty vessels were lying at the wharf, loaded with three million dollars worth of goods.[35] The *Advocate* described the Monongahela wharf during another rush season:[36]

The wharves present one of the most animated scenes we have witnessed in a long time. Twenty steamboats lie at the landing taking in cargo for Louisville, St. Louis, Nashville, New Orleans and "intermediate ports" as the phrase goes. The whole of our broad levee, from the bridge to Ferry Street, is closely dotted with drays and wagons, hurrying to the margin of the river from every point of access, burdened with the valuable products of our factories or with Eastern goods. Some half a dozen of the steamers are puffing away ready to start. The margin of the wharf is absolutely covered to the height of a man with freight in all its varieties, while higher up on the footwalks and streets the fronts of the great forwarding houses are blocked by piles of boxes, bales and barrels in beautiful disorder. Shippers, porters, draymen and steamboat clerks blend their hurried voices at once—one is actually deafened with their cheerful din and rush of business. Some idea may be formed of the magnitude of our manufactures from the fact that the larger iron houses have 800 some 1,000 and some as high as 1,200 tons each of iron and nails ready for shipment to the West.

An attempt was made by the city council to eliminate the confusion at the wharf by the ordinance of January 7, 1825. A wharfmaster was appointed to direct traffic, and landing places were designated for different types of boats. Family boats and farmers were directed to land between Grant Street and 150 feet below the Monongahela Bridge; from that point to the southeast end, Market Street was reserved for

[33] One of the most irritating problems of the merchants was the lack of boat schedules. Captains would promise to start at a specified time, and then refuse to leave if their boats were not filled. Ellen H. Blythe described her trip on the Ohio: "They stop frequently to receive fuel and other necessaries, or to take in freight. This is a provoking part of the business, for the delays are often long and yet the captains will flatter the passengers constantly with the hope of getting off in a few minutes. When we went down, we stopped at Steubenville, where my husband begged the captain to allow him 15 minutes to see his sister Jane, who was with in a few yards of the landing. The captain refused, on the plea that he must pass some miles below Wheeling that night. He proceeded to Wheeling, 25 miles from Steubenville, and there, notwithstanding his repeated promises and the solicitations of the passengers, he lay for 20 hours. We left him for one more accommodating; but with him we touched the bottom very frequently, and at last had the pleasure of striking a bar, on which we lay for ten hours when within 30 miles of our destination, and we had no way to better our conditions." Mrs. Ellen H. Blythe to John C. Green, July 22, 1834. *Blythe Mss.*
　　The *Gazette* announced, on January 31, 1835, "It has been a sore grievance to travellers on the western waters, that there was no dependence to be placed upon any assurance that steamboats would start at any particular hour. The commencement of a daily line will at once remove this source of annoyance."
[34] *Wheeling Times and Advertiser*, March 19, 1845. A common practice of western merchants, and hotel keepers, as well as steamboat operators, was to employ "runners" to bring customers to their places of business. Pittsburgh merchants decided to outlaw the practice in 1845 and agreed not to patronize steamboats who used "runners". Wheeling accused Pittsburghers of using the objectionable practice in Brownsville, and berated them for carrying on a practice which they would not permit in Pittsburgh.
[35] *Pittsburgh Gazette*, December 11, 1818.
[36] *Ibid.*, May 18, 1838.

keelboats, barges, and flatboats engaged in freighting; from Market
Street to Ferry Street was to be marked off for steamboats; from there
to Redoubt Alley, space was again designated for farmers and family
boats. The remainder of the beach to Penn Street was to be reserved
for boats undergoing repairs; for boats that were up for sale, and all
other boats that were not landing for the purpose of loading or unloading.[37] The ordinance also specified that fees collected by the wharfmaster were to be used for the improvement of the city's public landing places. Thus, guaranteed a source of income, the wharf was
gradually improved.

Much of the goods which arrived at the Pittsburgh wharves and
markets, however, were not accompanied by their owners or destined
for the shelves of a specific retail store. The practice of sending goods
to a market to be sold by a person who specialized in selling, became
more and more common, especially as business increased. The commission merchant was one of the most important pillars of a commercial town, and upon him rested the responsibilities of building up
a reputation for the town's integrity and honest dealing. The func-
tions performed by the commission merchant were not new services
to the western world, but before his advent each person handled his
own goods completely. When trade was in its infancy, there was no
need for commission merchants because the business was too small to
support a middleman. As business expanded and goods were sent on
longer journeys and in greater amounts, one man found that he could
make a living by distributing goods for merchants and manufacturers.
Probably the first local commission merchant in Pittsburgh was
Thomas Cromwell, who, on October 18, 1805, informed his "friends"
that he had opened a warehouse on the bank of the Monongahela
River, at the mouth of Wood Street, and that he was ready to receive
goods.[38] Cromwell promised that any goods which were directed to
him would be safely delivered to the boats; that he would take care
to secure good and honest boatmen; and that "he will also attend to
the commission business which Kentucky merchants or other persons
may have done on very moderate terms."[39] The advertisement also
added that Cromwell expected to do a good business because of his
knowledge of trade, the location of his house, and the moderate price
he charged for storage. Cromwell called his house the Pittsburgh

[37] Ibid., February 4, 1825.
[38] Pittsburgh Commonwealth, October 19, 1805. Previous to this advertisement, Pittsburghers were informed by a Charlestown advertisement from Pittsburgh Gazette,
May 7, 1802, that: "David M'Kibben respectfully informs the traders in this Western
Country that he intends in the course of a few days to set out for New Orleans. For
several years past he has been engaged in trade to that place, and has still made
it his study to become acquainted with whatever relates to that trade. He now intends to reside at New Orleans, and hopes to be serviceable to his countrymen and
himself by doing business on commission. Consignments of produce of every kind will
be carefully attended to, and the products remitted agreeably to instructions. His
charges will be moderate and always in proportion to the trouble. . . ."
[39] Pittsburgh Commonwealth, October 19, 1805.

Warehouse.[40] Ten years later Pittsburgh had 11 commission merchants, three of whom were glorified by the title of company.[41] By 1833 Pittsburgh supported 60 to 80 large wholesale establishments who were the successors to the commission merchant.[42] As the avenues of trade were improved, and as more and more goods were shipped both East to West and North to South, the commission merchants prospered. The coming of the railroad, however, reduced their importance because transient goods no longer required transfer. The railroad assumed the responsibility of caring for the goods until the final destination was reached, and trunk line eliminated the disjointed transportation system of the pre-1850 period.

The commission merchants held auction sales in order to dispose of their products quickly and profitably. Certain days were usually designated as sales days for a particular merchant. Ebenezer Denny, for example, held auction on Mondays and Thursdays "weather permitting"[43] while Anthony Beelen advertised his sales on Monday and Wednesday.[44] All kinds of goods from calicoes to furniture were sold in this fashion. Auctions were popular in Pittsburgh and they provided a satisfactory method of exchange. Customers could examine the goods before purchasing and be assured that the articles measured up to expectation. Goods were sold both for cash and on short term credit. Ebenezer Denny advertised that sales for less than one hundred dollars would have to be cash, but that over that amount properly endorsed notes for 60 days would be acceptable.[45]

Public sales were under the direction of auctioneers. In order to protect the seller and the buyer from frauds, the auctioneers were appointed by the governor of the Commonwealth. Furthermore, the State collected a percentage on all sales made at auction.[46] For every one hundred dollars worth of merchandise the State collected one dollar and fifty cents; on ships the rate was thirty-seven and one-half cents on each one hundred dollar sale.[47] The position of auctioneer was apparently very important. In 1833 Pittsburghers were considerably aroused over appointments and they flooded the governor's desk with appeals and testimonies on the various applicants'

[40] *Ibid.* The advertisement concluded with offering for sale Dorsey's Iron, and an advance announcement of an expected shipment of Probst's Castings.
[41] Riddle, *Directory*, 1815. According to the *Directory* there were also 85 merchants listed, who probably were also willing to undertake a commission.
[42] *Ebensburg Sky*, October 24, 1833.
[43] *Pittsburgh Commonwealth*, March 19, 1806.
[44] *Ibid.*, March 16, 1808.
[45] *Ibid.*, March 16, 1808.
[46] *Mss.* in Public Records Division, Pennsylvania Historical and Museum Commission, Governors' Papers. Letters addressed from W. C. Enoch to Governor Wolf, January 1, 1833; letter from P. Mulvany to Governor Wolf, December 21, 1832.
[47] Riddle, *Directory*, 1815, 115.

characters.[48] In 1842 the appointment of auctioneers was stopped and auctioneering became open to all who could afford to purchase a license.[49]

Auctioneers and commission merchants facilitated the distribution of goods in an era when business methods were in a state of transition. Trade had outgrown its local character due to inventions and improvements in transportation and in production, but the changes had been of too recent origin to effect a complete readjustment. Business had become too large for complete personal supervision, and yet absence of standards required it. Goods travelled greater distances than one man could supervise, but the disjointed transportation system necessitated a caretaker. Credit was extended, yet the system was too involved and confused to work smoothly. The commission merchant was the go-between, and upon him rested the responsibility of expediting the flow of goods.

Pittsburghers generally were concerned with business, and the local papers showed the town's importance as a commercial center. The *Gazette* carried a regular column devoted to steamboat news. This service appeared for the first time on August 18, 1818, and the columns contained the date of arrivals and departures of boats and incidental information pertaining to the state of river navigation. The papers continued to report the river news despite the difficulties in collecting the news. At one time the editor of the *Gazette* requested that:[50] "If freighters, commission merchants, and others concerned would communicate arrivals and departures to the clerk at Mr. Hart's warehouse,

[48] Among the numerous *Mss.* on the subject one of the frankest statements was from Thomas White, dated January 8, 1833:

". . . I have been an acquainted with McKennas for several years before his appointment of auctioner [sic] and have been for 7 or 8 years as head clerk in the auction business here until about last 6 years when [I] was appointed clerk in the bank and during the leisure time assisted Mr. Hanson in his business in a particular department also Mr. McK & Mr. H. during their copartnership until Mr. H's failure. Mr. McK became involved with him by the public presuming that he was a party concerned when by my knowledge by the articles of agreement he was to be exonerated from all responsibility for debts of his contracting, but under this presumption storys [sic] were commenced against him and the only dockett [sic] suits to my knowledge against him were those from those circumstances. The public lost confidence with him but from the services rendered and that gratuitously to him I was enabled to convince the public that he was not in any wise leagued with H. and now when he's beginning to get his head above water and enabled to make headway the envious malicious slanders must endeavor to destroy him which I hope will not succeed. In regard of the charge of habitual drunkardness I would ast [sic] what constituted to that name [?] [word illegible] is it not one who is given to that viece [sic] daily, but this is not the fact as I before observed having been acquainted with McK for several years yet during the last three years to my knowledge he had but twice given a short time away to it, he then abstained from liquor of any kind and he has assured me that he will not again be observed drinking of any kind. It is a query with me and believe I could point those malicious characters out whether they have and been more guilty than he ever was at the present time even more capable when the other is—

I have several times made out auction reports and consequently have had access to his books which I examined carefully and have always found them correct and they are always open for the inspection of the public if they are desirious [sic] of examining them." *Mss.* in Public Records Division, Pennsylvania Historical and Museum Commission, Governors' Papers.

[49] *Pittsburgh Mercury*, April 13, 1842.
[50] *Pittsburgh Gazette*, August 27, 1824.

he would keep a register of them which we could copy." After a wharfmaster was appointed in 1826, the news is more complete. Market reports also formed a large item in the newspaper, and the completeness of the reports increased year by year. From a very humble and unpretentious beginning, the market reports grew until they covered one-fourth of a sheet of newspaper. The state of trade for the particular season was noted in the later editions, and prices current were listed for the convenience of the visiting merchants. By scanning these reports, merchants and customers could get a good idea of prices and the quantity of goods on hand. Freight rates were also given after 1840 so that prospective customers could calculate their freight charges.

Today these reports tell the magnificent story of Pittsburgh's commercial and industrial development. In 1801 less than 20 items were quoted and the articles listed for sale were entirely farm products.[51] Flour was the only manufactured item included. By 1815 the market report consisted of a new list of articles, and the only products common to both lists were flour and butter. The list included the following items and prices quoted during the spring and fall seasons when trade was most active:[52]

		OCT. 14, 1815	Nov. 25, 1815	JAN. 6, 1816	MAY 11; 1816
Orleans cotton	lb	.29	.30 to .32	.33 to .34	.30 to .33
Tenn. Cotton	lb	.27	none	none	.28 to .30
Orleans Sugar	lb	.25	.25	.25	.25 scarce
Lead	lb	.14–.15	.15–.16	.15 to .16	.13 to .15
Tobacco leaf	lb	none	none	none	.14 to .15
Tobacco Ky. keg	lb	.18¾–.20	.20 to .22	.25 to .30	.22 to .25
Superfine flour	bbl	5.00–5.25	5.00–5.25	5.00 to 5.25	5.00 to 5.50
Bar Iron Juniata	Ton	200. scarce	210. scarce	210.	210. to 220.
Castings	Ton	125.	125.	125.	125.
American steel	lb	.18 scarce	.17 scarce	.17	.17
Whiskey	gal	.75–.80	.80 to .81½	.80 to .81¼	.62 to .68
Salt Kanawha	bbl	7.50–8.00	7. to 7.50	7. to 7.50	6. to 6.50
Flax seed	bu	.75–1.00	.75 to 1.00	.75 to 1.00	.75
Linseed oil		none in market		1.25 per gal	1.25
Tanner's oil	bbl	35.00	40. to 45.	40. to 45.	40. to 45.
Coffee	lb	.38–.40	.38 to .40	.38 to .40	.38 to .42
White Lead	lb	.17	.19	.19	.22
Keg butter	lb	.18	.14 to .15	.16 to .17	.20 to .25
Sumatra pepper	lb	.43–.45	.43 to .45	.43 to .45	.40 to .43
Bacon	lb	.12½ scarce	none	none	.13 to .14
Cheese	lb	.12½–.15	.10 to .12	.10 to .12½	.13 to .15

The prices of the two articles common to both lists show that prices had risen between 1801 and 1815. On January 9, 1801, superfine

---

[51] See page 131.
[52] *Pittsburgh Mercury*, October 14, 1815; November 25, 1815; January 6, 1816; May 16, 1816.

flour was quoted at two dollars per hundredweight, while in 1815 the prices varied between five dollars and five dollars and fifty cents, per barrel (196 lbs.); butter sold at 10 cents to 17 cents per pound in 1801, and in 1815 it varied from 14 cents to 25 cents. Several slight references were made also to the amount of goods on the market. On October 14, 1815, no leaf tobacco or linseed oil were available, and bar iron, steel, and bacon were "scarce." By May 11, 1816, the only item marked "scarce" was Orleans sugar.

In 1817 the market reports began to appear regularly each week from April to November and the list expanded noticeably. A total of 84 items were now enumerated indicating that Pittsburgh's market had tripled in size since 1801. The list included the following items:[53]

Ale	Grain, corn	Segar [sic] Spanish
Ashes pot	Grain, oats	Segar [sic] American
Ashes pearl	Gun powder, best	Shot, all sizes
Beef	Glue	Skins, deer
Bread, crackers	Hams, Ky.	Skins, bear
Bread, ship bread	Hams, country	Skins, Fox
Butter (keg)	Iron, Juniata	Skins, Muskrat
Coffee fine green	Iron Monongahela	Skins, Racoon
Coffee 2nd quality	Iron Hoop large	Soap, white
Coffee 3rd quality	Iron Hoop small	Soap, rosin
Candles, mould	Iron sheet, Am	Steel, Crowley
Candles, dipt	Iron sheet, foreign	Steel, American
Cheese N Connecticut	Lead, pig	Steel Blistered
Cheese country	Lead, barr [sic]	Sugar, N. O.
Cotton, Tennessee	Lead red	Sugar country
Corn Meal	Lead white, dry	Sugar loaf
Clover seed	Lead white, ground in oil	Sugar lump
Coal, stone	Leather, soal, [sic] Spanish	Tallow
Feathers	Leather, soal, [sic] country	Tobacco, country manu.
Flax, clean	Leather upper	Tobacco, Ky
Flour, sup	Nails, all sizes, cut	Whiskey, rye
Furr [sic] Beaver	Nails wrought	Wax, bus.
Glass 7 x 9	Nails spikes	Wool, Merino clean
Glass 8 x 10	Oil linseed	Wool, fleece
Glass 10 x 12	Oil fish	Wool, half breed
Grain, wheat	Porter bottled	Wool, quarter
Grain, rye	Porter	Wool common clean
Grain, barley	Salt	Wool fleece

Thus, in 1817 Pittsburgh merchants offered their customers coffee in three grades, all kinds of iron and steel; "segars" [sic] both Spanish and American brands; four kinds of sugar, and six grades of wool. According to the reports, prices during April and May remained unchanged; flour was quoted at eight dollars to eight dollars and fifty cents per barrel.[54] In June several items dropped in price, among which was flour then quoted at seven dollars to seven dollars and fifty cents

[53] *Pittsburgh Gazette*, April 11, 1817. In 1818 the list included 117 articles.
[54] *Ibid.*, April 18, 1817; April 25, 1817; May 2, 1817; May 9, 1817; May 16, 1817; May 30, 1817.

"IN THE DIAMOND," PITTSBURGH'S MARKET PLACE

From *History of Pittsburgh and Its Environs*, II, American Historical Society, Inc., 1922

per barrel;[55] other changes took place in price during July and August, and by October 31, flour had fallen to five dollars and fifty cents or six dollars per barrel.[56] No mention was made as to the state of the market.

The contents of the market reports between 1818-1839 remained fairly stationary, although the prices varied greatly depending upon the general business conditions. In 1824 a brief phrase was added to each quotation showing the market demand. The descriptions consisted of such remarks as "in demand," "plenty," "in fair demand," "little wanted," "scarce," "regular demand," and "dull sale." Flour in November, 1824, for example, was "in fair demand" at three dollars to three dollars and fifty cents per barrel; feathers were "scarce" at fifteen cents per pound, and hemp was "little wanted" at $90 per ton; rolled iron was "plentiful" at one hundred dollars per ton; and "crown wrap" paper was "in demand" at one dollar and twenty-five cents per ream.[57] In 1839 market reports became more informative. *Harris' Intelligencer* in reviewing the market on Friday, November 29, 1839, reported:[58]

Business continues rather improved and sales of small lots of goods are making, but no heavy transactions.

Money continues scarce and some houses are doing a good deal more for barter and exchange for produce, etc.

Flour from wagon is selling at $3.50 and a few small lots of very choice at $3.63½ a $3.75 barrel.

Whiskey has advanced, a good new is now selling at 30¢.

Salt—A good deal is selling from first hands at 2.00 a 2.12½ and from second hand at 2.35, and in small lots at 2.37½ a 2.50 per barrel.

Blooms—A few small lots have sold at $28. per ton at 4 months.

A good deal of Scorchings and Potashes have been sold in barter at 5 a 6¢ per lb.

During the 1840's the reviews became more numerous and increasingly more complete. On July 25, 1844, the weekly review included the following items: a summary of the week's business; a price list of commodities; reports of the cattle market, and the domestic market at the Diamond; a list of freight rates, and the conditions of the "Western Waters"; a comparison of the sales of provisions and of wool in July, 1844, with those of July, 1843; a review of the "Eastern Exchange and Money Market"; and a weekly summary of the amount of trade on the Pennsylvania Canal.[58]

55 *Ibid.*, June 6, 1817; June 13, 1817; June 20, 1817; June 27, 1817.
56 *Ibid.*, October 31, 1817.
57 *Ibid.*, November 19, 1824; November 26, 1824.
58 *Ibid.*, November 29, 1839.
59 *Pittsburgh Gazette and Advertiser,* July 25, 1844.

Thus, by 1850, Pittsburgh's commerce had recovered from its growing pains and was well established. Pittsburgh offered commercial opportunities and services comparable to those offered to merchants on the seaboard. The hit or miss element had been greatly reduced and business was conducted on a more even keel.

By comparison with present conditions, pre-1850 merchandising seems to have been crude and wasteful. Business methods, however, were adapted to the prevailing needs; they were adequate to meet the demands made by manufacturing and industry, and as such served their purpose. Methods improved as manufacturing and trading became enlarged, but the change was slow. Merchandising, on the whole, did not differ radically until after large scale production, unionism and government regulation forced an alteration. As transportation improved, as manufacturing developed, and as emigration extended beyond the Ohio Basin, Pittsburgh's exports increased and the trade area extended beyond the range of personal contact. Pittsburgh throughout the period was surging forward as a commercial city; business was beginning to specialize and to find a certain measure of orderly procedure. From 1800 to 1850 business did not experience as many revolutionary changes as resulted in the next half century, but the period was vital and important as laying the structural base for later development.

IX

Commercial Rivalries

PITTSBURGH'S outstanding commercial and industrial position was not attained without a struggle. Each advance was contested; each achievement was questioned; in fact, Pittsburgh merchants and industrialists had more than their share of competition. Commercial progress was made in various adjoining regions at the same time, and each community had specific advantages which also were clamoring for notice. Before 1830 the settlement and exploitation of the Ohio Valley proceeded at full-speed. Little settlements sprang up everywhere. Each one was vitally concerned with its economic well being and each one struggled to surpass its neighbor. The competition can hardly be described as friendly, because the stakes were high and the opportunities for expansion were easily recognized. On the other hand, the more destructive features were eliminated because of the wide scope of enterprise, the varied advantages peculiar to each, and the disparity in the time of settlement. Cincinnati found the pork industry her best economic undertaking; Louisville became the clearing house for tobacco and the port of exchange between the North and the South and St. Louis was the headquarters for the fur and lead trade. Cincinnati had a peculiar advantage in being the natural river outlet for the fertile agricultural region of central and southern Ohio. Louisville's treacherous Falls were responsible for her trade advantage becaue they made Louisville a natural point of transfer by necessity, and St. Louis was the outlet for the new western frontier.[1] None of these cities, however, offered serious competition to Pittsburgh merchants or industrialists because of the wide variety of their activities.

Pittsburgh's most serious competitor was Wheeling. Wheeling had been founded in 1769 by the Zanes on the site of an Indian crossing of the Ohio River.[2] Emigrants from the East had found that Wheeling was a good point for embarkation or for crossing into the territory of Ohio.[3] The town was also favored when Congress, by the Acts of 1802 and 1803, allotted one-twentieth of the proceeds of the sales of public lands in the new state of Ohio to the construction of a turnpike from the Atlantic seaboard to the Ohio River, and thence westward

[1] Cummings, Samuel, The Western Pilot. Containing Charts of the Ohio and of the Mississippi Rivers . . . and a Gazetter, (Cincinnati, Ohio, 1839), 40, 50, 78.
[2] Newton, J. E., (ed.) History of the Panhandle, (Wheeling, West Virginia, 1879), 60.
[3] Hulbert, A. B., The Old National Road, (Columbus, Ohio, 1901), 104.

to Indiana and Illinois.⁴ By 1818 the National or Cumberland Road
was opened to the Ohio. Wheeling was proud of this new highway,
built on the latest model of construction and supported by the power
of the Federal government.⁵ She had justification for hoping to
become the Gateway to the West. The latent rivalry between
Pittsburgh and Wheeling became active about the time the National
Road was opened to Wheeling, and continued in varying degrees
of intensity throughout the period. Both towns had too many things
in common to make congenial neighbors; both were rivals for the
same prizes; and their proximity made the competition keen. The
two towns seemed to differ on all major issues, and year by year the
rivalry flared up more frequently and more intensely until finally
it became chronic. The constant cause of contention was the struggle
for the leading position in the Ohio Valley; neither town was willing
to concede that each might share the western trade and still survive.

Their quarrel was centered around the control of the Ohio River, because both towns claimed the Ohio River as the principal artery of
trade and both claimed to be at the "head of navigation." All less
significant issues were subordinated, although none the less vigorously
prosecuted, to this bigger problem. As far as location, Pittsburgh was
above Wheeling, but Wheeling charged that the river was not satisfactory for navigation above her port. The Wheeling editors continually pointed out that five shoals existed between Wheeling and
Pittsburgh and that the river hazards were magnified by the lowness
of the water. The editor of the *Wheeling Times and Advertiser* attempted to prove his point by showing statistics for the number of
Pittsburgh boats, or boats laden for Pittsburgh, which had arrived in
Wheeling, and which were compelled to return without reaching their
destination:⁶

1838—72
1839—71
1840—72
1841—74
1842—84

Now these boats really wanted to go to Pittsburgh, reminded the
editor, and the fact that they did not was "evidence that they could
not." The editor concluded that only small boats could reach Pittsburgh—"little wet-tailed dinkey boats that a cart load of rock would
sink in their best days . . . ",⁷ or boats which continued northward because they could not turn back due to the narrow channel.

⁴ *Annals of Congress*, 7 Cong., 1 Sess., 1349.
⁵ Crall, F. Frank, "A Half Century of Rivalry Between Pittsburgh and Wheeling" in
   Western Pennsylvania Historical Magazine, (October, 1930), Vol. 13, 239.
⁶ *Wheeling Times and Advertiser*, August 10, 1843.
⁷ *Ibid.*, August 10, 1843.

Pittsburgh was visibly annoyed over Wheeling's attempt to discourage traders from her shops, but she put up a brave front. Under cover of a nonchalant attitude, tinged with contempt and sarcasm, Pittsburgh editors tried to minimize Wheeling's accusation. Jokingly, the editor of the *Pittsburgh Chronicle* wrote:[8]

We exceedingly regret that we cannot live at peace with our neighbors 'at the head of navigation'! Not our fault! We want to see our 'little sister' thrive and prosper. But she cannot let us alone. Like a half-starved, ill-natured mangy cur, she is constantly snarling and snapping at our heels.

But under the guise of bravado, Pittsburghers felt the darts. The entire Ohio River did need improvements, and Pittsburghers were well aware of that need. Their only response was that the river between Pittsburgh and Wheeling was no worse than any other part. Pittsburgh had campaigned actively, but not too successfully, for river improvements. An editorial in 1819 pointed out that the greater part, if not all, of the boats which were wrecked between Pittsburgh and Wheeling met disaster on three well-known rocks. The first was at the head of Montour Island in the Horsetail Ripples; the second in Lowrey's Ripple; and the third one nearly opposite the foot of Montour Island. The editor estimated that one hundred dollars would remove all of them, and that fifty or sixty men could do the job at once, having besides a good day's outing. He challenged his townsmen by asking them directly: "Fellow citizens, what say you?"[9] Pittsburghers responded and one month later the job was completed.[10] Pittsburgh unaided, however, could not do much to improve the river permanently, and the river project was hampered by lack of cooperation from other states and the reticence of the national government to become involved in activities which were considered out of her jurisdiction. During the interim all river traffic labored under the same difficulties, and the amount of agitation for improvement depended upon the depth of the water. In years when the water was extremely low, the cry for improvement was very loud; in years of normal navigation the efforts were relaxed. The improvement of the Ohio River was sporadically carried out and concerted action did not take place until after 1850.[11]

[8] *Pittsburgh Chronicle*, June 13, 1846.
[9] *Pittsburgh Gazette*, September 24, 1819.
[10] *Ibid.*, October 22, 1819.
[11] On January 27, 1817, the Ohio Legislature had passed a resolution calling upon the neighboring state to cooperate on river improvement. In 1819 the commissioners of Ohio, Virginia, and Pennsylvania met in Pittsburgh, and drew up a report to their several legislatures. The commissioners estimated that forty thousand dollars would be sufficient to clear the Ohio River of the most dangerous obstructions, and they also recommended a canal to eliminate the falls at Louisville. Nothing resulted from this attempt, however, until 1825 when a feeble beginning was made to clear the river. In 1830 the proposed Louisville Canal became a reality and in 1835 fifty thousand dollars was appropriated to clear the river. By 1844 obstructions amounting to 3,303 had been removed. Hulbert, *Ohio River*, 361-362. The Memphis Convention of 1845 outlined the national policy and made way for action by the Federal government. *Pittsburgh Gazette*, August 10, 1846.

The quarrel over the right to the "head of navigation" was gradually dropped as the Allegheny River trade increased. During the 1830's the steamboat had penetrated the Allegheny trade, and service was established in 1838 to Olean, 270 miles north of Pittsburgh.

Almost as serious an issue was the rivalry over each town's eastern connections. In 1834 the Pennsylvania State System was completely opened and Pittsburgh had a decided advantage over Wheeling. From 1818 Wheeling had held the trump card so far as eastern connections, because the National Road represented the nearest approach to successful overland travel. Pittsburgh, making the best of her handicap, improved her own turnpikes and tried to forget about the National Pike by concentrating on manufacturing. But the National Pike haunted Pittsburghers. The cost of transportation to Baltimore had been reduced as much as seven dollars per hundred pounds, and the time had also been drastically cut.[12] To make matters worse, Pittsburgh's manufacturing prosperity was also severely checked by the panic of 1819, and until 1825 Pittsburghers were struggling desperately to recover their lost prosperity. Economic conditions changed by 1826, and Pittsburgh was also considerably encouraged by the prospects of a canal to Philadelphia. For a few years, Pittsburgh editors were too busy writing on the proposed improvements and the growth of local industries to be much concerned with Wheeling. Pittsburgh was jubilant because the Pennsylvania System was the latest improvement in 1830, and the National Road was no longer the best route to the East. The Pennsylvania State System ushered in a new era of transportation for Pittsburgh, but Wheeling also felt the effect. It has been said that:[13]

By 1835 the change wrought on Wheeling business interests is perceptible, partly in the growing evidence of an 'inferior complex' pervading the editorial columns of her newspapers, partly in the frequent notices in the advertising columns of these same papers of dissolutions of partnerships involving withdrawal from New Orleans connections and the formation of new alignments with Philadelphia interest. While these moves by no means indicate changes detrimental to Wheeling, the facts do carry with them strong suggestions of increasing subordination to Pittsburgh.

Advertisements in the *Wheeling Times and Advertiser* bear testimony of Pittsburgh's penetration. Independent merchants such as J. G. S. Reily, Crangle and Bailey, Jacob and Mitchell, King and Crumbacker, and Lazier and Cox offered Pittsburgh merchandise. Numerous Pittsburgh products such as iron and nails, salt, textiles, yarns, oil, candles, scales, and machinery were most frequently advertised. Pittsburgh merchants also advertised in the Wheeling papers,

---

[12] Searight, *The Old Pike,* 108.
[13] Crall, "Rivalry between Pittsburgh and Wheeling" in *Western Pennsylvania Historical Magazine,* (October, 1930), Vol. 13, 244.

while others established agencies, although this method was considered less desirable. Pittsburgh transportation companies, likewise, advertised in the Wheeling papers, not only to deliver freight to Philadelphia but also to Baltimore. One of the most liberal of the advertisements was that of T. Devine, Commission Merchant, who offered:[14]

Canal and railroad transportation—Baltimore and Pittsburgh and United States Portable Boat Lines. For transportation of merchandise and produce to Baltimore and Philadelphia. Warehouse on Canal Basin Liberty Street, Pittsburgh. *I will pay River freight on all produce consigned* to me at Pittsburgh. I will make no charges for commission or drayage. I will receipt for all goods sent to me to be delivered in 2 days to Baltimore or Philadelphia at the following prices from Pittsburgh: Tobacco 85 cents per 100; Flour 130 cents per 100. All other freight at the regular established prices.

Another evidence of Pittsburgh's penetration is the fact that Pittsburgh market reports were included in the Wheeling papers, along with Pittsburgh prices. The advertisements, however, only tell one side of the story. Pittsburgh merchants had undoubtedly entered the Wheeling market, and much of Wheeling's trade was enticed to Pittsburgh, but Wheeling editors did not succumb so gracefully. The "inferior complex" was evidenced only in the pettiness of the criticism and in the bravado of the defense mechanism. Today these accounts seem humorous, but a hundred years ago they were serious and derogatory as the following example illustrates:[15]

The *Pittsburgh Gazette* says the improvements of Pennsylvania yield about one dollar tolls where they cost nine for repairs. We presumed they would yield about that much as all the travel is now coming through Wheeling. It will be but few years before the only travellers in that state will be tax-gatherers.

Not only did the editors watch Pittsburgh papers but they also quoted other sources, and whenever possible tried to deride the Pennsylvania System by publishing such reports as: "We hear by the *Philadelphia Sentinel* that the merchants and transportation companies have been compelled, owing to the neglect of the legislature, to advance the money to pay the hands for repairs on the canal."[16] After 1835 Wheeling editors watched the Pennsylvania State System like a hawk, and never missed an opportunity to cast aspersions upon it. Pittsburgh editors were constantly on the alert to correct or apologize for the accusations.[17] These apologists were in a bad position; they frequently found it necessary to complain for redress of grievances upon their own public works, and Wheeling was always able to make use of such information to show that the National Road was still the best

---

[14] *Wheeling Times and Advertiser,* January 16, 1841.
[15] *Ibid.,* March 30, 1841.
[16] *Ibid.,* April 1, 1841.
[17] *Pittsburgh Gazette,* March 29, 1837. Wheeling papers carried the news that there had been a break in the Pennsylvania Canal and that freight was piling up in Baltimore because of the shortage of wagons. The editor of the *Gazette* wrote that: "It is hardly necessary to say that this breach was entirely of Wheeling's manufacture, as the canal was not open until *after* the date of the *Wheeling* paper."

of trade channels. In 1846 the editor of the *Gazette* urged a reduction of tolls, and to prove his point, he wrote that the Pennsylvania tonnage was falling off. The article was lengthy, but Wheeling reprinted the larger part and observed:[18]

We have frequently called the attention of the public both at home and abroad, to the fact that the transportation of goods, either east or west, through Wheeling by the National Road and Baltimore and Ohio Rail Road was cheaper and more expeditious than any other accessible routes, and we are gratified in the fact that experience is proving the truth of our remark, and that the western merchants and produce dealers are increasing the trade through this route with every passing season. It is a fact that the transportation of goods over this road has increased immensely during even the last year, and there are very good reasons for it, viz: It is never closed by ice, low water or breakers; it is the more certain and speedy route; and when the whole expense is summed up, it is the cheapest route for a large majority of the goods transported either way.

Another element entered into the Pittsburgh and Wheeling rivalry—Baltimore and the State of Virginia also came in for a share of Wheeling's vituperation. Wheeling merchants frequently accused Baltimore and Baltimore merchants of selfishness and neglect; and at times like this, pointed to Philadelphia as a shining model of fostering consideration. The Wheeling editors warned the Baltimore merchants using the Monongahela Slackwater, instead of the National Road, that Baltimore would feel "the effects of the suicidal policy they have pursued for a few weeks past, in relation to their Western trade. The papers have puffed and puffed the Monongahela improvement, as though it was [sic] the 8th wonder of the world. . . ." The article concluded with the cheering observation that they were "cutting their own throats with a dull knife."[19] Wheeling also accounted for her misfortunes by explaining that:[20]

The difference is not created by any natural advantage that Pittsburgh possesses, but by the fact that it is located in a large, enterprising and free state, under whose fostering care she has grown and prospered, while Wheeling has had the disadvantage of northern prejudice, and no aid from an indolent and procrastinating state government.

And in this there was much truth.[21]

Along with the chronic rivalry over eastern arteries of trade, Pittsburgh and Wheeling carried on numerous minor struggles. One of the most amusing incidents revolved around the steamer *Josephine*, which was reputed to carry a burden of 150 tons. Pittsburgh listed the boat's

[18] *Wheeling Times and Advertiser*, February 18, 1846. The editor mentioned the Baltimore and Ohio Railroad. Wheeling had been keenly disappointed between 1835 and 1840 over the failure of the Baltimore and Ohio to utilize its Pennsylvania charter. By 1842 the Baltimore and Ohio was completed to Cumberland, and it did not reach Wheeling until 1853. Reizenstein, Milton, *Economic History of the Baltimore and Ohio Railroad*, (Baltimore, 1897), 45.
[19] *Wheeling Times and Advertiser*, April 7, 1845.
[20] *Ibid.*, July 31, 1846.
[21] Crall, "Rivalry between Pittsburgh and Wheeling" in *Western Pennsylvania Historical Magazine*, Vol. 13, 243. "Virginia lagged behind her neighbors in internal improvements. Her interests were those of the plantation South rather than the industrial North. Her political leaders were cautious and conservative."

manifest and Wheeling took issue. The editor of the *Wheeling Times and Advertiser* printed the manifest and his estimate of the weight of each article. According to the Wheeling editor the *Josephine* was carrying a load of 1,078,332 pounds or 539 tons. The questionable manifest included the following:[22]

2 Tierces Rice	800	1,600
10 sacks feathers	30	300
11 hhds, tobacco	1,200	13,200
2 box tobacco	100	200
58 hhds, sugar	1,200	69,600
2 casks Potash	800	1,600
3 cables	say	500
1 bbl. tools	say	200
1 casks Bacon		800
52 sacks Feathers	30	1,360
23,156 ps. shoulders	17	393,652
5,227 do sides	24	125,448
23,361 hams	15	397,137
1 keg alspice [sic]		25
10 bbl. Molasses	500	5,000
3 bbl. Sugar	270	810
5 half chests tea	75	375
32 half chests tea	75	2,400
1 cask rice		750
10 bbl. Grease	300	3,000
1 cask Grease		800
975 Shoulders	17	16,575
3 casks Bacon	800	2,400
1 bbl. Lard		320
1 bale Furs		50
5 sacks dried fruit	60	300
5 bales cotton	500	2,500
7 bags ginseng	say	300
6 bags feathers	30	180
3 bbl. beeswax	200	600
1 case prints		350
3 box merchandise	say	600
3 horses	800	2,400
41 hhds. bacon	800	32,800

1,078,332 lbs.
or 539 tons

The Wheeling editor also wrote a particularly cutting article on Pittsburgh built "war steamers" which had been supplied for the government:[23]

The Pittsburghers and Pittsburgh papers are great for grabbing at everything there is going. If a railroad is contemplated to the moon, they insist on a branch—if a canal is being dug thru Pawtuxent, they must connect—if govern-

22 *Wheeling Times and Advertiser*, February 21, 1845. Allowances must be made for variation in measurements. Beef and pork were usually packed in barrels weighing 200 pounds; hemp in bundles of at least 112 pounds, while tobacco hogsheads in Kentucky had to contain at least 1000 pounds. Baldwin, *The Keelboat Age*, 312.
23 *Wheeling Times and Advertiser*, June 10, 1846.

ment wants a war steamer, a barrell [sic] of pork, or a dozen buckets, Mr. Pittsburgh is ready for a push to get it, whether they can supply it or not. They are now in full cry for the privilege of building war steamers there, and seem to think seriously that the administration will give them the contract. They forget it seems, the war steamer built there some two or three years ago, which was so completely botched that it is still lying at Cincinnati for repairs and remodelling. Do they wish to give the government another such?

The editor of the *Pittsburgh Chronicle* answered the "paper notorious for its mean efforts to injure the prosperity of our city" and explained that Pittsburgh had built the boats according to governmental specifications.[24] But Wheeling was not convinced and replied that the boat "by her ordinary working of machinery knocked a hole in her bottom before she reached Marietta."[25] Another time the dispute was over wagons built for the Santa Fe traders, and Pittsburgh answered proudly that "our manufactures have never yet been surpassed in anything, and do not intend to be at this day."[26]

Even the great fire in Pittsburgh of April 10, 1845, did not deter the two cities from their quarrel. Less than two weeks after the great disaster, Pittsburgh accused Wheeling of being "unsympathetic", although the Wheeling editor insisted that all he had printed was that the *Swiftsure No. 3* could not get up to Pittsburgh due to the bad condition of navigation. The editor then proceeded at length to express his sorrow over Pittsburgh's misfortune,[27] but he added "why shouldn't we tell our advantages—even if they have grown out of calamity?" The editor added:[28]

That calamity must, for many years, change the business character and capacity of Pittsburgh. The present generation of people in that city cannot recover from it. Even when all its ground is occupied as it was before, or even with more valuable houses and where those houses are filled, which will not be in five years, she will not have recovered from her loss. She will not attain the same business that she has had. It must seek new channels. Attempt to bolster up as they may, use whatever energy they may, actual loss must be felt, and business must fall into new channels to a very great extent. Why should Wheeling neglect to endeavor to secure her share of it, by an announcement of her business facilities and advertisement as usual?

The editor asked, should we "sit down and fold our hands" just because Pittsburgh was suffering? Navigation above Wheeling was just as bad as it had been before the fire; the Monongahela Slackwater was still no good; and now Pittsburgh was playing on sympathy. The editor, referring to the Right of Way Bill for the Baltimore and Ohio Railroad, concluded: "Modest men would have thought this using up of the funeral baked meats to grace the wedding supper is rather too hasty a manner."[29]

---

[24] *Pittsburgh Chronicle*, June 13, 1846.
[25] *Wheeling Times and Advertiser*, June 16, 1846.
[26] *Pittsburgh Chronicle*, September 22, 1846.
[27] *Wheeling Times and Advertiser*, April 24, 1845.
[28] *Ibid.*, April 24, 1845.
[29] *Ibid.*, April 24, 1845.

Pittsburgh then realized that she had overplayed her hand. Immediately following the fire, newspapers had carried full accounts of the effects of the disaster. In their usual thorough manner the editors recounted the losses. Aid and sympathy were promptly sent to Pittsburgh—but her western customers stayed away. Pittsburgh was then truly stunned. The fire had certainly been a great catastrophe, but Pittsburgh was not exterminated. The editor explained that the fire "was so great and apparently overwhelming, that sufficient care was not taken, while dwelling upon it, to guard against the effects of those general statements upon the country."[30] Wheeling lost again, for Pittsburgh recovered rapidly and built a better city than the one which had been burned.

Pittsburgh and Wheeling carried on editorial warfare on anything and everything. Business methods, a case of smallpox,[31] the building of a bridge across the Ohio at Wheeling,[32] or a Marine Hospital, [33] all called for argument. But this was the day for active civic, as well as State, rivalry. Pennsylvania, and Philadelphia in particular, had New York as their arch foe, and both were rivals to Baltimore. Newspaper editors evidently had to have a grudge against someone. Parallel to the Pittsburgh-Wheeling struggle for supremacy, each had another chronic cause for complaint. Pittsburgh alternately berated and cajoled Philadelphia, while Wheeling scolded and wheedled Baltimore. The character of this competition was of a different nature from the Pittsburgh-Wheeling rivalry because Philadelphia and Baltimore were not competitors of their little western off-spring. Pittsburgh and Wheeling were more like obstreperous children who could beg and cry at the same time.

The one-sided rivalry between Pittsburgh and Philadelphia was the older of the two major competitive struggles and was the unconscious outgrowth of a once friendly connection. Many Pittsburghers had deep roots in the East, and to many settlers Philadelphia had sentimental bonds. Consequently, a friendly attitude existed during the early days of settlement, and Pittsburgh was grateful for the economic and social connections with the old established city. As long as Pittsburgh was totally dependent upon Philadelphia for manufactured goods and certain food stuffs, the relationship was intimate and satisfactory. In 1793, during one of Philadelphia's periodic epidemics of yellow fever, a letter was written to the "printer" of the *Gazette* outlining how Pittsburgh might help Philadelphia in her

[30] *Pittsburgh Gazette,* May 13, 1845.
[31] *Wheeling Times and Advertiser,* January 23, 1846. The editor accused Pittsburgh of not allowing a gentleman from North Carolina to land because he had the disease. Wheeling called it cruel and heartless.
[32] *Daily Wheeling Gazette,* August 20, 1849. "Our friends at Pittsburgh are groaning so piteously about the building of the Bridge across the Ohio at this point that some of our contemporaries have given it the name of "the *Bridge of Sighs.*"
[33] *Wheeling Times and Advertiser,* July 22, 1846; *Pittsburgh Gazette,* August 7, 1847.

calamity and misfortune.[34] The writer explained that while the fever
was raging in Philadelphia, economic activities had practically
stopped; much of the western trade went to Baltimore, or was delayed
because shopkeepers did not want to "desert their old friends in the
hour of their distress."[35] But he continued: "As soon as a connection
with Philadelphia is unquestionably safe, let our shopkeepers prefer
Philadelphia manufacturers and goods, and buy nothing from any
other place, which may be had there."[36] Every good citizen was
urged to do his bit by patronizing the shopkeepers who did buy at
Philadelphia.

But gradually this attitude changed and Pittsburgh began to show
an active animosity towards her big sister. The reasons for the
alteration are clearly discernible—Pittsburgh was no longer a dependent child. By the end of the first decade of the 19th century,
Pittsburgh had begun to supply many of her own demands. Textiles,
glass, pottery, and iron products could now be produced in Pittsburgh,
and the eager local industrialists no longer wanted eastern store goods.
Philadelphia now became a competitor to Pittsburgh instead of a
supplier of necessities. But not all Pittsburgh was equally anxious
to be rid of Philadelphia's leadership; and between Philadelphia's
superior advantage of priority and some Pittsburghers' reticence to
change, the fight became increasingly bitter. Many of the goods
were not of equal quality with those of Philadelphia; furthermore,
people had to be educated to the idea of local manufactures. An unfavorable balance of trade made it difficult for Pittsburghers to be
gracious towards this increasingly large drain on their purses. Pittsburgh had to pay eventually for almost every shipment which arrived
from Philadelphia; and as she became more and more established in
manufacturing, her animosity towards eastern merchants and manufacturers increased substantially.

Pittsburghers' feelings were injured further because they suspected
that they were being exploited by Philadelphia. A combination of
self-pity and jealousy complicated matters. Pittsburgh lamented
over her isolated position and alternately pleaded with and threatened
Philadelphia for help in improving the connecting roads. Why can't
Philadelphia be like New York? asked the editor of the *Gazette*.
Why does Philadelphia have to be bound up in a "fatal lethargy"?[37]
Pittsburgh always had some cause for complaint. After Philadelphia
had aided financially in the building of the Philadelphia and Pittsburgh Turnpike, the editor complained that the road "is trammelled
with such preposterous and narrow minded regulations as to destroy

[34] *Pittsburgh Gazette*, November 23, 1793.
[35] *Ibid.*, November 23, 1793.
[36] *Ibid.*, November 23, 1793.
[37] *Ibid.*, May 22, 1818.

every chance of its utility." He referred to the fact that western merchants were called upon to pay for the transportation of their goods in advance. A letter to Poulson's *American Daily Advertiser* signed "Z" took up the issue and threatened to use Wheeling instead of Pittsburgh. John Scull, the editor of the *Gazette,* retaliated by telling "Z" to go ahead, that Pittsburgh still had New York and Baltimore. He concluded by reminding Philadelphia, in general, that she made her wealth through the West.[38] Five weeks later the *Gazette* informed its readers that Philadelphia had gone "to the other extreme" —she wanted to build a canal to the Ohio River. The editor admitted that the idea was good, but not practical, and that a good turnpike would be better. He followed up with a two-edged compliment and admitted that the Philadelphia and Pittsburgh Transportation Company was satisfactory, that freight rates had been reduced to five dollars per hundred, *but* that "this could only continue if the road be made good."[39] Pittsburgh was a fair weather friend. As long as Philadelphia was doing something to aid her, the relationship was friendly and on a firm basis.

The intense interstate rivalry for the western trade which was so keen prior to 1850, also helped Pittsburgh because she was the only Pennsylvania town which qualified for the western terminus of the huge internal improvements program, necessitated by the competition of New York's Erie Canal and Baltimore's National Road. Relationships between Pittsburgh and Philadelphia improved considerably during the era of the building of the Pennsylvania State System. Both cities had the same objectives; both were aligned on the same side of the issue against the other sections of the State; both expected to benefit by improved trade conditions. Pittsburgh, yoked with Philadelphia, enjoyed the temporary relationship, and was grateful for Philadelphia's leadership and money. A twelve million dollar trade artery of the latest design was reason enough to make any city forget past differences! Pittsburgh was happy, for at last she had her much desired eastern connection and she was booming with commercial activity. In 1836 Pittsburgh found it necessary to employ 250 drays and carts to do the hauling between the canal basin and the wharves whereas formerly one had been sufficient.[40] One hundred teams of from four to six horses were also constantly employed in furnishing "stone coal to our manufacturers."[41] Furthermore, "upward of 250, 3-4-5 storey brick stores and warehouses, of which about 80 were commenced or finished this year," handled the products brought to Pittsburgh by river and canal. Fourteen regular lines transported freight daily over the Penn-

[38] *Ibid.,* June 23, 1818.
[39] *Ibid.,* July 31, 1818 ; See page 179.
[40] *Ibid.,* November 10, 1836.
[41] *Ibid.,* November 10, 1836.

sylvania State System,[42] while eight regular steamboat lines operated on the Ohio River.[43] Pittsburgh was fairly bubbling over with activity, and it was reported that:[44]

The manufactures and mechanical products, and sales of all kinds of goods, foreign and domestic by all our manufacturers wholesale and retail, and commission merchants may be estimated at from 20 to 25 million of dollars. The value of every description of foreign and domestic goods received in *transit* from the Eastern cities and passing through the hands of our commission merchants for all parts of the West and South may be estimated at between 60 and 70 millions of dollars, and perhaps it will not exceed the truth to say, that the whole of the goods manufactured, or imported and sold, in our city, or that are brought out annually from Boston, New York, Philadelphia and Baltimore, on the sea board, by the canals and turnpikes, and from New Orleans, St. Louis, Nashville, Louisville, Cincinnati, and all the intermediate ports on the several rivers, from the flourishing states of Ohio, by land and water, from the state of New York, and northwestern part of Pennsylvania, by the turnpike and Allegheny River; and from Virginia, Maryland and the southern part of Pennsylvania, by the Monongahela River, that is sold or passes through Pittsburgh, into all parts of the country East, West, North, and South amounts to the enormous sum of about 100 million of dollars. In this calculation two of our most extensive commission houses have been consulted, concur with the writer.

Merchants, manufacturers, and newspaper editors were in a fine humor, for they had envisioned Pittsburgh *at the center* of the large wheel whose spokes were reaching out farther and farther. Philadelphia, too, had visions of her own advantage at the head of a huge trunk line which extended westward, but to Pittsburgh the picture looked different. She, and not Philadelphia, occupied the favored spot—she, and not Philadelphia, was the center through which all trade must pass. Small wonder that Pittsburgh was happy and felt important. She could now afford to be gracious; she saw Philadelphia as a partner rather than an exacting creditor; she was anxious for closer trade relationships because the West was expanding and the East needed western raw materials.

Unfortunately, the novelty of the Pennsylvania State System wore off, and Pittsburgh began to see the handicaps and difficulties. Gradually she began to suspect that railroads might be better than canals. In January, 1838, a memorial was authorized by a convention of delegates from the western counties of Pennsylvania on the subject of a continuous railroad from Philadelphia to Cleveland.[45] Although the memoralists announced that they had no intention of entering into a discussion of the merits of either canals or railroads, they hurried to add that they did believe that heavy freight could be better moved

42 *Ibid.*, November 10, 1836.
43 *Ibid.*, November 10, 1836. In addition to the regular lines, the writer estimated that from March 1 to January of the following year, extra boats amounting to three per day arrived, or about a total of 1830 arrivals and departures with an average cargo of 80 tons each, or a total of 140,400 tons.
44 *Ibid.*, November 10, 1836.
45 *Pittsburgh Mercury*, February 7, 1838.

by canal, but that the canals also had serious deterrents.[46] Contrary
to promise, they listed the handicaps; canals were more susceptible
to frosts; canals were not opened in time to take away the heavy
spring river traffic and seasons were too short and too uncertain. Railroads, continued the memorial, would eliminate all these because they
were unaffected by seasons, and trade would be continuous and regular.[47] Philadelphia must act, urged the memorial because "Baltimore
is awake and Maryland and Virginia are exerting themselves to get the
Rail Road finished from Baltimore to Wheeling."[48] The memorial
facetiously reminded Philadelphia that wagon carriage from Baltimore
to Pittsburgh was one-half the price as from Philadelphia to Pittsburgh.[49]

But this was the beginning of the railroad issue which continued
between Pittsburgh and Philadelphia until Pittsburgh finally won the
fight. The beginning of the railroad question was of slight importance
because the enterprise was new and untried. Pennsylvania became
involved in 1828 when the legislature granted a 15-year charter to
the Baltimore and Ohio Railroad to construct a line through southwest Pennsylvania to Pittsburgh.[50] By 1843 when the charter expired
the line was completed only as far as Cumberland, and Pennsylvania
had now a system of internal improvements of her own. Consequently,
Pennsylvania, particularly Philadelphia, was not so liberal with her
aid to competing projects. When the Baltimore and Ohio Company
tried to get better terms,[51] Philadelphia was unapproachable although
Western Pennsylvania was more than anxious for the connection.
Pittsburgh alternately threatened and cajoled; she blessed and con-
demned Philadelphia in the same breath. In 1844 an editorial in the
Gazette on the chronic question of the respective merits of Philadelphia, Baltimore, and New York, sounded a new tone. At last, Pittsburghers had roused their courage and definitely asserted in black and
white that "we are necessary to you, but you are not indispensable
to us . . . we are the mountain, and you are Mohamet. . . ."[52] Continuing, the editor changed his tone:[53]

Philadelphia seems to have exhausted her energies and to recline at ease, con-
tent with the laurels which were green a dozen years ago, but are now so sadly
faded by the sunshine of other emporiums. . . . Why so much apathy in the
grand old city of Quakers? She has the bones and sinews to command victory

---

[46] *Ibid.*, February 7, 1838.
[47] *Ibid.*, February 7, 1838.
[48] *Ibid.*, February 7, 1838.
[49] Rates from Philadelphia and Baltimore were quoted from time to time in the local
papers but there was never a 50 per cent variation. Evidently the memorialists were
not too accurate.
[50] Godcharles, Frederic A., *Daily Stories of Pennsylvania*, (Milton, Pennsylvania, 1924),
36.
[51] *Pittsburgh Gazette*, March 31, 1845.
[52] *Ibid.*, December 20, 1844.
[53] *Ibid.*, December 20, 1844.

in the race of cities for commercial eminence. Why then, does she not rise from her lethargy and by a decided effort push on to Pittsburgh? She has long since accomplished half the enterprise, another effort would achieve the whole. . . .

By 1845 the railroad issue reached its climax. Sadly Philadelphia began to realize that the Pennsylvania System would never provide adequate transportation facilities to the West, especially since the railroads had become acceptable. The once proud Pennsylvania State System, which had cost twelve million dollars, presented a problem; however, Philadelphia hesitated to grant the right of way to the Baltimore and Ohio Railroad for it would surely prove the end of the System. Pittsburgh in the meantime fought desperately for the bill. Indignation ran high; so high in fact that a pledge was circulated which threatened to sever all commercial connections with merchants and dealers of Philadelphia if the bill were defeated.[54] An editorial in the *Pittsburgh Chronicle* asserted that "this is a severe measure, but we are by no means certain that it is not justifiable by circumstances. We, in connection with a larger portion of the State, have long suffered under the domineering diction of the Philadelphians."[55] The editor continued by adding that Philadelphia opposed everything that might injure its interests even though it would benefit the rest of the State. He concluded by saying that Pittsburgh did not wish to quarrel with any eastern city, least of all Philadelphia, and that he hoped it would not be necessary to keep the pledge.[56]

On February 23, 1846 the Right of Way Bill was defeated in the Senate by a single vote. Before any action could be taken by Pittsburgh, the Senate reversed itself on February 26. Pittsburgh was informed of the good news by the Good Intent Canal Boat Line on February 28.[57] During March and April Pittsburgh awaited with suspense and anxiety while the House decided how it would vote. The fight was half won, but this was no assurance for the final success of the bill. On April 8 a convention of western Pennsylvanians was held at the Public Square in Allegheny in favor of the Right of Way Bill.[58] Nearly 2,000 delegates from twenty counties attended the meeting which was called to order by the Honorable Walter Craig of Washington County. The gathering was addressed by the most outstanding and responsible citizens of Western Pennsylvania. The Honorable Walter Forward said that "no earthly power has a right to say that the people of Western Pennsylvania must trade alone with Philadel-

---

[54] *Pittsburgh Chronicle*, February 14, 1846.
[55] *Ibid.*, February 14, 1846.
[56] *Ibid.*, February 14, 1846. On February 17, 1846, a letter to the editor opposed the drastic action taken by Pittsburghers. The writer warned that such a threat could not be carried out because "the natural laws of trade always vindicate themselves, and resist the imposition of force. Men will always buy and sell wherever they find the greatest profits. . . ." *Ibid.*, February 17, 1846.
[57] *Pittsburgh Gazette*, February 28, 1846.
[58] *Pittsburgh Chronicle*, April 9, 1846.

phia"; to do so "was to usurp our natural rights, and render us serfs and slaves to Philadelphia. . . ."[59] The Honorable R. Coutler went even further and asserted that "if their interests are thus to be trampled upon it was their duty to go back to the first principles and shake off the shackles which bound us to the eastern end of the State."[60] The Honorable William Wilkins, so full of indignation that he could scarcely speak, said "we are refused justice."[61] William McCandless, Esquire, of Clarion County, praised the "hard-fisted people who would not bow down to the *Golden Calf* which the Chinese of Chestnut Street had set up."[62] The convention resolved not to use "the language of menace" but they were determined not to be oppressed. The delegates called only for justice, and likened themselves as suffering from the same treatment and abuse as did the Irish. The convention, having made plans to meet again on the 4th day of July, adjourned.[63]

On April 10 the House passed the Right of Way Bill with an amendment providing that the grant to the Baltimore and Ohio should be null and void if the Pennsylvania Railroad advocates[64] could obtain a subscription of three million dollars in capital stock, of which nine hundred thousand must be paid in cash by July 31.[65] The bill passed the Senate and was signed by Governor Shunk on April 21. Every effort was made to carry out the provisions of the amendment. Subscriptions were solicited throughout the State and the required down payment was met on time. Governor Shunk then issued a proclamation announcing the grant to the Baltimore and Ohio null and void.[66] Pittsburgh and Philadelphia were both satisfied—Pittsburgh had secured her improved trade connection and Philadelphia had saved her face.

Rivalries between cities and states were especially characteristic of the period and persisted until the Civil War. Keen competition can be expected when the race is open and the stakes are high. Furthermore, the competition is keen when the odds are great— when one side has nothing to lose and everything to gain. As Pittsburgh became better established in manufacturing and commerce, she joined the ranks of the "haves," and consequently had fewer causes for quarrels.

[59] *Ibid.*, April 9, 1846.
[60] *Ibid.*, April 9, 1846.
[61] *Ibid.*, April 9, 1846.
[62] The reference was made because the Philadelphia opposition met in Chinese Hall, and Pittsburgh used the term "Chinese" as one of opprobrium.
[63] *Pittsburgh Chronicle*, April 9, 1846.
[64] On January 14, 1846, a State Railroad Convention had been held in Harrisburg, and resolutions had been adopted favoring a Pennsylvania Railroad rather than to grant a charter to the Baltimore and Ohio. Certain Pennsylvanians felt that if a railroad had to be built it would be better to make it a Pennsylvania enterprise. Godcharles, *Daily Stories*, 37.
[65] *Pittsburgh Chronicle*, April 20, 1846.
[66] Schotter, H. W., *The Growth and Development of the Pennsylvania Railroad*, (Philadelphia, 1927), 4.

X

Finance and Credit

PITTSBURGH'S finance, closely allied to commerce and industry, experienced a retarded and haphazard development. Until the 19th century Pittsburghers were unable to effect a banking establishment simply because they lacked the necessary prerequisites of specie and credit. A newly developed region is usually handicapped by an insufficient amount of circulating medium. Pittsburgh in 1800 was no exception, and business for the most part was transacted on a paper basis. Credit was essential if merchants were to have any stock, and eastern houses realizing this, early established a credit arrangement with the frontier. The western trade was valuable to the East, and the profits derived were large, although usually slow to materialize. Eastern account books were kept open indefinitely,[1] and the West paid for the privilege of credit in high rates of interest. The "West" was always in debt.

In Pittsburgh a similar relationship existed between merchants and customers. The merchants were now the creditors and the credit circle engulfed the individual consumer and the smaller country merchants, who, likewise, lacked specie. Country products were exchanged for store goods, and the indebtedness usually acted to the advantage of the merchant. Local accounts were also rarely closed, and pleas for their settlement were seldom heard because there was no money with which to settle them.[2] Raw materials were exchanged for finished products, and the surplus was sent off to obtain cash to pay a part of the eastern debts.

By 1800 the frontier had moved westward, but the frontier's ideals and philosophy continued to influence the new generation at the forks of the Ohio. Independent and ultra-individualistic to an alarming degree, the average businessman was reluctant to establish combinations in business and banking. Any type of combination was frowned upon, but the hostility toward the banks was keenest; a hostility caused by the fact that the West was the debtor. Furthermore, because banks were eastern products, and exacting "monsters" at that, the West would have preferred to have none of them. Had the West been able to trade on a more equal basis with the East, the greatest obstacles to banking would have been removed, but, as the indebted-

---

[1] Reynolds, John, *Journals and Day Books,* 1813-1850.
[2] Notices appeared constantly in the newspapers pleading and demanding settlement. The story was always the same and only the dates vary.

ness grew and multiplied, the opposition to the monied East grew in
like proportion. Zadok Cramer as early as September 23, 1803, wrote
a gloomy account of the dangers of too many imports:[3]

Upon a rough calculation, we find that the imports of this place for the last
twelve months of merchandise of various kinds amount to $250,000 (two-hundred
and fifty thousand dollars) and the amount of the exports of flour, whiskey, bar-
iron, castings, etc. from the neighborhood of Pittsburgh, about $180,000 so that
we find ourselves in debt no less than $70,000. This year we are flattered with
the hope of a better market for our produce; the lightness of the crops however
will scarcely make up the deficiency. So that I see but little prospect of getting
rid of this already accumulated debt for two years to come. For every corner
and hole in this western country, if they be not ready filled with foreign extravagances, they cannot long remain so. To see miles together of the mountains
lined with wagons, you would be disposed to presume either that their contents
were lost to the right owners, or that the bowels of the country must groan with
mines of gold equal to that of Peru—it is known but to a few how so many
debts are paid off as really are. Where the money comes from God knows. To
visit the country—to hear the cries of the widows and fatherless—to see their
property torn from them by the rugged hand of the law—exposed to sale—the
cryer cries—who'll buy! and perhaps it is the last bed that a delicate female has
to sleep on—or a cow, the only support of a numerous and helpless family of
children—the picture is too alarming—we will let the curtain fall for a moment,
and wait the event of time.

To make up the deficiency in trade seemed impossible, and the process
of indebtedness went on until Pittsburgh manufacturing developed
and until internal improvements made possible cheap transportation.

Merchants were constantly on the alert to collect sufficient cash to
meet running expenses. Transportation costs and eastern merchandise
required payment, and merchants had to have a certain amount of
money to keep in operation. Accounts were paid as money was available, and the times were called good or bad depending upon the way
the accounts were settled. Individuals and merchants alike paid their
debts as they were able. This mutual dependence upon credit and
the prevalence of debt are keenly evidenced in the correspondence of
James, David, and John Dick, Meadville merchants. John and David
Dick maintained a general store and dealt in pot and pearl ashes in
Meadville, while James Dick handled their extensive business affairs
in Pittsburgh. The correspondence between the brothers dealt largely
with money matters and business prospects, and from their letters an
intimate picture of financial dealings from the 1830's to 1850 can be
found. As late as May, 1837, James Dick wrote to David that:[4]

Your letters of the 1st and 8th inst are at hand. We have transfd [sic] the a/c
of Bemus to you say 64.98/100—I have already written to Guy & Foreman that
some money would be acceptable on their account.

I succeeded after a good deal of trouble in procuring a d[ra]ft for the 450
am[oun]t at a half p[e]r c[en]t premium and have charged it to you the amt

---

[3] Cramer, *Almanack, 1804*, 18.
[4] Dick *Mss.*, James Dick to David Dick, Pittsburgh, May 11, 1837.

of the note given for the Sunday school books—Has he paid his a/c to you, and if not are you not going to collect it.

I have not yet paid the instalments on the Bank stock as the dividends are not payable before the 12th and I want them to go in part. Shall attend to the matter tomorrow. We have rec[eive]d an order from N & B [illegible] in your hand writing for some goods which are ready. They state that they have some pearl ash to come down. When they send it we will do the best we can with it, but I very much doubt whether ten tons could be sold now for 6½ c[en]ts at 4 mo[nths] I am sorry I did not offer yours at 7¢ which I think might have been had for most of it, but I really don't think you will get over 6½. Scorchings are or have sold at 4¢ and no quantity would command that price. We are beginning to feel the effects of the pressure, and there are a good many houses will have pretty tight squeezing to get through, and I suspect some of them will be swamped. It is really awful to read the acts [sic] from New York, New Orleans and many other places in the South.

Money "was acceptable" on accounts generally. Another letter also illustrates the urgent need for money:[5]

If you have received the last six months interest from All.[egheny] Coll.[ege] will you have the goodness to remitt [sic] it to me as I have not a dollar to use, and it has been due nearly a month. I should like to know your opinion about my getting the principal the early part of next month, I fear it not be forth coming.

I hope you have arranged your own business to your satisfaction. I am really grieved that you have so much trouble with that, which ought to have been nothing but honour, and profit, to you. Everything in this world is deceitful, we cannot calculate upon a possession from one week to another.

Business cycles were the only element in the economic field which moved with any degree of speed. A break in the credit chain meant widespread disaster and started a hurried retrenchment which resulted in ruin. Fortunately, business was elastic and survived the repeated shocks because of the extensive possibilities which accompany the filling in of a new country. Out of this remolding process, order and growth developed as the country became settled and its resources were utilized.

The development of banks, the increase of banking facilities and circulating medium, and the use of an improved credit system aided materially in the expansion of manufacturing and trade. Since merchants and manufacturers needed improved financial machinery, and since a few of them had acquired a little capital, they naturally were instrumental in founding banks in Pittsburgh. The initial step, however, to establish a bank in Pittsburgh was taken by the Philadelphia directors of the Bank of Pennsylvania who made a formal proposition to the business men of Pittsburgh. The public was informed through a notice published by the town clerk, William Christy, that:[6]

The free holders and other inhabitants, householders, are hereby requested to attend a meeting of the corporation at the court house on Saturday, the 26th of March, at four o'clock P. M. in order to take in to consideration a proposition

[5] Ibid., L. S. Alden to David Dick, Pittsburgh, October 30, 1850.
[6] Pittsburgh Gazette, March 18, 1803.

of the directors of the Bank of Pennsylvania for establishing a branch of their own within this borough providing it is approved by the corporation.

From the beginning, the people of Pittsburgh were consulted in matters having to do with the banking question, and the newspaper accounts are numerous, indicating the fact that Pittsburghers took their responsibilities seriously. Throughout the period, the people were bank conscious, and banking was benefited and hampered alike by general public supervision. The people were like children who talk loudly to overcome the fear of the dark. Never having complete confidence in the institution, but, having been forced by necessity and needs of the time, Pittsburgh established her bank.

The board of directors was comprised of sound, solid businessmen who were the builders and the leaders of the community.[7] Being merchants and manufacturers they, above all others, realized the need for a bank, and through their influence, the bank was successful from the beginning. Trade and manufacturing needed the stabilizing influence which a bank could provide, and the bank needed an active and expanding business. The commercial situation in Pittsburgh was definitely improved with the establishment of the branch bank in 1804, although conditions were not perfect by any means. Between 1804 and 1810 business in Pittsburgh increased, and the existing banking facilities were thought to be insufficient to meet the demands. A second bank was organized in February 1810.[8] This association was a Pittsburgh enterprise, and the capital was supplied by a group of local merchants. However, legislative obstacles prevented the bank from materializing, for the Act of March 18, 1810, required all banks to be incorporated under State law and forbade the banks incorporated under the Act of 1808 to lend money, to receive deposits, to issue notes, or, in short, to do a banking business. A memorial, pleading the need for increased banking facilities to take care of the growing trade and commerce, was sent to the legislature for the purpose of securing a charter. The legislature, however, refused to grant the charter and the organization was obliged to change its name to the Pittsburgh Manufacturing Company. On June 16, 1812, the company commenced a partial banking business and the sale of insurance. Thus, the financial business of Pittsburgh during the War of 1812 was handled by these two institutions—the branch of the Bank of Pennsylvania and the Pittsburgh Manufacturing Company. The restraining hand of the Bank of the United States had been lifted by the lapse of its charter in 1811, and the United States was de-

[7] *Ibid.*, January 13, 1804. "The Directors of the Bank of Pennsylvania have elected the following gentlemen Directors of the branch bank about to be established at this place: John Wilkins, Jr., Presley Neville, Oliver Ormsby, James O'Hara, James Berthoud, Ebenezer Denny, Joseph Barker, George Stevenson, John Wood, Thomas Baird, John Johnson and George Robinson. John Wilkins, Jr., was elected president and Thomas Wilson, cashier. John Thaw was chosen teller."
[8] Pennsylvania *Laws*, 1807-1808, (Philadelphia, 1808), 185-86.

prived of its guiding influence at a time when a strong fiscal agent
was needed.[9] The government and private business alike were in a
fool's paradise for almost three years. Shortsightedness characterized
many of the financial measures of the period. Specie was in active
circulation, large amounts of notes were issued, and credit was liberal.
American business prospered and naturally overreached itself. When
Congress refused to recharter the United States Bank in 1811, the
field was opened for state banks; nor were the states slow to seize
the opportunity. Lack of banking restrictions, demands for new
credit caused by the war, loose credit in public and private enterprise,
the exportation of seven million dollars to European investors upon
the dissolution of the United States Bank alone—all these forecasted
troubles ahead. When the British captured Washington in August,
1814, banking institutions everywhere south of New England were
forced to suspend specie payment.

The Act of March 6, 1814, passed by the Pennsylvania legislature
was an attempt to remedy the situation. The act provided for loans
to farmers and manufacturers, as well as providing for the organization of 41 banks throughout the State.[10] Two of these banks were
to be located in Pittsburgh. More drastic action was needed, however,
than the mere incorporation of new banking establishments to repair
the muddled financial deals of three hectic years. Furthermore, with
the cessation of the war, a reaction set in which intensified all financial
ills. Pittsburgh and the West were besieged by the usual peace
retrenchment, and the condition was aggravated by a drainage of
specie to the East. Every issue of the newspapers carried editorials
and letters on the banks and the general financial distress. The
attacks on the banks of the seaboard were especially bitter, and the
Pittsburgh bankers and merchants blamed them entirely for causing
the difficulties.[11] The western country correctly anticipated a general
bankruptcy which materialized not only for it, but for all sections.
Business and banking collapsed both in Pittsburgh and on the seaboard.[12]

National measures were inaugurated, but sectionalism and politics
delayed action. The Second Bank of the United States finally commenced operations on January 7, 1817, and while the banking system
was considerably improved, the currency problem was unimproved.

[9] The total loss to the government in disposing of its loans during 1812 to 1816 was
enormous; in 1830 the Committee of Ways and Means of the House estimated that
for loans of over $80,000,000, the treasury received but $34,000,000 as measured in
specie. Dewey, Davis R., Financial History of the United States, (New York, 1934),
134.
[10] Pittsburgh Gazette, March 18, 1814.
[11] Ibid., February 7, 1817; February 25, 1817; March 4, 1817.
[12] The Bank of Pittsburgh paid a 4 percent dividend, nevertheless, on May 16, 1816,
Pittsburgh Gazette, June 11, 1816; while the Farmers and Mechanics Bank declared
a similar dividend to be collected after November 16, Ibid., November 15, 1816.

Paper of the banks of Western Pennsylvania was at a discount of more than 25 percent.[13] On December 2, 1816, a group of Pittsburgh citizens with Ebenezer Denny as chairman, held a meeting and prepared a memorial praying for the establishment of a branch of the United States Bank in Pittsburgh.[14] Their petition answered, the branch of the Bank of Pennsylvania became a branch of the United States Bank in 1817, and its name was changed to the Office of Discount and Deposits of the United States. On March 20, 1817, when the Pittsburgh banks resumed the payment of specie,[15] the editor of the Gazette looked forward to a return of the "gold or silver age." He thought that resumption would restore the confidence which had been lacking, and that the exchange brokers would be forced out of business.[16] The exchange broker had arrived in Pittsburgh during the boom days of the War, and since that time his services had been accepted for a small fee. Few, if any, objected to the broker during the rush to gather in the war profits, for he had aided the precariously balanced financial setup to slide along smoothly. The broker unscrambled the mass of paper notes which had flooded the commercial world, and through his efficiency, facilitated the growth of the boomerang which circled around and finally returned to strike the creator. When the financial tower of paper began to tumble, the fall was rapid. Bankers, investors, merchants, farmers, and brokers were hard hit, and the West blamed Great Britain, the East, and the brokers for the unhappy times.

When the Second Bank of the United States was started, Pittsburghers thought that the day of the brokers was over, and that the eastern and western notes would be equal, but, wailed the Gazette: "We are brought back to a sad reality that the acts of a bank cannot restore prosperity to a country."[17] The editor realized that exchange must exist when the balance of trade of a country was unequal and that "every country that imports more in value than it exports must submit to a depreciation of its paper in the places from which it exports."[18] Pittsburgh, more than ever, feared the exchange brokers because their presence constantly reminded Pittsburghers that huge

[13] Thaw Mss., George Poe to John Thaw, January 6, 1815, and December 14, 1816.
[14] Pittsburgh Gazette, February 14, 1817.
[15] Ibid., March 25, 1817. "We omitted in our last to mention that the Banks in this city resumed the payment of specie on Thursday the 20th instant."
[16] Ibid., February 14, 1817. An article signed "Wood Street" denounced the system of brokers which had sprung up in Pittsburgh: "When we are compelled to pay from 17 to 20 per cent on notes taken currently in business to obtain 'bank money' it indicates 'something rotten in Denmark!' Will any one say that these notes cannot be collected in the usual course of trade from the different banks at a less loss than half this sum. I will admit that the high price of Pittsburgh and United States money amongst us, is owing in a great degree to its scarcity. But what causes the scarcity? Because the money is bought and withdrawn by brokers who transmit it backwards and forwards to the different banks, and brokers, eastward and westward at an enormous profit." Ibid., February 19, 1819.
[17] Ibid., September 15, 1818.
[18] Ibid., September 15, 1818.

quantities of their paper was questionable and that bankruptcy was too close for comfort. Pittsburgh was faced with a severe crisis during this postwar period for manufacturing had declined rapidly; exports had dropped with the return of normal trade conditions, and imports from the East had increased. Pittsburghers bemoaned their fate, and the prospects did indeed look very dark.

The East, however, had a similar catastrophe to face, and her nemesis was Great Britain. The actual warfare between England and the United States had ceased, it is true, but a commercial policy was instituted by Great Britain which was as ruinous as a war. British manufacturers dumped their goods upon American shores by the boatloads for sale at prices which were ridiculously low, and the balance, estimated at about $30,000,000, was against the United States.[19] For a time, it seemed as though America would be reconquered by the Manchester weavers and the Sheffield manufacturers. British goods flooded the country, and American merchants and manufacturers in all sections faced ruin.

Pittsburgh was extremely disturbed by the postwar conditions, and the situation tended to become more aggravated as time went on. In 1817 and 1818 the general public was stunned with amazement that the economic machine could buckle and collapse so quickly. At first, Pittsburghers blamed outside forces for the misery, but, as the hardships continued to multiply and become permanent, the "bank" began to lose standing.[20] Mumblings against the bank began late in 1818, and on February 16, 1819, a town meeting was held to discuss the propriety of petitioning for the removal of the United States Bank. At the meeting two resolutions were passed: the first demanded the repeal of the charter of the bank, and the second requested the removal of the branch bank from Pittsburgh.[21] Sounder judgment evidently prevailed, for the bank continued in Pittsburgh.

The fundamental difficulty was not that there were too many banks in Pittsburgh but rather that there was too much paper. Specie never had been too plentiful, and with the wholesale drainage all over the country, and with each individual's desperate rush to save his own integrity, the situation was made worse. Pittsburgh, along with other regions outside of New England, had made loans on improper securities and had overissued notes. "Freedom had triumphed with regard to money and banking, except freedom from the natural laws of trade; and before these laws all were equal."[22] Until loans were reduced and

---

[19] *Ibid.*, November 25, 1818. The anticipated exportation of specie to England for 1819 was expected to be $15,000,000; fearing that all specie would be drained from the country the *Gazette* urged that specie payment be stopped and that future importation from England be temporarily prohibited.
[20] *Ibid.*, February 2, 1819.
[21] *Ibid.*, February 19, 1819.
[22] Dewey, *Financial History of the United States,* 154.

note circulation was contracted to safe proportions, banking was precarious. After the re-establishment of the Second National Bank and the first shock of banking retrenchment, financial conditions became more stable.[23]

Pittsburgh banking suffered another unexpected shock on April 6, 1818, when the Farmers and Mechanics Bank was robbed.[24] One hundred thousand dollars in banknotes and six thousand eight hundred dollars in specie were taken; and although the robbers were captured and the money recovered, the credit of the bank was hopelessly shaken. On March 12, 1819, the bank began gradually to call in its notes in order not to embarrass the merchants,[25] and on July 23, 1819, it closed its doors.

Between 1818 and 1823 bankers in Pittsburgh had an uncomfortable time. Bankers and businessmen were brought down to earth, so to speak, and banking, like business and manufacturing, had to be rebuilt on a sound foundation. As the rigorous commercial pressure began to ease up from 1823 to 1828, an interval of calm ensued in financial affairs.[26] Trade and manufacturing made a remarkable recovery, and banking was sound and under control. The dumping of English goods had been halted and specie was no longer leaving the country in a wholesale fashion. Loans were made on a more secure basis, and note issue was based on more than the available amount of paper and printing presses. The banking establishments which handled Pittsburgh business were the Branch Bank of the United States,[27] the Bank of Pittsburgh, the City Bank of Pittsburgh,[28] and the private house of Nathaniel Holmes.[29] The period was a welcome calm after the turbulent postwar period. The calm, unfortunately, was short-lived.

About 1828 a flair for speculation, unparalleled in the history of the United States, sprang up among all classes. Good times had brought widespread profits. Prosperity in peacetime usually means internal development, and America began to build roads and canals. Influenced by the inherent desire to produce results, the program was

[23] *Pittsburgh Gazette,* December 28, 1819. J. Town's Exchange Office listed the bank note exchange, and the discount for the various Pittsburgh banks on December 28, 1819, was as follows:
    United States Bank and branches—½ and 1 per cent.
    Bank of Pittsburgh—par.
    Farmers and Mechanics Bank—4 per cent.
[24] *Ibid.,* April 7, 1818. The bank had been chartered on August 2, 1814.
[25] *Ibid.,* March 12, 1819.
[26] Day, *Historical Collections,* 51.
[27] The Pittsburgh branch was known as the Office of Discount and Deposit.
[28] In 1817 the City Bank of Pittsburgh was opened for business by the Reverend Robert Patterson. The bank was not incorporated, but it issued its own notes which circulated at par, and which were eventually redeemed by Mr. Patterson after the suspension of the bank in 1824. Thurston asserted that the bank made only one discount and then, for some unknown reason, closed; the notes were redeemed, however. Thurston, George H., *Allegheny County's Hundred Years.* (Pittsburgh, 1888), 253.
[29] Nathaniel Holmes was the oldest private banking house west of the Alleghenies and was established in 1822.

wide and too extensive. Internal improvement had been lacking for a long time, but suddenly every section realized an urgent need and began to build at a furious pace. States and individuals alike made loans either at home or abroad. New banks sprang up and old ones enlarged; paper increased and the demand for roads and canals continued to grow. Manufacturing expanded, real estate boomed, and the price level rose; in short, "all the world was getting rich, and that without labor."[30] The states in which internal improvements were especially needed were those of the frontier where capital was scarce. The temptation was strong to take advantage of the freedom of action allowed to the states to create their capital, and "this generation in the vigor of its exuberant youth, unable to coin its dreams, many states printed them and then discounted them in the money markets of the East or Europe."[31] The entire United States felt the excitement, and the fever spread to all classes of business and finance.

During the period of expansion, four new banking houses opened for business in Pittsburgh. In 1830 George A. Cook opened a banking house, and combined banking with the selling of lottery tickets, which was a legal business, and, in keeping with the times, extremely popular.[32] The Merchants and Manufacturers Bank, chartered by the State, began business on June 4, 1833, with a capital of $600,000.[33] As its name implied, the Merchants and Manufacturers Bank was closely concerned with commerce and industry, and the bank played an important role in Pittsburgh development. The Pittsburgh Saving Fund Company also was organized in 1833. The company consisted of ten men, each of whom paid ten dollars to the fund and added two dollars weekly.[34] In 1844 the company became known as the Farmers Deposit Company. The Exchange Bank was chartered by the Act of March 2, 1836, with a capital of $1,000,000.[35] Within the years 1834 and 1835 the amount of money invested in bank buildings alone exceeded $360,000, and during the year 1835, bank business had doubled.[36]

The economic conditions in Pittsburgh began to tighten early in 1834. The newspapers and businessmen lamented and called the situa-

[30] Day, *Historical Collections*, 51.
[31] Fish, *The Rise of the Common Man*, 37.
[32] Thurston, *Allegheny County's Hundred Years*, 253.
[33] The first board of directors were: Michael Tierman, President, Isaac Lightner, T. B. Dallas, Jacob Forsythe, Thomas S. Clark, George A. Cook, Fred Loverz, Samuel Church, Thomas Scott, Francis G. Bailey, Samuel Smith, Samuel Fahnestock and John Shoenberger. White, *One Hundred and Fifty Years of Unparalleled Thrift*, 45.
[34] The original company consisted of the following: James Fulton, President, James Anderson, Reuben Miller, Jr., James Marshall, James Armstrong, Nathan Carlisle, Huey Sweney, Robert Galway, Samuel George, and Gabriel Adams. Thurston, *Allegheny County's Hundred Years*, 255.
[35] The first board of directors were: William Robinson, Jr., President, Sylvan Lathrop, James Lidlie, George Wallace, Tobias Meyers, B. A. Fahnestock, Samuel Darlington, John Grier, John Freeman, W. G. Alexander, James W. Brown, Samuel Baird, Harvey Childs. Pennsylvania *House Journal*, 1835-36, I, 670.
[36] *Pittsburgh Gazette*, February 22, 1836; March 3, 1836.

tion "the 'experiment' of our wise financiers." Commercial transactions were seriously curtailed even in March, 1834:[37]

. . . our business, like all others, here, has felt the baleful effects of the late Executive measure, [Bank charter refused] and consequent pressure in the money market, and we have therefore been obliged to suspend operations and discharge our hands—and intend lying upon our oars until the gale has passed. When that much desired event shall occur we cannot foretell, and we are therefore unable to say whether we shall be at all able to go on—much less to quote any prices for future operations.

Further light is thrown on the subject:[38]

Your letter covering Judge Vincent's note for $2,000 came to hand and was discounted last night by my indorseing [sic] it as the rule is here By Mr. Hunter I Enclose proceeds $1978.67. In Erie notes which if necessary I new [sic] you could get Exch[ange]d into such funds as w[oul]d. suit you.—The B[an]k. of P.[ittsburgh] was hard work to supply all the wants she is called on for and probably in no other than such a use could the Loan this time be renewed on any other account. It is necessary to send Jno. Vincent's check by 1st opp[ortunit]y. for this sum $1978.67 as it passd [sic] to his cr.[edit] on the Books. I hope you are well and are not so much annoyed with politicks [sic] and their awful affects [sic] as we are—the very name of Jacksonism makes me *sick* and ere five years I am of the opinion a respectable man will dislike so much to have belonged to that gang of Robbers and plunderers as ever *Nugens* band of *Horse* thieves was to belong to their name—a disgraced dishonoured Country of innocent people are however principally sufferers.

Despite repeated danger signals, the period of expansion did not cease. The country was steeped in a financial chaos which had begun shortly after 1832 and which continued to grow worse at intervals until the climax in 1837. The panic of 1837 was the direct result of overexpansion and political machinations. "The construction of public works outran the needs of the country and tied up millions of borrowed capital in enterprises that would for many years be unproductive."[39] Speculation had been based largely on bank credit and paper money of doubtful value, and when politics had become involved, the catastrophe resulted.

The commercial interests of Pittsburgh were hard hit by the panic of 1837, but Pittsburgh was not prostrated as much as the eastern

[37] Dick *Mss.*, Maitland and Brother to J. D. Dick, Pittsburgh, March 10, 1834.
    Maitland quoted these prices:
       Sketch of the Effects of the Experiment in Pittsburgh:
       On 1st Jan. of 1834 Flour sold at $4½; on 15th Feb. was selling at $2.⅝
       On 1st Jan. of 1834 Wheat sold 77 @ 80¢; on 15th Feb. was selling 56 @ 60¢
       On 1st Jan. of 1834 Rye sold at 56¢; on 15th Feb. 40 @ 45¢ is only offered
       On 1st Jan. of 1834 Corn sold at 50¢; on 15th Feb. 33 @ 35¢ is only offered
       On 1st Jan. of 1834 Barley sold at 50¢; on 15th Feb. we are begged to take 35¢
       On 1st Jan. of 1834 Whiskey sold at 25 @ 26¢; on 15th Feb. it sold at 16¢
    "So the farmer has benefited by the 'experiment' with a loss of 40 per cent on flour and an average of 25 per cent on his other grain. Yet this is a war 'in favour of the poor and against the rich.'
      In Wheeling the highest price given for wheat is only 50¢ per bu., but most of the mills refuse to give more than 44¢. On 1st Jany. it sold at 75¢!
      Accounts from New Orleans of date 20th Feby. State that flour there is held nominally at $4. ! ! ! ! ! & no sales on demand & Rectified Whiskey at 17¢."
[38] *Ibid.*, J. N. McKee to D. Dick, Pittsburgh, April 9, 1834.
[39] Kline, Harriet, The Financial and Industrial Aspects of the Panic of 1837 on Pittsburgh, (Master's Thesis, University of Pittsburgh, 1933), 3.

cities. The panic was not a sudden overnight occurrence. Pittsburgh had suffered from almost unparalleled pressure for six months before the downfall of the financial centers.[40] The stringency in the money market became so serious in late January, 1837, that a committee was selected from the Board of Trade to investigate conditions.[41] The committee reported that:[42]

There was too great disparity between the banking capital invested and the business operations of the city: that owing to this fact the system of credit has been too extensively relied on, thus greatly endangering enterprises in times of monetary agitation, that the business of Pittsburgh per annum amounted to $45,000,000 while the banking capital was less than $5,000,000; that the branch of the Pennsylvania Bank of the United States had proved a 'broken reed,' though great benefits had been expected from it by reason of the representation of its directors; and that as a measure of relief, they would recommend that another representation of the needs of the community for greater banking capital should be made to the Pennsylvania Bank of the United States, with the request that the Branch here should be capitalized for $3,000,000.

The committee favored increasing the capital of the established banks rather than to charter new ones, but the Board of Directors of the Pennsylvania Bank of the United States replied that they were unable to meet the proposal.[43] "Nick" Biddle and the bank both fell in the estimation of the people.

As always happens when pressure is brought to bear on any part of a credit system, the disturbance began to bring ruin. Pittsburgh's industrial development had progressed to the point where she was able to extend credit to the country and western merchants, but these men were now unable to pay their debts due to the stringency of the money market.[44] Pittsburgh merchants who were likewise indebted to the East, were forced to ask for an extension of time from their creditors. Furthermore, merchants who did come to Pittsburgh to buy did not have cash, or if they did have money, Pittsburgh brokers could not exchange it.[45] Merchants hardly knew where to turn:[46]

At present we have quantities of money in the shape of Ohio Bank notes that we cannot use. The very devil is to pay about money matters and I don't know how we Pittsburghers are to get along. I am discouraged at the threatening aspect of affairs and have no desire to do much business under present circumstances—you may depend there are squally times coming and I do hope you and John will bring your matters to a close and try to collect your debts while there is any money in the country to pay them. It is impossible that the present difficulties can be long confinded [sic] to the cities, and it must sooner or later reach the country. There will most certainly be a great come down in real estate and I hope you will make no more engagements for land purchases. Flour

[40] *Saturday Evening Visitor,* January 7, 1837.
[41] *Pittsburgh Gazette,* February 3, 1837.
[42] *Ibid.,* February 3, 1837.
[43] *Ibid.,* February 12, 1837.
[44] Wilson, *Standard History of Pittsburgh,* 171. "In February 1837, it was estimated that there was due the local merchants in money which they could not collect $10,000,000."
[45] Dick, *Mss.,* James Dick to David Dick, Pittsburgh, June 29, 1837.
[46] *Ibid.,* James Dick to David Dick, Pittsburgh, April 26, 1837.

will certainly be down to 6 dollars and probably lower here, but I do not think
that it would be any object for you to borrow money to purchase any. At all
events wait awhile to see what turn things will take. I fear your ashes will not
bring over 7 cents as we have had no more offers to buy at 7½¢ and none of the
glass men will purchase any more than they can get along with. Gene Mards has
just stepped in and wishes very much to have the taxes for 1836 paid on lot no.
1679 8th donation list. . . .

In an attempt to alleviate the difficulties, the businessmen of Pittsburgh memorialized the legislature to establish another bank, but the
legislature failed to respond. A local bank was, nevertheless, organized in Pittsburgh[47] under the name of the Mechanics Bank, and although never incorporated, the bank issued notes and carried on a
general banking business. This attempt was insufficient, however, to
meet the emergency, and manufacturing, as well as business generally,
was greatly curtailed because money was scarce; "the pressure" became more and more severe.[48]

On May 13, 1837, Pittsburgh received the news that the banks of
New York, Philadelphia, and Baltimore had suspended specie payment. After holding a meeting, Pittsburgh bankers decided that the
only course open for them was to do likewise[49] in order to prevent
"the entire abstraction of the precious metals from Pittsburgh."[50]
James Dick described the condition:[51]

You will have heard before this reaches you, the disastrous news of the banks
in New York, Phila,[delphia] and Baltimore having suspended specie payment.
Our Banks have followed suit this day having been obliged to come into the
measure, as the only means of saving them from immediate and absolute ruin.
There were persons arrived here a few minutes after the hour of closing the Banks
on Saturday with paper to the amt of 80 thousand doll[ar]s to get the specie.
The city has been in greatest fear for these two days but every one acquiesces
in the poor propriety of the act. This morning at seven o'clock there was a
town meeting held at which several hundreds were present, who recommended by
a very unanimous vote the suspension of the specie pay[men]t by our Banks was
recommended. The fact is there was no alternative left, for if they had not done
so, now before Saturday night they would have been obliged to do so from

[47] *Pittsburgh Mercury*, October 18, 1837.
[48] *Pittsburgh Gazette*, April 17, 1837.
[49] *Pittsburgh Mercury*, May 17, 1837. The resolutions were unanimously adopted:
    Resolved that under the existing circumstances . . . it has become expedient that the
    banks of this city . . . should suspend specie payments.
    Resolved, that we have implicit confidence in the stability of all the banking institu-
    tions of the city of Pittsburgh. . . .
    Resolved, that we pledge ourselves to receive the notes of the Banks of Pittsburgh in
    all payments and business transactions. . . .
    Resolved, that an immediate application be made to the Governor to call the Legis-
    lature together with all convenient speed, that measures may be adopted suitable to
    the present exigencies.
    Resolved, that a committee of ten persons be appointed to communicate the above
    resolutions to the banking institutions in the city. . . .
    Resolved, that the banks be requested to take immediately into consideration the pro-
    priety of making arrangements for the creation of circulating medium of a denomina-
    tion less than five dollars.
    Resolved, that the city council be requested to take into consideration the propriety
    of issuing small bills to fill up and supply a circulating medium during the suspension
    of specie payments.
[50] *Souvenir of the Bank of Pittsburgh*, (1810-1896), 25.
[51] Dick *Mss.*, James Dick to David Dick, Pittsburgh, May 15, 1837.

inability to meet the calls that would have been made on them—A meeting of the city council is already called to consider the propriety of issuing by the corporation small bills or shin plasters to supply the purposes of exchange. So we are to have the scenes that followed the late war reenacted much sooner than we dreamed of. What this state of matter will lead to time only can develop. Many think that the times will be better for a while, but this way of improving the state of the times is a most desperate remedy. I do not know what notes will be received hereafter by our Banks, but presume very few western ones will, and those that are rejected, I expect will be at a discount of from 5 to 25 per c[en]t discount. This will operate very severely upon country places situated as yours is where there is such a mixed description of notes in circulation I send you by this mail a New York Express in which you will see something of the state of feeling in that city—John Anderson has just returned from New Orleans and brought us some rotten oranges from Mr. Smith besides some other things not rotten. He says Mr. S has suffered to the tune of about sixty thousand dollars by the failures in that place. So much the worse for me. He has however not been obliged to yield to the storm and I hope will be able to get through.

Banks in all parts of the country suspended payment, and the uneasiness was nationwide. James Dick wrote: "We are in dreadful state at present about money affairs. Nothing will be taken in our banks but city notes and even then they reserve the privilege of paying out the particular kind that are taken."[52] Again:[53]

Times continue pretty tight and I see little prospect of them being better. A good deal of complaint is made against our Banks for not discounting more liberally, these are doing scarce any new paper, but renewing discounted notes generally. If they expect to renew specie payment soon this course is necessary to be adhered to. No money but Dg[?] or Eastern is received by them on deposit.

A request was sent to Governor Ritner to call a special session of the legislature,[54] but the Governor declined to do so because he considered that the measures it proposed to adopt would be mischievous. Consequently, Pittsburgh was forced to act for itself. One of the greatest hardships was the lack of specie of small denomination, so local notes were issued under the name of "shin plasters."[55] By the ordinances of May 16, 1837, July 8, 1837, and January 29, 1838, the city of Pittsburgh issued small notes to the amount of almost $100,000.[56]

By 1838 conditions appeared to be improving although the specie was still hoarded, and "shin plasters" were much too plentiful. Pittsburghers accepted the situation as gracefully as was possible under the circumstances.[57] On July 10, 1838, Governor Ritner issued a proclamation requiring all State banks to resume specie payment on and after August 13, 1838. By the end of the year, the financial dis-

---

[52] *Ibid.*, James Dick to David Dick, Pittsburgh, May 22, 1837.
[53] *Ibid.*, May 31, 1837.
[54] *Pittsburgh Gazette*, May 15, 1837.
[55] *Ibid.*, May 27, 1837.
[56] *Pittsburgh Mercury*, August 23, 1837.
[57] *Ibid.*, January 4, 1838.

tress seemed to be diminishing and public confidence in banking institutions returned. "Shin plasters" began to disappear, and currency was gradually restored to its former position.[58]

Pittsburgh recovered slowly, and her commercial and financial business did not function normally until 1841.[59] Banking was by no means completely restored, and the 1840's witnessed frequent fluctuations. Pittsburgh suffered with the rest of the country and snatched brief periods of prosperity whenever possible.

But the national banking "experiment" continued. President Van Buren attempted to remedy the situation by his independent treasury system. The Whigs, coming into power in 1840, decided that the system was not good, and so the law was repealed on August 13, 1841.[60] While the government legislated, one way or another, Pittsburgh tried to get along as well as she could under the circumstances.[61] Conditions being too unsettled for safe commercial ventures, merchants were surprised to find themselves still in business. James Dick before leaving Pittsburgh for New Orleans wrote:[62]

We will I hope have a pleasant trip, as the weather is very pleasant, and everything favorable except money matters. I had a letter since I came down from Mrs. Smith who represents New Orleans as in a deplorable condition, failures occurring everyday among the strongest houses. A great many heavy failures have taken place recently in Philad.,[elphia] and God only knows when we are to see the end of these disastrous times. I hope you will be able to rub along untill [sic] you get your Pearl Ash to Market. The prospect of making sales then in the spring is dull and I think you will be obliged to send a part of yours to New York. Bakewells are unwilling to make contract for any, but I think [they] will buy some in the Spring.

Bank notes continued to be issued in large amounts, although not so recklessly as in the years before 1837. The greatest handicap to trade was that all banks were not conducted on an equally safe basis;

---

[58] *Pittsburgh Times*, December 10, 1838.
[59] *Pittsburgh Gazette*, March 2, 1841.
[60] The plan for an independent treasury system was first proposed by President Van Buren in his message of September, 1837. In this message Van Buren stated that the constitution had not intended that the government should assume the management of domestic or private exchange any more than it should provide for the transportation of merchandise; that the previous experiments in the employment of local banks for the care of government funds had proved unsatisfactory; that the early practice of employing the banks was a measure of emergency rather than of sound policy, that the emergency no longer existed, for instead of a large national debt there was a large surplus which the government should adequately protect. He pointed out that the use of government funds by banks led to pernicious results in the expansion of credit, rashness of enterprise, and speculation. He proposed that the government should take care of its own fund, and return to the practice of requiring the payment of all dues in specie with no exceptions whatever in favor of bills of specie-paying banks. A bill was introduced in the Senate, September 14, 1837, without the specie clause: both Van Buren and Calhoun objected, so it was added and passed the Senate by a vote of 26 to 20. The House failed to pass it by a vote of 120 to 106. The bill was reintroduced in the 1837-1838 session and again in 1838-1839 session, but failed both times. The election in 1838, however, brought new men to Congress and the bill finally passed and was approved by the President on July 4, 1840. Dewey, *Financial History of the United States*, 235-236, 239-240.
[61] Legislative measures were:
    1. Independent Treasury System, July 4, 1840-August 13, 1841.
    2. State Depositories, 1841-1846.
    3. Independent Treasury System, August 1846-1863.
[62] Dick *Mss.*, James Dick to David Dick, Pittsburgh, March 3, 1842.

consequently, trade was highly uncertain. Pittsburgh banks were satisfactory, but all neighboring State and country banks were not equally safe. A good illustration of what Pittsburgh businessmen had to worry about is seen in the following letter:[63]

Your favor of the 14th Inst. is at hand this morning, enclosing 105$ in notes of the Berks Co. Bank.

We have tried our Brokers to exchange at same price. They, however, refuse to buy unless at a rate much greater, than you perhaps would wish to pay viz. 50 p[e]r c[en]t discount.

The notes of the Bank are quoted in Philad[elphia] 40 to 50 p[e]r c[en]t disc[oun]t.

Shall we sell them here—return them to you, or remit them to Philadelphia to be sold there on the best terms which can be had?

It was our intention at one time today to sell them at 50 p[e]r c[en]t disc[oun]t. but as they will probably not depreciate more within a few days, will wait until we hear from you.

Our currency is sadly deranged—We hear today of the failure of several long established firms in Philad[elphi]a.

From 1841 until 1850 Pittsburgh banking was more regular, and the financial business was handled by the already established five banks and two private institutions.[64] There were few, if any, sweeping changes in banking during this decade, although business in both banking and trade increased.

Generally speaking, banking in Pittsburgh from 1800 to 1850 was not able to keep pace with commercial development. Handicapped by ignorance and the inherent western philosophy, Pittsburghers them-

---

[63] *Ibid.*, D. S. Stockton & Co. to David Dick, Pittsburgh, March 17, 1842.
[64] Pittsburgh banks established between 1800 and 1850:

Name	Chartered	Capital	Comments
Pittsburgh Branch of Bank of Pennsylvania	1804		Became Office of Discount and Deposits of U. S. in 1817. Rechartered as branch of U. S. Bank of Pennsylvania in 1837.
Bank of Pittsburgh	1814	$600,000	Began in Feb. 1, 1810 as Pittsburgh Manufacturing Co.—banking and insurance.
Farmers & Mechanics Bank	1814	$450,000	Liquidated late in 1819.
City Bank of Pittsburgh....	1817		Not incorporated; suspended 1824.
N. Holmes & Sons........	1822		Private house.
George A. Cook	1830		Private house; also real estate, lottery; 1837—E. Sibbett & Co.; 1840, Sibbett and Jones.
Mercants and Manufacturers Bank	1833	$600,000	Pittsburgh enterprise.
Pittsburgh Saving Fund Co...1834		$25,000 to $200,000	Became Farmers Deposit Company, 1844.
Exchange Bank of Pittsburgh 1836		$1,000,000	
Mechanics Bank	1837		Not incorporated.

selves were not kindly disposed towards banks, especially Federal banks which had their roots in the East. This hostility was accentuated because of the unfavorable balance of trade, and because there was no real money in the West to pay for the difference. The greatest difficulty, however, lay in the fact that banking throughout the country was in an experimental stage and currency was as equally unsettled as banking. Until that time when credit could be regulated and until currency meant something more than the printing of paper, it was physically impossible for a financial system to function calmly. Banking was largely a gamble, through no fault of its own. Personal integrity might be intact, but circumstances were at great odds. Politics, always willing to help the financier, was the step-father of pre-1850 banking. To live through such a period was far from comfortable and business cycles changed too rapidly for good business. By 1850, however, Pittsburgh's financial structure had developed to a point of safety and, although far from perfect, the succeeding period had brighter prospects.

XI

Pittsburgh's Attempts at Economic Organization

ECONOMIC organization in Pittsburgh experienced a similarly reluctant development as did banking. Prior to 1830 the accepted business philosophy and the keystone for success apparently demanded little more than honest industry, and according to the established standards, a man willing to work possessed the most necessary requirement. If problems were too big for one individual, the problems were broken down; early industrialists were not favorably inclined toward large scale economic organization. The opposition to organized capital and the fear of monopolies were carried to the point of fetishness. The struggle against them was a losing battle; gradually, but steadily, the West discovered that organization was imperative. After years of trying to handle problems individually, they found it more successful to organize and to tackle problems jointly. But the road between these periods was strewn with dismal failures of brave, ambitious, but premature, undertakings.

Probably the most persistent problems that annoyed Pittsburgh were the freight rates and marketing difficulties. Despite the energy and money expended, the problems grew and multiplied. Consequently, the first organizations were formed to deal with marketing problems.

The earliest known attempt to organize the river trade was proposed by John Wilkins, Jr., on August 31, 1802. In an appeal to the "Farmers, Millers, Traders and Manufacturers of the Western Country who are concerned in its prosperity and improvement" Wilkins presented the difficulties:[1]

> You are not ignorant of the many disadvantages under which the Mississippi trade has laboured since its commencement, chiefly for the want of competent information of the extent of the demand at the Orleans market, the means of exportation by sea, and the proper destination of our produce so exported. Hence it happens that sometimes unusual profits are made by a few, and unusual losses suffered by a few, sometimes by many. To compute moderately there cannot be less than Sixty Thousand Dollars lost in that trade this year in this country. This, and the consequent discouragement must sink the value of our produce, and of course of our farms. Many embark on this trade who are unacquainted with the navigation of the river, and strangers to the climate and the inhabitants whom they go to deal with and their government, their customs and their language. When they arrive at Orleans they are obliged to sell for what may be offered for want of vessels to carry their produce to another market, or knowledge of a proper market. And they cannot remain long there on account of the expense, the risk of sickness, the anxiety to return home to attend to their families and their farms.

---

[1] *Pittsburgh Gazette*, September 17, 1802.

Cautiously and tactfully, Wilkins urged an organization "to combine the interests of the inhabitants of the Western Country in general" so that the losses would be scattered and that they would not ruin any one person. Naturally distribution of losses would mean also distribution of profits, but, by this plan, no one individual would be entirely ruined. Wilkins pointed out: "If this could be done, our trade would no longer be fluctuating, but as steady as at seaports, the farmer could get a just price for his grain and be encouraged to go on with his improvements, and the trader would not be ruined and hurt the farmer in his fall."[2]

The suggested plan for stabilizing the Mississippi trade called for a large company backed by sufficient capital and drawn from the entire area. The management of the company was to be entrusted to a few designated and elected members; agents were to be located at New Orleans, Philadelphia and other necessary seaports to personally supervise the marketing. Wilkins proposed that:[3]

... a company be formed and erected into a corporation with a capital of, say, One Hundred Thousand Dollars or more divided into shares of, say, One Hundred Dollars each, payable by installments, and some portion of it in produce, this capital put under the direction of a President and manager, with power to appoint proper agents for information and transaction of their business. Regular books will be kept and dividends made at stated times, yearly at least. Let any man consider what a happy and steady effect this would have in promoting the circulation of money and insuring the increase and sale of produce and manufactures.

Having made this proposal, Wilkins suggested that neighborhood meetings be held by all those who were interested in discussing the matter. A general meeting would then be held at Pittsburgh on Wednesday, September 29, "to confer together and consider and digest the most proper scheme for establishing a company of the nature which has been proposed."[4]

The month of September must have been a busy one for John Wilkins and his fellow workers, although the newspapers fail to indicate their course of action. The next publicity that his almost staggering proposal received was an account of the actual meeting on September 29.[5] To the courthouse at Pittsburgh came leading citizens of the western parts of Pennsylvania and Virginia. The counties of Fayette, Westmoreland, Ohio, Beaver, Washington, Crawford, Brooke, and Butler were represented. Colonel Ebenezer Zane presided and Dorsey Pentecost, Esquire, was elected secretary. After the routine business of organization was disposed, the actual work of forming a company was undertaken. The general meeting then agreed that a committee

[2] Ibid., September 17, 1802.
[3] Ibid., September 17, 1802.
[4] Ibid., September 17, 1802; Tree of Liberty, October 9, 1802.
[5] Pittsburgh Gazette, October 8, 1802.

should be selected to draw up the plans of association. Two members from each county represented, comprised the committee.[6] Colonel Zane was again selected as chairman.

The committee agreed that a company to export the produce of their country was absolutely needed because agriculture and manufacturing had grown beyond "previous calculation," and that both were able to be enlarged to still greater proportions. In order to maintain the rapid strides, the committee decided that certain improvements are "indispensably necessary" because "the embarrassment and fluctuation of this trade checks both our agriculture and manufactures rendering price precarious, retards industry."[7] Marketing handicaps were the underlying causes for this "embarrassment and fluctuation." The problem must have been a trying one for the committee used strong language to show that if a country could not have access to the "best market then it must be at the mercy of those who have, must be subject to their impositions of terms, and thus must surrender to them as much of the fruits of its industry as they can extort."[8] As no individual exertion could remedy the matter, the committee was convinced that there was nothing left to do but to unite the capital and effort of the entire western country to cope with the problem. The plea of necessity, it was hoped, would lessen the objections to such an organization.

The proposed company was to be known as the Ohio Company. No definite capitalization was determined, but sufficient stock was to be sold at one hundred dollars per share to provide a working capital "for the purchase and exportation to the best markets of the commodities of our country at the joint risk and for the joint benefit of all the subscribers to this stock according to the amount of their subscription."[9] A president and 12 directors were to be elected by the stockholders[10] to conduct the business of the company, and subscrip-

---

[6] The committee was comprised of the following representatives:
   Allegheny: John Wilkins, Jr.; John Findley
   Fayette: William Hodge; Samuel Jackson.
   Westmoreland: John Denniston; Colonel John Irvin
   Ohio: John Clark; Ebenezer Zane.
   Beaver: John Baird; David Drennan.
   Washington: Craig Richie; John Patterson
   Crawford: Francis B. Holmes; Jabez Colt.
   Brooke: James Marshall; David Offley.
   Butler: Abdiel M'Clure; John Cunningham.
[7] *Tree of Liberty*, October 9, 1802.
[8] *Pittsburgh Gazette*, October 8, 1802.
[9] *Ibid.*, October 8, 1802.
[10] *Ibid.*, October 8, 1802. Stockholders were to meet annually on the first Monday in June and "at such other times as they may adjourn to." Stockholders could also vote in person or by proxy, and their number of votes depended upon their shares of stock. The fear of monopoly is evidenced by the plan for determining the votes to which each stockholder was entitled. A mathematical scale was determined allowing so many votes for various share holdings, and no stockholder was to be entitled to more than 21 votes.

tion books were to be opened on November 1 at various towns.[11] In order that the price of the stock might be within the reach of all people, a very liberal plan was allowed for payment. One dollar in cash was to be paid at the time of subscribing and the remainder was to be paid in instalments, of which one-fifth (or $20) was to be paid in cash, and four-fifths (or $80) was to be paid in produce.

Such was the proposed company presented to the inhabitants of Pittsburgh and its environs in 1802; a company to be capitalized at one hundred thousand dollars in a region which rarely saw specie. The meeting was hardly adjourned before the opposition, led by the editor of the *Tree of Liberty*, began to cry "Monopoly," and "Speculation."

The Republican *Tree of Liberty* attacked the proposal as a Federalist electioneering scheme, seeing nothing but chicanery and ruin for all concerned. The plan could not be carried out, warned the editor, because:[12]

The most advantageously situated, will not, nor cannot be, bound to any agreement. You can have no compulsion over them. But suppose a company to be formed thus by a considerable number of millers, farmers, etc., I beg leave to repeat the question, What will the consequences be? I dare to answer 1st, disappointments; 2nd, loss and 3rd, altercation among the parties. . . . No English adage is more pertinent than 'let the cobbler stick to his last' so the farmer to his plough, the miller to his mill and the merchant to his commerce; thus can trade become simplified, easy and certain. Much might be added, but a word to the wise is sufficient.

The *Gazette*, on the other hand, defended the plan and also the author, and bemoaned the country's situation when such a good scheme was attacked.[13] "A Westmoreland Farmer" wrote that nature had been good to them and asked "why not take advantage of it?"[14] He pointed out that "we deserve to be slaves if we don't," and then he proceeded to show "the necessities which should make us wake up from our lethargy." Pittsburgh needed a good permanent market because of her present unfavorable balance of trade. Money was scarce because the army, which had circulated large sums of cash, was now reduced or removed entirely, and because the emigrant trade had temporarily ceased. The writer could not understand why objections would be raised to a plan which would solve marketing difficulties. He added: "It is but too well known what difficulty and distress our traders suffered at that place for want of storage, advice and assistance, when markets were dull or rather no markets at all."[15]

---

[11] Subscription books were to be opened at: Pittsburgh, McKeesport, Elizabeth Town, Noblesburg, Georgetown, Beavertown, Whelen, West Liberty, Uniontown, Brownsville, Geneva, Connellsville, Washington, Williamsport, Canonsburg, Middletown, Fredricktown, Erie, Meadville; also in Westmoreland County and Butler County, and in Brooke County, Virginia, now West Virginia.
[12] *Tree of Liberty*, October 9, 1802.
[13] *Pittsburgh Gazette*, October 22, 1802.
[14] *Ibid.*, November 5, 1802.
[15] *Ibid.*, November 5, 1802.

Local disputes over the question were abruptly quieted by the stunning blow that the New Orleans market itself was no longer open to their products. Pittsburgh merchants now had other problems more serious to consider than the propriety of forming an exporting company. The right of deposit had been curtailed on October 16, 1802; neither "corporations" or individuals would have to worry about ways and means.[16] World events moved rapidly; and Pittsburgh was only a spectator. Suddenly on May 18, 1803, the right of deposit was restored, and before merchants became readjusted the situation was changed again. This time the problem of a foreign dominated market was removed entirely—the United States had purchased Louisiana, and New Orleans was no longer a foreign market. Pittsburgh's basic reason for establishing the Ohio Company was now eliminated and the task of organizing was delayed. The Ohio Company expired before having had an opportunity to show its value. Probably its demise cleared the way for later organizing attempts. At least, the company did not have an opportunity to fail and its aims may have been too ambitious.[17] The Mississippi trade was a big undertaking even for a company and Whitaker is of the opinion that:[18]

The export trade in produce from the Ohio Valley to New Orleans was indeed of too recent origin and was expanding too rapidly to lend itself to organization, and geographical factors prevented any merchant or group of merchants from getting control of it. On the Ohio and its tributaries, every river farm was a potential port, every man who could use hammer and saw was a boat builder, and every farmer was an exporter.

Thus, after 1803, Pittsburgh no longer needed to cope with foreign nations at New Orleans, but political domination did not remove the physical obstacles in the Mississippi trade. River losses became greater as trade was accelerated, and in December, 1811, a second organization was proposed.[19] The Pittsburgh Manufacturing Company was actually organized before the newspaper took notice, and on December 20, the *Gazette* carried the articles of association.[20]

---

[16] The *Tree of Liberty*, February 26, 1803, reported that "Not a word is saying in or out of Pittsburgh about the Ohio Co. . . . it appears that shutting Orleans has shut the mouths of the speculative Ohio navigators."

[17] Ambler reported that an alliance had been made between the Ohio Company and the Bank of Pennsylvania, (Philadelphia), and with this backing, the Company may have been able to withstand the variability of the market. Ambler, *A History of Transportation in the Ohio Valley*, 94.

[18] Whitaker, *Mississippi Question*, 142.

[19] Cramer, *Magazine Almanack*, 1811, 55. Cramer reported that a company had been formed to navigate on the Ohio between Pittsburgh and Louisville "in large boats to be propelled by steam." Nothing appears to have resulted; evidently that too was premature and occasioned by the first optimism of the Roosevelt success. In 1811 Nicholas Roosevelt had built at Pittsburgh the first steamboat to navigate the Ohio and Mississippi Rivers. This was the *New Orleans*, and in addition to being the first steam ship to be built for western waters, it was also the first steam ship to make a round trip from Pittsburgh to New Orleans. Pittsburghers were jubilant over the prospects of being able to make a return trip by way of the river.

[20] *Pittsburgh Gazette*, December 20, 1811; *Pittsburgh Commonwealth*, December 23, 1811.

The company was formed because:[21]

We the subscribers believing that insurance is necessary on houses, stores, furniture, goods, utensils of trade, and material for manufactures, against loss of damage by fire; on boats . . . together with their cargoes, against perils of navigation; for raising a fund for the purpose of assisting farmers, mechanics and merchants in purchase and sale of articles they raise, manufacture, or deal in. . . .

The Pittsburgh Manufacturing Company, despite its name, was an insurance company capitalized at $500,000. Stock was sold on the instalment plan at fifty dollars a share, and William Wilkins was the company's first president, and Thomas Cromwell was its secretary. The president and managers were empowered to offer insurance on boats, cargoes, houses, stores, merchandise, and furniture, and "to receive on deposit articles of growth, manufacture or produce, and to loan money on such deposits."[22] Such an undertaking the organizers of the company thought:[23]

Will materially tend to bring into active operation the resources of the Western country—to encourage the spirit of improvement, and enterprise in commerce, and manufacturing and the mechanic arts, by affording to all, facilities in the persecution of their business and indemnity against those accidents which often sweep away the fruits of industry. . . .

Nine years' time had lessened Pittsburghers' fears of monopolies, and the fact that the company had intended originally to organize for banking saved it from opposition.

Stock sold readily; Fayette County alone subscribed to "upwards of 4,000 shares. . . ."[24] By March 20, 1812, the entire amount of stock had been sold, and three payments had also been made on each share.[25] All details were completed by June 16, 1812, and the company was ready for business.[26] The company prospered and declared a dividend in 1814.[27] During the same year the company received its banking charter, dropped the insurance feature, and became the Bank of Pittsburgh. Thus, the corporate enterprise was advanced slightly, but too much emphasis must not be laid on its acceptance by the people. The years from 1812 to 1814 were unusual in many ways for Pittsburgh; and urgency, war frenzy, and the flush of good times almost transfigured the struggling little borough of Pittsburgh.

The third attempt at organization came from an unexpected source.

[21] *Pittsburgh Gazette,* December 20, 1811. The original intention of this company had been to organize a bank, but due to a change in the banking laws, it failed to secure a charter. Under the name of Pittsburgh Manufacturing Company, a partial banking business was carried on.
[22] *Ibid.,* December 20, 1811. The Board of Managers had met on December 18, and elected officers. The managers were prominent businessmen: James Riddle, James Morrison, Wm. M. M'Candless, C. Cowan, F. B. Holmes, Jeremiah Barker, John Darragh, Thos. Hoge, (Greensburg), John Hoge, (Washington), James W. Nicholson, (Geneva), George Anshutz, George Sutton.
[23] *Ibid.,* December 20, 1811.
[24] *Ibid.,* February 17, 1812.
[25] *Ibid.,* March 20, 1812.
[26] *Ibid.,* June 12, 1812.
[27] *Ibid.,* January 14, 1814. The company paid a dividend of 4½ per cent, and on July 4, 1814, another dividend of 4½ per cent was declared. *Ibid.,* July 8, 1814.

In 1817, the merchants of Philadelphia, who were concerned in the western trade, formed a company for the purpose of speeding up transportation. The organization became known as the Philadelphia and Pittsburgh Transportation Company, and was capitalized at $100,-000.[28] The money was "to be employed in the establishment of lines of waggons [sic] to travel day and night between Philadelphia and this city: to perform the journey in seven days, and at a uniform rate throughout the year considerably lower than at present."[29]

Whether Pittsburghers were canvassed to subscribe to this undertaking is uncertain, but not unlikely. The next notice of the company which appeared in the local papers was addressed "to citizens and traders" interested in wagon transportation, and an invitation was issued for all interested persons to meet on May 3, at seven o'clock at the Pittsburgh Hotel.[30] Plans were formulated and a notice appeared the next month to the owners of horses to call for their contracts.[31] Wagons were to carry four-thousand-pound loads from Philadelphia to Carlisle; from Carlisle to Pittsburgh the loads were to be 3,500 pounds, reduced to 3,200 in bad weather; the proposed rate of travel was to be two miles per hour. An agency was established in Pittsburgh under the direction of John Harper.

Operations were scheduled to begin on April 1, 1818. Two wagons were to start daily from Pittsburgh and from Philadelphia and they were expected to travel day and night "when roads will permit" changing horses every ten miles.[32] The journey was to be accomplished in ten days. The freight rates were not to be lowered because the contracts were averred to have been made favorable to the drivers and not to the company. The drivers owned the horses, and the company supplied the wagons. Forty new wagons "on the new plans" were to be used.

The company had hopes for great developments and kind treatment from the legislature.[33] Evidently neither materialized for the next notice of the company reported: "To be sold at Auction on August 4, 1819, 19 Road Waggons [sic] with covers—complete and well built. Have been very little used, some of them nearly new. At your own terms."[34] In these few lines the whole story of the undertaking is told. The problem was too big even for a corporation. Public support was evidently lacking for the company never realized its capital, and instead of selling one hundred thousand dollars worth of stock, only forty thousand dollars were subscribed.[35] The Philadelphia and Pittsburgh Transportation Company is another evidence of prematurity.

---

[28] Ibid., April 15, 1817.
[29] Ibid., April 11, 1817.
[30] Ibid., May 2, 1817.
[31] Ibid., June 20, 1817.
[32] Ibid., March 31, 1818, quoting the *Philadelphia Gazette*.
[33] Ibid., March 31, 1818.
[34] Ibid., July 23, 1819.
[35] Ibid., March 31, 1818.

Pittsburgh may have been indifferent to the transportation company, but concerning the succeeding enterprise, advocates and opposition alike hastened to print their views. An editorial in the *Gazette* of February 19, 1819, announced that the Western Navigation and Insurance Company had been formed for the purpose of facilitating transportation from Pittsburgh to "all countries below us watered by the Ohio and its tributaries." The editorial pointed out that the company was brought into existence in order to do away with the embarrassments of the previous season, "a season that will long be remembered by the Western merchant; a season which will not pass entirely unmarked by either Philadelphia or Baltimore."[36] The year 1818 had been an unusually low water year. The river trade had been severely interrupted. Merchandise was delayed from two to four months in reaching its destination; boats loaded with heavy cargoes were tied up in harbors or fastened high and dry on the river bars; trade throughout the valley was suspended for lack of supplies. Faced by these problems, certain Pittsburgh leaders turned to cooperation.

By their joint efforts Pittsburgh merchants hoped to eliminate the delays and the risks which hampered the river trade. The company planned to obtain boats of various sizes so that low water would not tie up trade; low draught vessels of small size were to be purchased which would permit trade to be carried on long after the regular Ohio boats were detained for want of sufficient depth. Rates were to be uniform, despite the water level, and the company promised that low water would no longer be an excuse for exorbitant rates.[37] The company also hoped to cut down the long delays in making up a cargo. This had always been a sore spot in the river trade. Freighters would usually not start until they had a full cargo and these delays meant money to the merchants and commission houses. In 1818 the freighters had continued this policy, despite the contingency, and the majority of them had refused to lighten their boats. "A Stockholder" discussed the situation:[38]

In the month of November last, when many goods had been detained at our shores for two months, a small rise of water took place, it however, began to fall, and at this crisis a meeting of commission merchants and gentlemen from the

[36] *Ibid.*, February 19, 1819.
[37] In the battle which ensued after the company was proposed, the question of rates was a high spot of contention. The freighters had evidently mulcted the merchants in 1818, and on the pleas of low water, legitimate or otherwise, had charged exorbitant rates. The advocates of the company asserted that the freighters had charged $2 per one hundred pounds for freight to Maysville. The freighters refuted the statement saying that $1.50 was the maximum rate. The company then produced evidence of the fact that one commission house had arranged to send goods to Maysville at 62½¢ per hundred, and afterwards, having received orders to send them immediately, had engaged freight in another boat at $2.25. In order to force the first freighter to release the goods, the house had to pay the 62½¢ per hundred charges. The commission merchants asserted that $2.25 was the rate charged by all freighters at that time. Commission merchants also offered $3.00 per hundred pounds for goods to Louisville, but none of the freighters would take the goods. *Pittsburgh Gazette,* March 5, 1819.
[38] *Ibid.*, March 2, 1819.

West having goods detained here, was held and the freighters being sent for, were requested to name the terms on which they would lighten their boats and start, after consultation, some of them declined altogether, but the majority gave in their terms, which were $2 per hundred pounds to Maysville, and a proportionate freight to other places. Some Kentuckians were very anxious to get on their goods, and complied with the demands, but the commission merchants here, considering them as exorbitant in the extreme declined. . . .

The company also expected to be able to protect the river trade by assuming a complete responsibility for goods entrusted to it. The freighters, lacking capital, had made the laws of bailment entirely useless and the merchants were unable to obtain redress. In short, the company expected to vitalize the river trade and to conduct it on a respectable and also a very reliable basis.[39]

The articles of association and the names of the officers of the company were presented to the public on March 5, 1819. The name had been slightly altered to the Pittsburgh Navigation and Insurance Company. The capital stock was set at one hundred thousand dollars with power of increasing it to five hundred thousand dollars whenever necessary.[40] Two thousand shares of stock were offered to the public at fifty dollars per share, of which five dollars was to constitute a down payment. The company was to be managed by seven directors chosen by ballot by the stockholders. The first board consisted of Thomas Cromwell, Anthony Beelen, William Robinson, Jr., George G. Bowen, George Grant, Robert Patterson, and Isaac Bean. Thomas Cromwell was named as president of the board. The articles of agreement also took steps to guard against monopolizing control by rationing the votes to which each stockholder was entitled. Businessmen themselves were still not converted entirely to the principle of corporate control, but once again the problem had become overwhelming, and necessity had forced a sacrifice of principle. The directors indicated the reasons for the undertaking in the same account in which they published the articles of association. Their story was very convincing:[41]

The directors aware that misrepresentations have been circulating representing the objects and views of the association feel it their duty to state what the real objects and views of the company are—the public cannot be ignorant of the great (and to many individuals ruinous) delays which occurred in forwarding goods the last season, and which has induced many western merchants to look for other channels, through which to get their goods in the future. The delays complained of, may in a great measure be attributed to the unusually large boats, provided by the freighters and the want of public spirit on their part to encounter the difficulties of low water. Our rivers have been low in former years, but never before have such delays been the consequence; and the fact, that boats from this to Wheeling, did continue to take freight, on reasonable terms, nearly the

[39] Ibid., February 19, 1819. The editor asserted that the river business had been monopolized by individuals who had been rewarded; that "due to lack of capital, this business has not been conducted in that manner which a business of such magnitude requires."
[40] Ibid., March 5, 1819; Riddle, Directory, 1819, 118.
[41] Pittsburgh Gazette, March 5, 1819.

whole of last season is proof, independent of the example of former years, that the navigation is practicable at the lowest stages of water and that the company will be able to redeem the pledge they have made to receive and deliver goods at all seasons of the year except when the rivers are obstructed by ice. As to the price of freight, although the company has as yet started but three boats, a very considerable reduction has taken place, especially on articles of the manufacture of the country, which will always be taken at as low freight as can be afforded. It is not the intention, nor does it comport with the means put in operation, to engross the whole carrying trade from this place, nor is it their wish or design to take the bread from the mouth of honest industry, but they solicit so much support as will enable them to effect the contemplated objects, and which they consider themselves entitled to ask from their fellow citizens. As the carrying of goods when the water is low, is expected to be a loosing [sic] business, a liberal support at other times is thought to be but fair.

Insurance being one of the objects contemplated in the association due notice will be given when sufficient capital shall have been paid in to warrant the company in receiving proposals; but at present, it is their intention to confine themselves to the freighting business.

Unquestionably the need for reform was great, but it is a matter for conjecture whether the opposition was motivated by general animosity towards corporations or by the fear of loss of private gain. The vested interest group, at any rate, appears to have taken the lead of the opposition in the newspaper controversy. Articles signed by "The Boatmen" were addressed "To the Public," appealing to them to oppose the attempted monopoly. The public was warned that the Navigation Company would ruin them and business in general by depriving them of their daily bread.[42] The freighters reminded the public that they had handled the river trade to the best of their ability; that they had gone "through the worst difficulties and borne the heat and burden of the day."[43] The boatmen who led the opposition refused to join the company, and they maintained that they had a combined capital of $85,000 while the company was estimated to have only $4,000.

Newspaper articles defending the company were usually signed "A Stockholder," and they disclaimed any ideas of monopoly. Stock was said to have been purchased in small quantities with the hopes that the boating business would be reformed and not with the idea of making a profit.[44] The company was formed by:[45]

Those whose interest it is to foster and preserve the trade between this place and the country West of us, from persons, who cannot for a moment, be supposed to be actuated by other motives than what they will profit, for no rate of

[42] Ibid., February 26, 1819. The article was signed by the following boat owners of Pittsburgh: S. and A. Hart; McCullogh and Young; [Isaiah] Scott and Co.; Jos. Ferguson and Stedum; Knox Holderman and Co.; Nesmith and Rollings; Srodes and Johnson.
[43] Ibid., February 16, 1819.
[44] Ibid., March 2, 1819. In another article signed by a "Boatman" some members of the company were accused of having boasted that their stocks would net them fifty to one hundred per cent profit, and the "boatmen" threatened to expose some of the members' dealings if another attack was made by them. Ibid., March 9, 1819.
[45] Ibid., March 2, 1819.

interest, be it what it may, on the amount of stock they have severally taken
could weigh against the loss scarcely of a single customer from the westward.

The company also denied the charge of trying "to take the bread
from the mouths of the old freighters"; citizens were called upon to
unite "not to pull down good freighters, but to raise a barrier against
unreasonable encroachments and exorbitant demands. . . ."[46] The company argued that the boatmen themselves had generally acknowledged
the necessity of reform, and that:[47]

. . . one of the freighters and a signer to the appeal to the public in the last
Gazette [February 26] acknowledged at a meeting of the Navigation and Insurance Company where he was present, that in former years, and he instanced 1813,
the Ohio had been as low for a length of time as the last season, but that he had
notwithstanding continued to take and deliver goods at the place of destination
at the rate of 50 cents per hundred pounds to Maysville and that same person
then stated that he had the last year, unfortunate as the season was, doubled the
capital he had employed in the freighting business. . . .

After the first heat of the battle over the formation of the company
had subsided, newspapers were silent, and uncertainty shrouds the
results. Apparently the company failed. The year 1819 was an un-
desirable time for any new undertaking because the postwar effects
were taking their toll of all business undertakings. Times continued
to grow steadily worse until 1821, and normality was not restored until 1825. Consequently, it would not be surprising that such a radical
innovation as the Pittsburgh Navigation and Insurance Company
should fail. Transportation was a difficult problem and taxed the
ingenuity of each succeeding generation of businessmen even in times
of prosperity.

In 1819 another problem which had faced Pittsburgh merchants and
manufacturers was attacked, and the outcome was surprisingly successful considering the unfavorable times. Another corporate enterprise was started under the name of the Pittsburgh Manufacturing
Company. This organization was wholly unrelated to the banking
establishment of the same name. The title belied its purpose for this
enterprise was organized for the "Buying and selling, receiving and
forwarding and disposing of, on commission, all articles of American
produce and manufacture."[48] Specifically the company was formed
by the manufacturers to better themselves and to advance Pittsburgh's
manufacturing spirit which was beginning to lag. The company
represented a part of Pittsburgh's lifeblood, and was the result of a
demand which was too urgent to be overlooked if Pittsburgh was to
take advantage of its position as a manufacturing center. The Pittsburgh Manufacturing Company, instead of being a producer, was
almost similar to the modern department store. The company was

[46] *Ibid.*, March 2, 1819.
[47] *Ibid.*, March 2, 1819.
[48] Jones, *Directory*, 1826, 91.

organized to market Pittsburgh manufactures large and small. Pittsburgh needed such a middleman for "it was soon perceived that there was no place of general deposit in the city, where the western merchants and others, might have an opportunity of viewing at once, the various articles fabricated within Pittsburgh and its vicinity."[49] Pittsburghers realized that to be a manufacturer one had to have customers; everyone was concerned in this problem, and the lull in business may have somewhat frightened the merchants into a greater degree of cooperation than would have been possible if times had been booming and profits more general.

The company began operations cautiously and was a success from its inception. A manufacturer had literally nothing to lose by the attempt, and the possibility of gain was great. The organization was more cooperative in features than corporative, for stock was sold at $25 a share *payable in manufactured articles*.[50] A warehouse was opened on Wood Street "for the reception not only of the stock subscribed, but to receive domestic goods for sale."[51] Business at first was confined to bartering and exchanging, and was under the direction of George Cochran. The company made no profits the first year, but neither had it gone into debt. A committee of investigation made a favorable report on the company affairs, and a vote of approval was also given to Cochran.[52]

After the first year of probation, the company effected a more regular organization. A charter of incorporation was obtained for ten years, and capital stock was limited to thirty thousand dollars.[53] Stock was always to be sold at $25 in gold, silver, or products, and shares in the company were always to be limited to people in the business of domestic manufactures. The articles of association provided for managers to be elected annually, and only one-third could be reelected. Stockholders were to meet on the first Tuesday of February, May, August, and November. The holder of one share of stock was to be entitled to one vote, although no stockholder was allowed to control more than four votes even though he did possess more than four shares of stock.[54] Dividends were to be declared only after 10 per cent over and above the capital stock had been realized; until that time, profits were to be turned over to the contingent fund.

The company prospered, and at the end of the first year of incorporation was able to declare a dividend of five per cent. During the

[49] Riddle, *Directory*, 1819, 116.
[50] Jones in his *Directory* for 1826 reported that by April, 1819, about four thousand dollars' worth of stock had been paid.
[51] Riddle, *Directory*, 1819, 116.
[52] Jones, *Directory*, 1826, 92. Other officers were George Sutton, President; James Arthurs, Vice President; Jeffry Scaiff, Secretary; A. Updegraff, Treasurer.
[53] *Ibid.*, 92.
[54] Provisions were also made to prevent "absentee ownership" by specifying that no votes of proxy would be received. The Pittsburgh Manufacturing Company was definitely a product of and for Pittsburgh.

next two years the company paid no dividends, although a nominal profit was realized. By 1823 the business in general had revived sufficiently so that the company was able to declare another five per cent dividend. Between 1824 and 1826 the company paid ten per cent dividends. Jones, in his *Directory*, estimated that the company sold sixty thousand dollars worth of Pittsburgh merchandise yearly and that the amount was increasing.[55] The amount of increase can be appreciated by a notice of 1830 to the stockholders notifying them that "a dividend of 20 per cent on the capital stock, will be payable in goods of the association, at cash prices, to those who choose to avail themselves of it, on or after the first Monday in June."[56] The next year a similar dividend was declared.[57]

The company acted as retail and wholesale agent for the entire Pittsburgh area. Goods of all types were sold at the company's warehouse. Cash or produce was taken in exchange. Early advertisements carried a great variety of household items such as chairs and cabinets, cutlery and coffee mills, copper and iron teakettles, tinware and waffle-irons. Advertising emphasis was also placed heavily on tools which were so necessary to an expanding society. The company noted that it carried axes, adzes and augers, hatchets and hammers, as well as plows and mould boards. Glass of various sizes, paper, cloth and a few items of wearing apparel were also listed. Advertisements show that the company carried items much in demand in Pittsburgh such as bridles and bits, stirrups and saddles. Frequently, the company invited Pittsburghers to inspect its stock because the advertisement could not enumerate all the products manufactured in the community.

The Pittsburgh Manufacturing Company served Pittsburgh businessmen faithfully. It successfully bridged the gap between the period of individual enterprise and the beginning of corporate methods, and acted as commission merchant in the days before business could support a middleman. By 1830 commerce and manufacturing had become sufficiently established and had developed to an extent that demanded organization and control. As business expanded and as commercial methods improved, the need for the company declined; furthermore, the charter of the company expired in 1830, and application was not made for its renewal. A committee was appointed to close the company's affairs and to settle its debts.[58] The company was the first successful Pittsburgh business corporation, and had shown that organization could be made without inflicting ruin and without the loss of individual rights.

---

[55] Jones, *Directory*, 1826, 92.
[56] *Pittsburgh Mercury*, June 2, 1830.
[57] *Ibid.*, June 15, 1831.
[58] *Ibid.*, April 28, 1830. In this same article notice is given that George Cochran, the agent for the Pittsburgh Manufacturing Association, also had his own stock of goods. After the company closed its affairs, Mr. Cochran went into the commission business.

Business expanded or halted according to the business cycles which changed so rapidly in the 1830's. The need for cooperation became more and more pressing as Pittsburgh became a commercial emporium. A major event in this direction occurred in January, 1836, when the Board of Trade was organized. The purpose of this organization was to extend the trade of Pittsburgh; "to give proper direction to all commercial movements; to encourage and to extend facilities of transportation; to provide a public exchange for the general transaction of business; to settle controversies between members; and to register the arrival and departure of steamboats and other items of commercial importance."[59] The Board of Trade was an association of Pittsburgh businessmen who were all vitally concerned in the city's commercial betterment; no one member had a private ax to grind, nor was the association formed for the advancement of any individual or any special group. The association was a group movement for group achievement, resulting from the realization that cooperative action could accomplish results otherwise impossible. Membership was open to all who were engaged in business enterprises, and dues were five dollars per year.[60] A president, two vice-presidents, a secretary, a treasurer, and 21 directors were elected annually.

The Board of Trade was a much needed business improvement. Newspapers contained numerous articles on their achievements, for the board maintained a strict vigilance over what was, or was not, good for Pittsburgh. Tariff, commission rates, inspections of ashes and flour, reduction of tolls on the Pennsylvania State System, the Right of Way Bill, the fight for the Marine Hospital, the building of an armory; all were problems which were considered by the Board of Trade. The organization grew in strength and was constantly on the alert for Pittsburgh interests. Apparently no one objected to its formation, and nothing but praise for its accomplishments appeared in the newspapers. The nature of this association was different in the scope of work undertaken from the earlier associations, but the mere fact that a Board of Trade was deemed necessary by Pittsburgh merchants and businessmen illustrated a decided change of outlook. Rugged individualism had outlived its usefulness, and a modified form of cooperation had taken its place. Business was no longer deathly afraid of monopoly.

Pittsburgh was interested mildly in another form of organization, but she was so destitute of capital that the interest did not materialize into a local undertaking until after 1830. Pittsburgh could not afford the luxury of an insurance company, although the need for protection was urgent. The growth of insurance companies in Pittsburgh and

[59] *Pittsburgh Gazette*, January 12, 1836; Harris *Directory*, 1837, 107.
[60] *Pittsburgh Gazette*, January 12, 1836.

elsewhere in the United States was slow, retarded everywhere by the opposition to monopolies and by a lack of surplus capital. The principle of win or lose was the accepted business philosophy. Developing new country was more or less of a risk for all involved. The degree of security reached by a frontier can be measured by the establishment of "shock absorbers." On the seaboard the first American insurance corporation was founded at Philadelphia in 1792, thereby lessening the commercial risks by fire and marine insurance.[61]

Scattered news items relating to insurance appeared in the Pittsburgh papers prior to 1808, but Pittsburgh was merely an outsider looking in. On February 19, 1802, the *Gazette* copied an article from Frankfort, Kentucky which congratulated their fellow citizens who were engaged in the exportation of produce on the establishment of an insurance company at Lexington, with a fund of twenty thousand dollars. Such an establishment said the editor "is truly desirable . . . already, although our rivers have not been in navigable order more than 40 days, have several boats with valuable cargoes been entirely lost."[62] Whether or not Pittsburgh, prior to 1808, used this company is undetermined.[63] Another notice appeared on March 3, 1804, which informed Pittsburghers that two new insurance companies had been incorporated in Philadelphia.[64] But it was not until 1808 that Pittsburgh had its own company. The company was not of local origin, but was a branch office of the Insurance Company of North America. Thomas Wilson was made the Pittsburgh agent.[65]

The first local insurance attempts were made by the Pittsburgh Manufacturing Company in 1811, and again in 1819 by Pittsburgh Navigation and Insurance Company. But neither company was in business a sufficient length of time to have produced any permanent results for Pittsburgh. Long gaps appear in Pittsburgh's insurance development, and the first definite statement of establishments appears in Jones' *Directory of 1826*. Four fire insurance companies were reported to be located in Pittsburgh: the American Fire Insurance Company, George Cochran, agent; Aetna Fire Insurance Company, N. Holmes, agent; Traders' Insurance Company, R. Bowen, agent; Protection Insurance Company, M. B. Lowrie, agent.[66] These com-

[61] This company was known as the Insurance Company of North America, and was located at Philadelphia. The company's history is closely allied with the history of the nation. The company met with reasonable success, despite the uncertainty of the times, and the idea of insurance companies spread. During the first ten years, the company charged 12 per cent average premiums, but the payment of losses absorbed 91 per cent of the premium income. The War of 1812 brought disaster to the insurance business in general, and it was not firmly re-established for 30 years. This period was the testing time for insurance companies. Following the panic of 1837, the companies which survived entered a period of prosperity for the next 20 years. Winter, William D., *Marine Insurance; Its Principle and Practice*, (New York, 1919), 21.
[62] *Pittsburgh Gazette*, February 19, 1802.
[63] Baldwin, *The Keelboat Age*, 299-300.
[64] *Tree of Liberty*, March 3, 1804.
[65] *Pittsburgh Commonwealth*, May 25, 1808.
[66] Jones, *Directory*, 1826, 91.

panies were apparently outside undertakings with only branch offices in Pittsburgh. Each agent had other interests in Pittsburgh business for insurance was not a full time job. The extent of business, however, is not known. The next local attempt was not made until 1832, at which time the Pittsburgh Navigation and Fire Insurance Company opened books for subscription.[67] Evidently the undertaking was readily received, because by May 3, the company began to sell fire insurance on buildings, merchandise, vessels, and cargoes.[68] Details of organization were not made public, although by 1837 the company was reputed to be capitalized at $250,000, and stock was valued at one hundred dollars per share.[69]

By 1837 Harris listed five fire insurance offices in Pittsburgh, but four of the names differed from those listed by Jones in 1826. Harris named the following companies, three of which were local companies:[70]

1. George Cochran, agent for fire insurance for the American Fire Insurance Company of Philadelphia
2. Philadelphia Fire and Inland Navigation Company (also possessed marine privileges)
3. Pittsburgh Navigation and Fire Insurance Company
4. The Beaver County Insurance Company (fire and marine insurance)
5. Firemans' Insurance Company

The Beaver County Company was capitalized at four hundred thousand dollars and the Firemans' Insurance Company at $250,000. All five companies survived the panic of 1837, and continued in business.[71] No new enterprises were started until 1843, when, in September of that year, the Penn Insurance Company under the presidency of Josiah King, was incorporated.[72] Business conditions continued to improve in Pittsburgh after the panic of 1837 and the depression of 1842; transportation became more regular, and the element of chance was largely reduced. Merchants accepted and even demanded insurance, and certain transportation companies advertised that "all goods shipped will be fully protected at no extra charge."[73] The extent of the demand for insurance can be measured by the fact that two local companies were incorporated in Pittsburgh in a two-year period, and on April 10, 1844, another company was chartered under the name of the Allegheny County Mutual Insurance Company.[74]

On April 10, 1845, insurance companies in Pittsburgh received a staggering blow. The "Great Fire" which occurred on that day, wiped out a large section of the business district, and losses were estimated

[67] *Pittsburgh Mercury*, March 2, 1832.
[68] *Ibid.*, May 4, 1832.
[69] Harris *Directory*, 1837, 104-105.
[70] *Ibid.*, 104-105.
[71] *Ibid.*, 1839, 5.
[72] *Pittsburgh Chronicle*, August 11, 1843.
[73] *Pittsburgh Mercury*, April 20, 1844; *Pittsburgh Gazette and Advertiser*, October 24, 1844.
[74] *Pittsburgh Gazette and Advertiser*, July 25, 1844.

at nine million dollars.[75] Only seven hundred thousand dollars in property was covered by insurance,[76] but the immediate call for even this amount was too sudden a drain for the insurance companies. The local companies, with the exception of the Pittsburgh Navigation and Insurance Company, were forced to suspend business for a short time.[77] But by September the companies were able to resume operations and to issue policies on both fire and marine risks.[78] The American Fire Insurance Company of Philadelphia was able to meet its obligations and to continue all branches of business *without* interruption.[79] No reaction was noted in the newspapers against the companies, so obligations must have been met in a fairly satisfactory manner, although the companies were not able to settle their indebtedness completely.[80] The demand for insurance by the public grew immeasurably after the fire, and Philadelphia companies hastened to establish agencies. Many complaints were heard in Pittsburgh, however, against the high State tax which prevented companies from other states from opening offices,[81] and which gave Philadelphia a monopoly. A bill was introduced into the Pennsylvania Senate which would permit insurance companies from other states to enjoy the same privileges as those chartered in the State.[82]

Local insurance companies recovered slowly after the fire, and a feeling of support was developed for the home institutions, accompanied by a sense of opposition toward other companies. In 1849, when the Citizens Insurance Company was incorporated by the legislature, citizens rejoiced because the profits would remain in Pittsburgh.[83] Evidence of this was found even in the Western Insurance Company's (incorporated also in 1849) advertisements in the Wheeling papers:[84]

Western Insurance Company of Pittsburgh. . . . Will insure against all kinds of risks, fire, marine. . . . A home institution—managed by Directors who are well known in the community, and who are determined by promptness and liberality to maintain the character which they have assumed as offering the best protection to those who desire to be insured.

---

[75] White, *One Hundred and Fifty Years of Unparalleled Thrift*, 15.
[76] *Pittsburgh Gazette*, May 13, 1845.
[77] Thurston, *Allegheny County's Hundred Years*, 280. Slightly different evidence is given in a letter, dated April 18, 1845, from D. C. Stockton to David Dick: "The Pittsburgh Navigation and Fire Insurance Company will pay its losses in full, and is now doing business as usual. The Mutual Fire Insurance Company will pay in full and will I understand continue to do business. The Penn Insurance Company can pay 90% and with authority from the Legislature to increase their capital will go on.
The Firemens office (Mr. Gormly's) the most popular in the city has lost more than its capital. Can pay 75%. I have not yet learned, what the Directors propose to do." Dick, *Mss*.
[78] *Pittsburgh Chronicle*, September 5, 1845.
[79] *Pittsburgh Gazette*, April 22, 1845. From April to September this company was the only agency in Pittsburgh which was able to assume marine risks.
[80] *Pittsburgh Chronicle*, April 12, 1845.
[81] A tax of twenty dollars on each one hundred dollar premium had been placed on out of state companies, and, consequently, they were not able to do business in Pennsylvania, Hazard, *Register*, 1829, III, 319.
[82] *Pittsburgh Gazette*, March 28, 1846.
[83] *Ibid.*, November 13, 1849.
[84] *Wheeling Daily Gazette*, July 25, 1849.

By 1850 six companies were advertising in the *Pittsburgh Gazette*. Of this number three were local institutions, two were from Philadelphia, and one was from Hartford, Connecticut.[85]

Parallel to this development was also a quieter one. Slowly Pittsburgh business was organizing on a larger basis. Partnerships and individual enterprises were giving way to company organization. Necessity for larger resources had forced Pittsburgh merchants to band together to meet the larger problems in economic life. Little by little, the people became accustomed to corporations, and familiarity with them made the people lose their fears. By 1850 the newness of organized undertakings in business had worn off, but the development was a long way from the era of mergers and consolidations. The significance of the progress made, however, was notable, and the development of the succeeding half century was possible only because of this testing period.

---

[85] *Pittsburgh Gazette*, January 15, 1850.

XII

Pittsburgh in 1850

PITTSBURGH in 1850 was a very different place from the little borough of 1800. During the half century she had grown from a small isolated town of 2,400 people to a manufacturing and commercial center with a population of 46,001.[1] Furthermore, by 1850 Pittsburgh was solidly established as the Iron City, and her economic activity was completely dominated by the production of iron products. Nor were her mills and foundries small individual "shoestring" enterprises operated by the owner, assisted by a few apprentices. Now the mills and foundries were large factories which employed over five thousand men.[2] At mid-century, Pittsburgh and the vicinity had 13 rolling mills, among which were the Birmingham Iron Works owned by Wood, Edwards and M'Knight, who had their warehouse at 7 Wood Street; the Lyon, Shorb and Company's Sligo Iron Works, whose warehouse was located at the corner of Wood and Water. The Pennsylvania Iron Works, owned by Miltenberger and Brown, should also be mentioned because it was reputed to be the only manufacturer of Patent Wrought Spikes. The warehouse was located at the foot of Wayne Street on the Allegheny River. H. S. Spang and Son were operators of the Etna Iron Works; their warehouse was at 55 Front Street; G. and H. H. Shoenbergers operated the Juniata Iron Works with their warehouse located at 27 Wood Street.[3] Pittsburgh's rolling mills were capitalized at five million dollars. They used annually about sixty thousand tons of pig metal and produced four million dollars worth of bar iron and nails.

In addition to the rolling mills, Pittsburgh in 1850 had 30 large foundries, together with many smaller ones, which employed 2,500 men and which were capitalized at two million dollars.[4] These foundries consumed 20,000 tons of pig metal annually and produced articles valued at about two million dollars. The Pittsburgh Foundry, one of the largest of the foundries operated by Bollmans and Garrison, located at the corner of Fifth and Smithfield, advertised that they "always had on hand Stoves and Grates, Wagon Boxes of all sizes, Hollow Ware, Tea Kettles, Plough Casting of all sizes, Sad, Tailors' and Hatters' Irons, Waffle Irons, Counter Weights, &c., Mill Casting &c., made to order."[5] The foundries too had greatly increased in size

---

[1] *United States Census Report, Seventh Census,* 1850.
[2] Fahnestock, Samuel, *Directory for 1850,* (Pittsburgh, 1850), 118.
[3] Harris, Isaac, *Directory for 1847,* (Pittsburgh, 1847), 54.
[4] Fahnestock, *Directory, 1850,* 118.
[5] Harris, *Directory, 1841.*

as well as in production. The *Pittsburgh Post* listed only six foundry warehouses in 1850, but the editor explained that his list was not complete, although "perfect as far as it goes." The *Post* included the following foundries:[6]

Quinn, McBride and Co., Seventh and Liberty Street
Nicholson and Payne, 181 Liberty Street
William Irwin, Athenian Building, Liberty Street
Pennock, Mitchell and Co., 160 Liberty Street
Alexander Bradley, 19 Wood Street
John Anderson and Son, Water and Grant Streets

Pittsburgh, by 1850, was able to supply iron products of all description and size from steam engines to tacks. Great amounts of locks, latches, coffee mills, patent scales and other malleable iron castings were offered for sale by two factories which employed 500 men and whose output was valued at $200,000 annually.[7] A beginning had also been made in the manufacture of steel, and Fahnestock reported that cast, shear, and blister steel were being produced.

Thus, by the middle of the century, Pittsburgh was producing iron valued at almost six and a half million dollars annually, while at the beginning of the century her iron industries were valued at $56,548.[8] Forty-five large establishments and numerous smaller plants produced the various iron products, and employed at least 5,500 laborers. Seven and a quarter millions of Pittsburgh's capital were invested in iron.

Although the production of iron dominated Pittsburgh's industrial scene, other manufactures were not excluded. Fahnestock reported:[9]

There are 5 extensive cotton factories, besides many smaller ones, with a capital in all amounting to about $1,500,000, and employing 1,500 hands; these establishments consume some 15,000 bales of cotton, and produce yarns, sheeting, batting, etc. amounting to upwards of $1,500,000.

The cotton factories were located principally across the river in Allegheny City, or in the present day North Side.[10] Lewis Peterson's Globe Factory, however, was located in the Golden Triangle, and the Hope Factory, operated by M'Cormick and Company, maintained a Pittsburgh warehouse. The textile industry had developed haphazardly, but by 1850 was able to boast of progress despite the fre-

[6] *Pittsburgh Daily Morning Post*, January 12, 1850.
[7] Fahnestock, *Directory*, 1850, 118. The factories were capitalized at $250,000 and they worked about 1,200 tons of pig metal annually.
[8] *Ibid.*, 118; Cramer, *Almanack*, 1804, 21.
[9] Fahnestock, *Directory*, 1850, 118. Harris, in his *Directory* for 1841, 64, listed the five cotton factories reported by Fahnestock as follows:
   1. Arbuckles and Avery, Eagle Factory, Sandusky Street
   2. Blackstock, Bell & Company, Pittsburgh Factory, Federal Street
   3. M'Cormick & Company, Hope Factory, West end of Aqueduct; warehouse corner Water & Market Streets
   4. Morehead, J. K. & Company, Union Factory, Saw Mill Run
   5. Peterson, Lewis, Globe Factory, Corner Ferry & Second
[10] Five hundred employees were engaged in these factories, and raw materials amounting to 150 tons of lead and 200 tons of pearl ashes were used annually. Fahnestock, *Directory*, 1850, 118.

quent reversals. In 1803, textiles produced in Pittsburgh and its vicinity were estimated at a value of $46,825, and a half century later the value of textile products had increased to a million and a half. Fahnestock also listed eight flint glass factories, capitalized at three hundred thousand dollars, whose products were valued at $400,000. Seven phial furnaces and eleven window glass factories employing 600 persons produced goods valued at $600,000.[11] Thus, the total value of Pittsburgh's glass industries was placed at one million dollars in 1850, while at the beginning of the century the glass production was valued at $13,000. The name of the original glass maker, Bakewell, was still among the factories listed, although the personnel had changed, and the house had been reorganized under the name of Bakewell, Pears and Company.[12]

Pittsburgh also manufactured wire, rope, tin, and copper products, leather products of all types, a great variety of wood products, snuff, cigars, and liquor. Fahnestock valued "manufacturing and other business" at not less than fifty million dollars;[13] iron, glass, textiles, lead, and copper industries produced eight and one half million dollars of the total estimate; one million dollars was also designated as the value of the coal trade. The great variety of small unidentified industries each contributed an unknown part of the whole, while the remaining amount was evidently the result of commercial pursuits.

While Pittsburgh was developing her manufacturing, commercial undertakings were not being neglected. In fact every turn of the factory machine, every stroke of the hammer, strengthened Pittsburgh's commerce, and, year by year, as more goods were produced the trade area became larger. The extension of Pittsburgh's trade area was aided immeasurably by the improvement of the channels of trade. Each decade broke down Pittsburgh's isolation, and as mechanical improvements came in transportation each decade emphasized the importance of Pittsburgh's favorable location. Pittsburgh, the City of Three Rivers, one-time Gateway to the West, was now naturally approached from all directions and securely linked with the financial and commercial nerve centers of the East. Improved rivers, roads, canals, railroads, and the telegraph had made Pittsburgh the center of a commercial wheel.

Improved channels of transportation radiating from Pittsburgh gave her a great choice of markets. The mighty Ohio River continued to carry off increasingly large amounts of manufactured products, not only to New Orleans, but to many parts of the rapidly growing West.

[11] *Ibid.*, 118.
[12] *Pittsburgh Daily Morning Post*, January 12, 1850.
[13] Fahnestock, *Directory*, 1850, 118. Fahnestock valued the coal trade at one million dollars. "There is consumed about 12,000,000 bushels of coal annually in our manufacturing establishments, valued at $500,000 and an equal number of bushels exported to the lower markets, giving employment to upwards of 4,000 hands."

As the settlers pushed farther and farther West, Pittsburgh merchants supplied them with iron products and manufactured goods. In addition to providing the West, Pittsburgh also found the internal trade of the Mississippi Valley increasing, due to the fact that all the southern area was specializing in cotton.[14] As the South was devoting itself to cotton culture, Pittsburgh, as a part of the North, was doubling her efforts in industry, and the rivers facilitated the exchange between the two regions. Pittsburgh's surplus products were now in demand at New Orleans, Memphis, and Natchez; no longer were they faced with competition from other agricultural communities. Her river trade had expanded beyond the wildest hopes of the merchants of the 1800 era. Furthermore, instead of clumsy flatboats, the river trade was now carried in steam propelled boats which started on schedule and whose cargoes were insured against losses. The steamboats could travel both ways on the river and current was no longer a deterrent. Consequently, freight rates were cheaper and western products found the Pittsburgh markets satisfactory. By 1850 the physical difficulties of river transportation, likewise, had been considerably reduced, although much remained to be done. In 1830 the dangerous falls at Louisville had been eliminated by the building of the Louisville Canal. Thus one of the serious bottlenecks had been almost removed, although the smallness of the canal and the high rates of toll left much to be desired. During the 1840's the Federal government had taken initial steps to improve the Mississippi waterways. Thousands of snags had been removed, which greatly reduced the river hazards and made navigation less of a risk. A concerted national program of river improvement, however, did not take place until after 1850. But despite that fact, looking backward to the beginning of the century, Pittsburgh's river trade had become bigger in quantity, wider in scope, more regular in method and more dependable in character.

Just as the Ohio River had become a better trade channel by 1850, so did the Monongahela and Allegheny rivers show improvements. The Monongahela and its principal tributary, the Youghiogheny, had both been slackwatered, and the coal and iron trades were greatly aided by the change. By way of the Monongahela, Pittsburgh had also easy access to the famous National Pike. The Monongahela Valley was thus a complement of Pittsburgh, and her economic value increased with the years. The river continued to serve Pittsburgh; likewise, Pittsburgh served the river. The same was true for the Allegheny, the twin river of the Monongahela. Her trade had also expanded and enlarged during the fifty year span, although no sweeping improvements had taken place in the river. The Allegheny had

---

[14] Way, "The Commerce of the Lower Mississippi in the Period 1830-1860," in Mississippi Valley Historical Association, *Proceedings*, X, (1916-1917), 58.

not presented the same hazards as had the Monongahela, and navigation was safer. The river was not so deep, and a smaller type of boat was used. The principal cause of the improvement of the Allegheny trade was due to the increased number of people who had settled and who were potential customers. As the trade area became enlarged, improved boats plied the river regularly, and trade relations were strengthened. The Allegheny River and the Erie-Waterford Turnpike had made possible a satisfactory lake connection for Pittsburgh. This channel was another evidence of Pittsburgh's enlarging trade area.

Rivers, however, were not the only trade arteries which had been improved by 1850. Pittsburgh's eastern connections had also undergone a complete change. The Pennsylvania State System had considerably reduced the freight rates and time between Pittsburgh and Philadelphia; and although the System was outmoded by 1850, its earlier beneficial effects upon Pittsburgh should not be overlooked. The Pennsylvania State System had contributed effectively in breaking down the trade barriers between Pittsburgh and the East. This improved trade artery had arrived at the time when the economic changes between Pittsburgh and the more southern areas of the Ohio-Mississippi valleys were becoming increasingly evident. The State System had tended to absorb the slack in Pittsburgh's tacit economic transfer from the Mississippi Valley to the ranks of the industrial North—a transfer which was gradual and unostentatious although teeming with future possibilities. When Pittsburghers became aware that the Pennsylvania System was no longer an adequate trade channel, they began to campaign vigorously for railroad connections. After a bitter fight, Pittsburgh was guaranteed such a connection in 1845 when a charter was granted to the Pennsylvania Railroad. Trains did not arrive in Pittsburgh until 1852, but the road was assured at the turn of the mid-century mark.

Along with these major trade arteries were numerous small spokes, each radiating from the trunk lines. Local roads were improved; new roads were opened, and all contributed to strengthen Pittsburgh. Pittsburgh was more than ever the hub of the wheel, and the spokes were considerably strengthened by 1850. Each factor had worked intermittently in strengthening the other; both were responsible for the results. Neither factor unaided could work successfully. Manufacturing and commercial facilities were necessary before a substantial trade could take place; the hub had to be strong to support the wheel. Trade arteries were essential if commerce were to flourish; the spokes had to be adequate to carry the weight of the burden. At mid-century Pittsburgh manufacturers were flourishing, and the improvement of channels of trade had kept pace with the development in manufacturing.

Thus, by 1850 Pittsburgh was a commercial emporium with no apologies to the West or to the East. Her importance is illustrated by the increased number and variety of stores and especially by the specialized aspects of her stores. The general store of 1800 had disappeared and the modern department store had not yet arrived.[15] The following types of, and number of stores were listed for 1850:[16]

Type of Stores	Approximate Number	Type of Stores	Approximate Number
Bankers and Exchange Brokers	9	Cabinet and Chair Makers ...	4
Watch Makers and Jewelers...	5	Insurance Company	4
Wholesale Grocers, Commission & Produce Dealers	33	Wall Paper and Bordering ...	3
		Tinners and Copper Smiths ...	9
Commission Produce and Forwarding Merchants	8	Emigrants Lines	2
		Hotel and Taverns	7
Wholesale Grocers and Dealers in Liquors	9	Foundry Warehouses	6
		Bakers and Confectioners	5
Saddle, Harness and Trunk Makers	8	Milliners and Mantua Makers.	4
		Fancy and Variety Goods	8
Looking Glasses and Varieties.	3	Cotton Manufacturing	1
Queensware and China	3	Boat Stores	6
Booksellers and Stationers	9	Brush Manufacturing	1
Patent Medicine	2	Family Groceries	11
Clothing Stores	20	Triming [sic], Hosiery and Variety	4
Gun and Pistols	4		
Merchant Tailors	2	Tobacco, Snuff, and Cigars ...	7
Cheap Publication	3	Glass Manufacturing	6
Dry Goods Merchants	15	Music Stores	1
Wholesale Dry Goods	4	Lumber Merchants	3
Boots and Shoes	23	Soap and Candle Manufacturing	1
Wool Merchants	3		
Planing Mills and Sash Factory	1	Fruit and Candies	3
Hardware and Cutlery	12	Plough Manufacturing	2
Leather Stores	7	Mustard and Spices	2
Drug and Medicines	14	Tea Stores	2
Hats, Caps and Furs	10		

A great number of Pittsburgh stores were also definitely classified by 1850 as wholesale or retail trade. The dividing line, however, was not absolute. Robert H. Hartley, for example, still advertised that he would sell saddles, harness, or trunks either wholesale or retail,[17] and probably there were many more like him. But the tendency toward specialization and large scale organization was evident. In 1850 Pittsburgh's business directory listed thirty-three wholesale grocers, commission and produce dealers; nine wholesale grocers and dealers in liquors, and four wholesale dry goods merchants.[18] At least these forty-six

[15] Joseph Horne and Company, 63 Market Street, was listed as a "Triming, [sic] Hosiery and Variety" store in 1850; Kauffman and Boyles, 88 Wood Street, was classified as "Fancy and Variety Goods." *Pittsburgh Daily Morning Post,* January 12, 1850.
[16] *Ibid.,* January 12, 1850.
[17] *Ibid.,* January 12, 1850.
[18] The business directory also listed retailers in the same line of goods:
Family grocers—11.
Dry goods merchants—15.
Commission produce and forwarding merchants—8.

establishments were definitely wholesalers. The process was further developed by the iron manufacturers who had local warehouses in the Triangle, or specifically designated commission agents who handled their retailing. Large scale organization had also taken place among these wholesale establishments and the following chart shows the extent of corporate enterprises:[19]

	COM-PANY	PARTNER-SHIP	INDI-VIDUAL	TOTAL
Wholesale grocers and produce dealers..	7	14	12	33
Wholesale grocers and liquor dealers	1	3	5	9
Wholesale dry goods merchants	3	1	0	4

Probably a still more important change of the 1850 stores was the improvement in quality and in size of the stock of goods. Goods of all descriptions, grades, and sizes were now offered for sale; and instead of a few bolts of cloth, a few barrels of sugar and coffee, and a thin scattering of household goods, the shelves of Pittsburgh stores were loaded to capacity. Pittsburgh merchants carried eastern merchandise as well as local products. A. A. Mason and Company, wholesale dry goods merchants, advertised a "Great Arrival of New Goods," among which were:[20]

105 dozen French Wrought Collars and Caps
 16 pieces rich Dress Silk
100 pieces Alpacas, from 20 to 50 cents per yard
  5 cases Mous De Laines, from 10 to 25 cents per yard
 25 cases Merrimac Prints, all styles
  5 cases Mourning Prints, from 10 to 12½ cents per yard
 10 cases Checks, from 10 to 14 cents per yard
  5 cases Ginghams, good styles, at 12 cents
Also sheeting, shirting and housekeeping goods in great variety—all of which will be offered at extremely low prices.

A later advertisement by the same company throws additional light on the merchandising process in 1850:[21]

Semi-Annual Sale of Dry Goods. At the One Price Store of A. A. Mason and Company will commence on New Years Day, 1850, and continue through the month of January during which time the whole of their immense establishment (including all their Wholesale Rooms) will be thrown open for Retail trade and their entire wholesale stock will be offered at retail on this occasion, at fully one fourth less than usual prices. Their Shawl Saloon [sic] contains more than three thousand Shawls, comprising every description of Long and Square Wool Shawls, Cashmere, Broche &c. Also Vizettes, Cloaks, Mantillas, Sacks &c. at an immense reduction from usual prices.

Dress and Cloak Goods—their stocks comprising more than one thousand pieces, Thibet cloths, Merinos, Paramettas, Alapacas, Lyones Cloths, Opera and

[19] *Pittsburgh Daily Morning Post,* January 12, 1850. Among the retailers one company existed in the "Family Grocers," no partnership; among the 15 dry goods merchants, one company and two partnerships were advertised.
[20] *Ibid.,* January 12, 1850.
[21] *Ibid.,* February 22, 1850.

Pelisse do. will be sold from 20 to 40 per cent, less than usual also, 300 pieces rich, plain, and fig'd Silks, reduced 30 per cent.

20 Cases Cashmeres and De Laines, entire new styles, also, White Goods, Mourning do., Embroideries, Laces, Ribbons Gloves and Hosiery, Trimmings, &c.

20 Cases flannels; 70 cases new style Calicoes; 70 bales Ticking; 60 cases Bleached Muslins; 100 bales Brown Muslins. Also Cloths, Cassemeres, [sic], Jeans, Cassinets, &c. at extremely low prices together with an immense variety of other goods making an assortment one of the most extensive in the country— all of which have been marked down at much lower prices than their extensive annual sale in January last.

They invite an early call, as many of their choicest Goods will soon be sold. The lowest price named first.

Silks, opera cloaks, mantillas, trimmings, laces, ribbons, and vizettes for sale at "one price" and "the lowest price named first" at a semi-annual sale! Strange shop talk for a community brought up on "country produce taken in exchange" for such and such an article, and a promise of liberal credit. Equally modern innovations were the advertisements for ready-made clothing and the frequently appearing "one price cash system." Advertisements were becoming also more detailed, spectacular, and informative.

By 1850 Pittsburgh had 20 clothing stores, two of which were corporate enterprises and six were on a partnership basis. The clothing stores had gradually appeared during the 1840's, and a few establishments, such as those of J. Boobyer, P. Delany and William Leonard, had grown out of the tailoring shops.[22] These merchants usually continued to make tailor-made clothes, and in addition, they offered a new line of goods which had a great appeal due to their reduced price. The Pittsburgh ladies were not the only ones who were demanding more than a Sunday silk or wool and homespun dresses for work days. The men were also becoming better dressed. An advertisement entitled "Plain Questions: Correctly Answered" shows what the Pittsburgh men were wearing:[23]

Who has the most handsome Vestings in the City?..........Boobyer & Gribble
Who has the best Black Satins in the city?...................Boobyer & Gribble
Who has the best Assortment of Beaver Cloth in the city?....Boobyer & Gribble
Who has the best Black Cassimere in the city?...............Boobyer & Gribble
Who has the best Fancy Cassimeres in the city?..............Boobyer & Gribble
Who has the best Ready-Made Clothing in the city?..........Boobyer & Gribble
Who sells the Cheapest Clothing in the city?.................Boobyer & Gribble
Who makes the Best Fitting Clothes in the city?..............Boobyer & Gribble
Where is B & G's Bee-Hive Clothing Store?   No. 257 Liberty Street
3 doors above Irwins.

Pittsburghers were not only dressing better in 1850 but they had also begun to beautify their homes. Wall paper and carpet were fre-

---

22 Harris, *Directory*, 1841, listed two ready-made clothing stores. Only eight of the twenty clothing merchants were listed in 1841.
23 *Pittsburgh Daily Morning Post*, February 22, 1850.

quently advertised; pianofortes and other musical instruments were also offered for sale, as well as modern and antique furniture for the *nouveau riche* who lacked family heirlooms. Pittsburghers in 1850 also had a more varied diet, and the Pekin Tea Store at 70 Fourth Avenue advertised in January the following articles:[24]

5 doz cans fresh Peaches	3 doz bottles Tomatoes		
5 doz bottles do	3 doz half-gallon bottles Pickles		
5 doz bottles Pine Apples	3 doz quart do do		
3 doz bottles Cherries	3 doz fancy do do		
3 doz bottles Strawberries			

One wonders what verdict was passed on the housewife who did so completely neglect her family as to buy these store products.

The ladies were being bombarded from all sides by tempting advertisements. By 1850 newspapers became so bold as to advertise cosmetics, but the appeals were subtle and cautious. Nevertheless, the ground was broken for later expansion, although the lady would probably have needed smelling salts upon reading present day advertisements. The advertisements in 1850 also used the present day overworked, but never failing health and beauty angles of approach. The *Elizabeth Arden* of 1850 was a chemical producer by the name of Jones, who offered[25] "A fine set of teeth for 25 cents—white teeth, foul breath, healthy gums—clean it with Jones' Amber Tooth Paste." On the same page appeared an advertisement for Jones' Italian Chemical Soap: "Will you Marry and get a rich husband, lady? Your face is your fortune . . . Be sure you get the genuine." But the best one offered:[26]

Ladies are cautioned against using Common Prepared Chalk, they are not aware how frightfully injurious it is to the skin! how coarse, how rough, how sallow, yellow and unhealthy the skin appears after using prepared chalk! Besides it is injurious, containing a large quantity of lead! We have prepared a beautiful vegetable article, which we call Jones' Spanish Lilly White. It is perfectly innocent, being purified of all deleterious qualities and it imparts to the skin a natural healthy, alabaster, clear lively white; at the same time acting as a cosmetic on the skin, making it soft and smooth. . . .

Pittsburgh in 1850 was also flooded with patent medicine. If Pittsburghers bought all the remedies which were offered, they must have been constantly on the verge of epidemic diseases. William H. Denny, author of an article on the "Salubrity of Pittsburgh and Vicinity" wrote: "We have less hepatic disease than the West, and less pulmonic disease than the East . . . On the whole, with regard to the health of Pittsburgh, it may be said that no city in the union is more healthy . . ."[27] Nevertheless, Pittsburghers were offered[28] Howes Cough Candy,

[24] *Ibid.*, January 12, 1850.
[25] *Ibid.*, February 22, 1850.
[26] *Ibid.*, January 12, 1850.
[27] Craig, *The History of Pittsburgh*, 309-310.
[28] All these appeared in one issue of the *Pittsburgh Daily Morning Post*, February 1, 1850.

which was good for whooping cough and "general affections of the Lungs"; Dalley's Magical Pain Extractor; Petroleum or Rock Oil for chronic bronchitis, consumption ("in its early stages"), asthma, liver complaint, diarrhea, gout, etc., etc., McDowell's Cholera Mixture, and Scarpa's Oil for Deafness (for sale at Pekins Tea Store, 4th Street), and many other miracle workers.

Had Zadok Cramer been living in 1850, he would probably have taken his quill and scratched off a scathing tirade against the addiction of the inhabitants to foreign merchandise. He had predicted in 1803 that "every hole and corner of the western land would be soon filled with foreign extravagances," and he pleaded constantly for Pittsburghers to patronize their own local manufacturers.[29] But times had changed since Zadok Cramer wrote, and Pittsburgh could now trade on an equal basis with the East. Her iron, coal, and glass products were in demand both in the East and in the West; her stores were visited by western merchants who needed supplies; her people had accumulated money, settled down, and wanted personal adornments and luxuries. During the half century, the frontier had moved far beyond the Ohio Valley; Pittsburgh merchants and industrialists had capitalized on their favorable location and abundant natural resources, and had joined the ranks of the moneyed and industrial East.

---

[29] Cramer, *Almanack,* 1804.

APPENDIX I

Value Of Pittsburgh's Manufactures
1800-1850

	1803	1810	1815	1817	1819	1826	1836	1839	1850
Iron	$56,548	$94,890	$764,200	$525,616	$166,500	$1,155,094	$6,290,000 / 5,878,500†	$4,946,800	$6,300,000
Glass	13,000	63,000	235,000	240,000	35,100	199,804	1,260,000 / 430,000†	520,000	1,000,000
Textiles	46,825	14,248	115,500	82,080	16,150	288,032	500,000 / 770,000†	536,400	1,500,000
Pottery	3,500	3,400	10,000	8,000	Closed	6,180	......	1,000	......
Leather	34,165	81,378	215,600	276,860	85,000	245,000	......	341,768	......
Hat & cap	14,675	24,507	122,000	44,640	50,200#	......	......	189,560	......
Liquor	32,100	......	91,050	72,000	35,000	48,000	......	108,000	......
Rope	2,200	2,500	30,000	15,000	15,000	15,000	80,000 / 250,000†	......	......
Wagons	1,500	2,872	40,000	28,500	18,500	25,000	......	203,450	......
Paper	1,000	......	40,000	23,000	30,000	37,440	20,000	25,000	......
Milling	8,400	......	......	50,000	......	72,000	......	103,110	......
Boat building	40,000	43,000	......	......	......	62,000	......	......	......
Wood products	33,900	19,674	144,900	141,700	48,000	90,000	......	249,400	......
Brick & stone	17,500	22,400	......	......	......	27,750	......	......	......
Tobacco	3,000	11,500	45,850	21,000	27,550	53,000	......	......	......
Brass & tin	15,600	25,500	249,633	200,000	56,700	58,000	241,200 / 206,000†	......	......
Soap & chandler	5,600	14,500	......	32,600	......	......	......	......	......
Red lead	......	13,100	110,000	40,000	35,000	23,100	......	......	......
Gunsmith	1,800	2,400	......	13,800	......	......	......	......	......
Miscellaneous	14,580	49,500	404,100	510,670	213,300	225,000	6,224,000 / 4,071,250†	580,535	......
Totals **	$350,000 Estimate	$1,000,000 Estimate	$2,617,833	$2,266,366	$832,000	$2,553,549	$15,575,640§	$14,000,000 Estimate	$50,000,000‡ Estimate
Corrected***				$2,325,466		$2,630,400	$11,606,350†§		

*Compilation made from the following sources:
1803—Cramer, Almanack, 1804, 21.
1810—U. S. Census Report, 1810.
1815—Pittsburgh Gazette, January 1, 1820.
1817—Cramer, Almanack, 1818, 49.
1819—Pittsburgh Gazette, January 1, 1820.
1826—Jones, Directory, 1826, 49.
1836—Lyford, Directory, 1836, 94.
1836-37—Harris, Directory, 1837, 185.
1840—Wheeling Times and Advertiser, November 14, 1840.
1850—Fahnestock, Directory, 1850, 18.

** These totals are usually estimates given by the compiler of the directory. They do not always balance with the breakdown. In 1803, Cramer's estimate is "upwards of three hundred, fifty thousand ($350,000.00) dollars," including Pittsburgh and county. In 1810, the figure is also an estimate. The Pittsburgh Council's Report for 1815 and 1819 are correct and balance. In 1817, Cramer's figures do not balance again. The same is true for Jones in 1826. In 1836, Lyford and Harris each made widely varying estimates—part of this can be explained by the fact that Harris had included the early months of 1837 in his account, and the panic had already demonstrated its effect. The years 1839 and 1850 are also estimates.

*** Errors apparently due to incorrect addition, or to misprinting in some of the various component figures.

See Hazard's Register, Vol. IV, 169, for correct amount i.e., $50,200, the Gazette gives $30,200.

† Harris.

§ Corrected $14,615,200, $11,605,750.

‡ Value of manufactures and "other business."

APPENDIX II

Tonnage of Monongahela Slackwater, 1845-1850

MANUFACTURED ARTICLES SHIPPED WESTWARD AND EASTWARD ON THE MONONGAHELA SLACKWATER, 1845 TO 1850

(Compiled from the ANNUAL REPORTS, 1846-1851)

	West 1845	East 1845	West 1846	East 1846	West 1847	East 1847	West 1848	East 1848	West 1849	East 1849	West 1850	East 1850
Beer, ale ....bbl.	......	228	......	516	......	......	......	......	......	......	......	......
Bricks ....no.	760,100	37,094	205,600	92,819	627,500	86,628	1,200,700	78,570	2,074,000	133,545	1,132,400	115,578
Carriages ....no.	......	......	33	19	38	21	49	30	37	23	43	42
Empty bbl. ...no.	1,164	2,171	1,193	4,951	268	4,511	1,002	13,138	2,398	7,674	2,800	7,046
Flour ....bbl.	27,839	557	51,225	362	79,933	......	60,110	1,452	54,599	1,317	38,421	2,341
Glass ....box	47,331	......	62,118	......	60,285	......	55,186	......	72,752	......	84,911	......
Hoop Poles ...no.	45,350	2,000	55,135	6,400	16,626	7,200	16,300	8,000	42,950	8,775	17,187	8,600
Hulls ....no.	......	......	29	......	22	......	29	......	27	......	27	......
Iron ....lb.	998,052	367,140	1,583,430	......	1,184,377	......	697,296	......	159,504	......	386,710	......
Lath ....no.	......	54,215	142,000	261,950	......	362,900	49,000	331,900	2,500	351,500	40,100	564,100
Lime ....bu.	49,037	248	36,800	......	38,155	......	13,839	......	12,081	......	26,394	......
Molasses .....bbl.	......	916	......	2,111	......	......	......	......	......	......	......	......
Nails ....lb.	1,343,800	105,586	1,479,200	......	988,000	......	1,209,300	......	1,387,400	......	1,340,900	......
Pig Iron ....ton	386	1,205	903	1,117	846	1,251	547	1,206	177½	1,716	288¾	1,590½
Ploughs .....no.	......	118	33	78	......	......	......	......	......	......	......	......
Shingles ....no.	347,000	......	......	806,650	......	1,129,300	......	1,760,500	......	2,532,500	28,500	1,798,750
Staves ......no.	4,000	45,834	68,250	300	81,940	......	81,610	......	35,350	2,200	20,950	148,660
Tobacco ....lb.	245,603	......	312,250	......	1,240,347	......	549,294	......	342,106	......	......	......
Wagons .....no.	......	29	86	26	147	45	195	44	58	63	73	105
Whiskey ....bbl.	5,753	622	4,518	1,286	6,092	2,193	4,908	2,515	3,796	3,895	3,217	4,352

AGRICULTURAL PRODUCTS AND LIVESTOCK SHIPPED WESTWARD AND EASTWARD ON THE MONONGAHELA SLACKWATER 1845-1850.

(Compiled from the Annual Reports, 1846-1851)

	West 1845	East	West 1846	East	West 1847	East	West 1848	East	West 1849	East	West 1850	East
Apples ......bbl.	12,061	......	13,511	85	15,544	......	17,969	......	15,021	773	3,665	564
Bacon ......no.	18,674	249,625	......	415,375	......	1,187,721	......	3,032,044	......	1,532,272	......	1,384,914
Beeswax ......lb.	......	......	......	......	......	42,217	......	16,378	......	9,065	......	29,234
Butter & Lard .lb.	......	......	......	233,040	......	1,304,960	......	1,102,521	......	559,338	......	276,491
Cider ......bbl.	123	......	363	......	287	......	631	......	150	......	229	......
Dried Fruit ...bu.	2,189	81	......	......	......	256,014	......	73,780	......	241,354	......	150,040
Leather & Wool lb.	......	......	......	......	......	278,347	......	128,552	......	102,159	......	437,420
Hay ......ton	......	......	205	......	93	......	124	......	108	......	140½	......
Hemp ......lb.	......	......	......	......	......	......	......	37,642	......	......	......	475
Oats ......bu.	......	......	50,794	......	71,887	......	35,110	......	51,874	......	41,830	......
Potatoes ......bu.	16,090	403	318	193	904	192	631	2,506	630	4,250	753	6,770
Seeds ......bu.	3,326	460	......	......	......	......	631	......	......	......	......	......
Wheat ......bu.	......	......	15,161	......	16,787	......	3,206	......	3,281	......	6,611	......
Livestock												
Hogs	154	......	423	1,588	106	3,185	168	5,315	476	13	308	1,287
Horses	82	62	118	61	79	39	88	105	83	65	127	127

EXTRACTIVE PRODUCTS SHIPPED WESTWARD AND EASTWARD ON THE MONONGAHELA SLACKWATER, 1845-1850

(Compiled from the Annual Reports, 1846-1851)

	West 1845	East	West 1846	East	West 1847	East	West 1848	East	West 1849	East	West 1850	East
Bark ....cord	57	......	......	......	......	......	......	......	......	......	......	......
Boards ....ft.	331,720	792,395	359,845	2,150,360	617,612	3,400,856	702,722	4,000,231	410,322	4,306,738	422,447	5,047,988
Coal ....bu.	4,605,185	......	7,778,911	......	9,645,127	......	9,816,361	......	9,708,507	......	12,297,967	......
Copper Ore ..ton	......	......	......	......	......	......	......	268	......	992	......	......
Iron Ore ....ton	......	......	587	......	105	......	149	......	150	......	386	683
Posts ....no.	3,848	......	......	......	2,525	......	1,189	......	220	......	2,485	......
Salt ....bbl.	1,958	5,971	2,325	12,246	787	10,155	50	11,063	1,748	11,416	1,065	15,436
Sand ....bu.	33,550	......	197,161	......	199,413	......	196,250	......	89,620	......	127,700	......
Stone ....perches	4,371	......	1,922	......	2,243	......	3,184	......	3,228	......	5,981	......
Timber ....ft.	169,417	20,973	111,086	176,406	169,926	140,753	87,512	265,520	89,525	393,894	34,827	246,720
Wood ....cord	103	......	108	......	109	......	139	......	164	......	225	......

APPENDIX III

A Compilation of the Tonnage carried over the Pennsylvania State System, 1835-1850

Author's Note: Figures for certain commodities vary greatly from year to year. A close study of the *Annual Reports* reveals that trade fluctuated greatly due to the uncertain state of transportation, breakdown of its own or competing routes, changes in rates of toll, epidemics along the trade routes, and the effect of famines in Europe. There is also the possibility that the *Annual Reports* may err in some instances, as for example, the unexplained rise in 1836 in the shipments of corn and wheat. Then, too, in 1844 the classifications changed drastically; new items were added, such as, dry goods, hardware, queensware, etc., thus eliminating the inclusive item of merchandise and other similar categories.

EXTRACTIVE PRODUCTS SHIPPED EASTWARD AND WESTWARD FROM OR TO PITTSBURGH OVER THE PENNSYLVANIA STATE SYSTEM, 1835 TO 1850

(Compiled from the Annual Reports, 1835-1851)

		East 1835	West 1835	East 1836	West 1836	East 1837	West 1837	East 1838	West 1838
Ashes	lb.	......	......	......	......	......	......	......	......
Board	ft.	212,987	1,000	5,950	......	110,294	47,290	85,000	......
Coal	ton	836	......	2,656	......	875	2,980	530,000	1,001
Fish	bbl.	352	9,774	44	......	65	11,191	55	7,294
Fur & Peltry	lb.	277,070	......	110,364	......	81,588	......	159,656	......
Gypsum	ton	......	13	547	......	......	29¼	......	22
Iron Ore	ton	......	12	......	......	......	......	......	......
Mahogany	lb.	......	......	......	......	......	......	......	......
Oil	gal.	9,526	50,363	26,311	......	1,251	77,226	44,540	76,381
Potash	lb.	......	......	......	......	......	......	......	......
Salt	bu.	......	215,352	......	......	......	156,623	......	140,935
Slate	bu.	......	......	......	......	......	......	......	3,500
Stone	perches	......	......	......	......	......	......	......	......
Timber	ft.	......	2,220	......	......	......	7,500	......	......
Wood & Bark	cord	......	......	......	......	......	......	......	......
Marble	lb.	......	72,870	......	......	2,310	874,922	......	1,385,608
Posts & Rails		3,140	......	......	......	......	......	......	6,900

EXTRACTIVE PRODUCTS SHIPPED EASTWARD AND WESTWARD FROM OR TO PITTSBURGH OVER THE PENNSYLVANIA STATE SYSTEM, 1835 TO 1850—Continued

(Compiled from the Annual Reports, 1835-1851)

	East 1839	West	East 1840	West	East 1841	West	East 1842	West
Ashes ....lb.	......	......	......	......	......	......	......	......
Board ....ft.	94,966	26,198	253,557	47,607	......	......	......	......
Coal ....ton	1,816	707	551	245	......	......	......	......
Fish ....bbl.	146	11,731	230	7,228	......	5,387	......	6,760
Fur & Peltry ....lb.	217,749	......	61,398	......	297,507	......	56,595	......
Gypsum ....ton	......	12	......	6½	......	485	......	196½
Iron Ore ....ton	......	......	......	......	......	......	......	......
Mahogany ....lb.	......	......	......	......	......	......	......	......
Oil ....gal.	2,578	91,147	3,023	55,006	2,244	75,860	10,130	16,353
Potash ....lb.	......	......	......	......	......	......	......	......
Salt ....bu.	250	206,202	148	171,604	......	240,621	......	188,508
Slate ....bu.	......	......	......	......	......	......	......	......
Stone ....perches	......	......	......	......	......	......	......	......
Timber ....ft.	......	600	......	18,100	......	......	......	......
Wood & Bark ....cord	......	......	......	......	......	......	......	......
Marble ....lb.	700,536	......	6,196	442,426	......	337,982	......	235,302
Posts & Rails	......	9,410	......	10,743	......	......	......	......

EXTRACTIVE PRODUCTS SHIPPED EASTWARD AND WESTWARD FROM OR TO PITTSBURGH OVER THE PENNSYLVANIA STATE SYSTEM, 1835 TO 1850—Continued

(Compiled from the ANNUAL REPORTS, 1835-1851)

		East 1843	West 1843	East 1844	West 1844	East 1845	West 1845	East 1846	West 1846
Ashes	lb.	......	......	277,220	......	772,269	......	569,720	......
Board	ft.	52,580	133,733	171,425	164,500	......	612,932	13,900	214,240
Coal	ton	1,297	......	350½	8	2,311¾	35½	659½	30¼
Fish	bbl.	68	7,065	116	8,506½	......	17,240	18	19,609
Fur & Peltry	lb.	76,773	......	103,007	1,528	91,066*	......	110,969	......
Gypsum	ton	......	......	......	781	......	......	......	19
Iron Ore	ton	......	......	......	......	......	......	......	......
Mahogany	lb.	45,651	......	......	74,693	......	16,092	......	50,532
Oil	gal.	......	33,610	38,319	58,905	31,551	42,014	......	35,066
Potash	lb.	......	......	217,220	123,000	......	......	......	......
Salt	bu.	913	211,392	......	41,295	......	190,265	......	166,415
Slate	lb.	......	......	......	73,368	......	254,800	......	889,968
Stone	perches	......	......	......	1,851	......	1,374	......	......
Timber	ft.	......	......	......	......	......	......	......	......
Wood & Bark	cord	......	......	......	422	......	......	686¾	......
Marble	lb.	......	232,494	......	391,419	......	374,642	......	502,377
Posts & Rails		......	4,494	......	3,000	......	4,789	......	2,558

* In 1845 deer and beef skins were added to the *Annual Reports*. These are not included in the above figure but are listed separately:

1845	641,477 pounds		1848	878,139 pounds
1846	993,378 pounds		1849	467,660 pounds
1847	510,672		1850	1,072,561

EXTRACTIVE PRODUCTS SHIPPED EASTWARD AND WESTWARD FROM OR TO PITTSBURGH OVER THE PENNSYLVANIA STATE SYSTEM, 1835 TO 1850—Concluded

(Compiled from the ANNUAL REPORTS, 1835-1851)

		East 1847	West	East 1848	West	East 1849	West	East 1850	West
Ashes	lb.	......	230,300	147,719	2,049,053	......	......	44,000	6,665,500
Board	ft.	246,936	294,311	78,900	299,960	6,000	77,841	163,800	85,200
Coal	ton	4,691	52,570bu	61,131	16,300	2,512	......	16,217	......
Fish	bbl.	7,254*	5,977,891*	......	4,745,115*	......	13,343	......	21,566
Fur & Peltry	lb.	203,925	......	166,425	......	182,712	......	183,137	......
Gypsum	ton	......	1,700	......	......	......	......	......	......
Iron Ore	ton	......	......	......	......	......	......	......	......
Mahogany	lb.	......	......	......	25,150	......	......	2,800	30,200
Oil	gal.	52,642	32,668	3,069	90,486	......	97,760	......	118,655
Potash	lb.	......	100,023	......	......	192,750	......	407,260	......
Salt	bu.	385	137,240	......	140,695	17,440	495,324	115,140	128,225
Slate	lb.	......	515,435	......	539,800	......	411,000	......	770,200
Stone	perches	......	1,374,529*	......	34	......	2,610	220	......
Timber	ft.	......	......	......	......	......	......	1,006	......
Wood & Bark	cord	14	410	......	688	......	819	387	578
Marble	lb.	6,000	590,012	28,582	961,980	......	1,308,700	......	1,147,200
Posts & Rails		......	1,280	......	245	......	8,375	2,100	......

* lb.

MANUFACTURED ARTICLES SHIPPED EASTWARD AND WESTWARD FROM OR TO PITTSBURGH OVER THE PENNSYLVANIA STATE SYSTEM, 1835 TO 1850.

(Compiled from the ANNUAL REPORTS, 1835-1861)

		East 1835	West 1835	East 1836	West* 1836	East 1837	West 1837	East 1838	West 1838
Bricks	no.	197,250	......	......	......	41,350	38,000	3,500	......
Copper & Tin	lb.	18,986	312,374	248	......	1,190	390,848	1,595	493,192
Drugs & Dyestuff	lb.	3,668	313,493	60,294	......	13,608	264,850	22,951	230,244
Flour	bbl.	37,515	7	45,587	......	71,536	......	101,725	......
Furniture	lb.	258,202	845,353	51,337	......	170,700	2,146,757	330,221	1,691,137
Groceries	lb.	696,917	4,877,686	158,540	......	403,972	6,512,188	315,680	7,456,634
Iron Pig & Castings	lb.	1,070,733	1,079,132	337,683	......	366,715	1,132,738	409,814	1,193,312
Iron, Blooms, Bar, Sheet	lb.	2,997,478	22,428,098	176,557	......	816,441	25,425,868	1,880,357	15,172,607
Lead—Pigs & Bars	lb.	11,934	5,360	4,581	......	7,394	......	......	12,195
Lime	bu.	......	......	......	......	......	......	......	......
Leather	lb.	49,962	145,829	4,450	......	11,656	222,407	6,492	212,420
Merchandise	lb.	660,141	30,280,506	495,977	......	844,977	20,394,638	690,702	14,932,410
Paper	lb.	......	......	......	......	......	......	......	......
Rags	lb.	211,194	7,149	114,881	......	45,901	......	41,493	......
Raw Hides	lb.	20,862	61,086	......	......	39,955	236,741	36,886	66,669
Tobacco	lb.	5,840,011	74,378	4,336,372	......	2,410,232	176,480	4,880,915	......
Tar & Pitch	lb.	......	......	......	......	......	......	......	......
Shingles	no.	283,750	......	3,300	......	23,500	6,000	7,000	5,250
Staves, Hoops, etc.	no.	347,066	13,200	......	......	38,360	132,360	......	244,680
Sundries	lb.	1,112,667	2,031,884	1,062,259	......	1,030,260	1,497,112	1,707,764	2,716,155
Whiskey	gal.	45,937	......	424,299	......	70,684	76,419	252,910	70,023
Window Glass	box	5,908	838	5,589	......	6,650	55	362,560	......

* The *Annual Report* for 1836 does not give figures for goods shipped westward from Philadelphia.

MANUFACTURED ARTICLES SHIPPED EASTWARD AND WESTWARD FROM OR TO PITTSBURGH OVER THE PENNSYLVANIA STATE SYSTEM, 1835 TO 1850—Continued.

(Compiled from the Annual Reports, 1835-1851)

		East 1839	West	East 1840	West	East 1841	West	East 1842	West
Bricks	no.	34,803	149,400	36,950	79,000	......	706,193	......	180,676
Copper & Tin	lb.	......	278,869	3,356	384,621	......	920,121	......	182,193
Drugs & Dyestuff	lb.	6,753	592,657	7,125	506,115	18,629	......	117,834	......
Flour	bbl.	55,229	......	139,637	47	109,878	......	114,103½	......
Furniture	lb.	248,957	1,444,759	225,076	1,450,531	327,375	1,637,856	446,820	956,484
Groceries	lb.	525,524	10,813,116	678,612	9,345,638	954,777	11,104,818	1,263,006	4,952,577
Iron Pig & Castings	lb.	449,127	872,786	709,127	601,091	......	......	......	......
Iron, Blooms, Bar, Sheet	lb.	585,237	32,958,817	1,658,261	20,953,244	......	22,468,706	......	14,106,698
Lead—Pigs & Bars	lb.	4,988	32,957	29,696	19,353	113,961	......	250,722	......
Lime	bu.	......	......	94	......	......	......	......	......
Leather	lb.	15,099	464,186	68,368	236,309	75,225	239,142	108,958	30,642
Merchandise	lb.	325,204	30,821,331	339,072	15,638,200	429,517	18,547,603	611,585	14,540,412
Paper	lb.	......	......	......	......	......	......	......	......
Rags	lb.	109,841	......	176,501	9,070	279,663	15,280	194,599	28,499
Raw Hides	lb.	31,412	79,589	31,370	13,039	103,260	16,608	221,710	27,532
Tobacco	lb.	3,011,400	378,887	10,179,618	589,142	11,501,846	777,381	13,998,348	368,618
Tar & Pitch	lb.	......	......	......	......	......	......	......	......
Shingles	no.	62,000	8,000	145,500	34,000	......	......	......	......
Staves, Hoops, etc.	no.	......	167,625	......	787,846	......	......	......	......
Sundries	lb.	1,360,357	10,244,224	......	11,612,794	......	......	......	......
Whiskey	gal.	34,652	......	66,666	105,820	118,086	116,096	65,076	48,081
Window Glass	box	1,675	......	6,144	......	9,901	......	9,123½	......

MANUFACTURED ARTICLES SHIPPED EASTWARD AND WESTWARD FROM OR TO PITTSBURGH OVER THE PENNSYLVANIA STATE SYSTEM, 1835 TO 1850—Continued.

(Compiled from the Annual Reports, 1835-1851)

	East 1843	West 1843	East 1844	West 1844	East 1845	West 1845	East 1846	West 1846
Bricks ....no.	26,950	270,760	84,408	110,000	......	1,230,000	......	1,045,688
Copper & Tin ......lb.	5,334	472,329	5,502	765,399	......	1,265,753	3,760	1,458,927
Drugs & Dyestuff ...lb.	40,916	769,091	80,634	1,721,778	16,004	848,745	18,862	622,293
Flour ....bbl.	130,858	......	100,454	......	82,092	139	156,412	316
Furniture ....lb.	361,031	992,375	250,744	1,049,718	290,936	......	216,659	1,427,885
Groceries ....lb.	1,357,836	4,445,705	1,379,780	5,108,266	1,063,472	5,118,460	1,571,889	6,933,856
Iron Pig & Castings ..lb.	1,447,090	2,473,505	2,646,167	5,094,724	3,956,728	7,374,738	2,675,341	15,410,966
Iron, Blooms, Bar, Sheet ...lb.	2,426,047	22,703,704	778,840	18,824,166	......	15,332,782	319,736	13,890,707
Lead—Pigs & Bars ...lb.	4,312	1,570	15,810	......	......	......	325,985	35,131
Lime ....bu.	......	......	......	......	......	......	......	......
Leather ....lb.	96,554	372,402	69,791	415,775	104,383	478,926	185,200	386,225
Merchandise ....lb.	566,608	28,368,868	324,318	42,798,671*	224,135	38,498,926	518,997	34,272,460
Paper ....lb.	......	......	11,979	15,152	26,342	207,391	27,405	109,946
Rags ....lb.	409,876	10,120	669,742	7,614	417,537	7,167	423,415	2,113
Raw Hides ....lb.	171,362	14,758	492,684	119,991	117,571	1,222,750	454,146	784,172
Tobacco ....lb.	18,173,849	431,238	17,303,415	763,465	24,015,613	451,645	24,696,742	542,145
Tar & Pitch ....lb.	......	......	......	215,040	......	......	......	......
Shingles ....no.	33,900	24,100	......	......	......	......	71,000	......
Staves, Hoops, etc. ...no.	......	66,853	......	55,000	......	139,090	......	31,400
Sundries ....lb.	958,200	1,875,968	597,539	485,142	1,007,336	708,640	2,605,142	350,241
Whiskey ....gal.	115,242	38,886	77,591	37,337	112,841	28,786	130,332	19,412
Window Glass .....box	5,595	......	3,009½	......	3,794½	......	3,281	......

* After 1844 the term *merchandise* no longer appears in the *Annual Reports*. Figures for 1845-50 have been obtained by adding the following items: chinaware, drygoods, muslin, earthenware, glassware, hardware, hats and shoes.

MANUFACTURED ARTICLES SHIPPED EASTWARD AND WESTWARD FROM OR TO PITTSBURGH OVER THE PENNSYLVANIA STATE SYSTEM, 1835 TO 1850—Concluded.

(Compiled from the Annual Reports, 1835-1851)

		East 1847	West	East 1848	West	East 1849	West	East 1850	West
Bricks	no.	54,000	953,438	......	748,233	......	131,500	80,000	737,558
Copper & Tin	lb.	......	1,472,846	104,547	931,818	925,470	430,200	853,920	948,600
Drugs & Dyestuff	lb.	14,673	1,171,500	......	1,426,380	139,203	1,552,473	118,600	1,489,964
Flour	bbl.	297,944	1,279	182,527	396	......	......	121,319	4,295
Furniture	lb.	89,721	1,390,767	196,140	1,318,433	63,500	835,050	352,505	680,400
Groceries	lb.	1,978,822	7,833,925	4,109,086	8,506,898	3,471,385	9,180,396	2,757,817	10,752,036
Iron Pig & Castings	lb.	316,447	22,104,015	3,479,703	26,159,481	187,240	21,957,567	4,104,542	23,879,968
Iron, Blooms, Bar, Sheet	lb.	563,252	19,339,658	544,782	18,191,782	242,349	14,466,504	5,458,000	15,862,482
Lead—Pigs & Bars	lb.	188,078	14,755	......	20,500	......	......	......	......
Lime	bu.	......	28	......	403	......	4,346	452	320
Leather	lb.	146,048	312,239	118,940	583,221	......	69,400	531,887	120,864
Merchandise	lb.	......	40,471,581	......	40,243,414	......	38,871,356	......	48,460,228
Paper	lb.	116,157	83,163	31,284	150,653	17,840	221,450	15,300	415,400
Rags	lb.	260,018	......	308,385	......	382,638	......	687,307	......
Raw Hides	lb.	397,831	3,965	79,539	......	......	......	113,750	4,300
Tobacco	lb.	14,778,059	1,613,876	8,925,500	2,475,280	13,118,447	3,080,600	15,387,994	2,688,989
Tar & Pitch	lb.	1,183	390,313	18,500	996,415	......	671,400	......	1,309,200
Shingles	no.	28,500	......	......	......	......	......	......	50,000
Staves, Hoops, etc.	no.	2,986	12,276	......	65,100	......	66,000	2,300	208,300
Sundries	lb.	2,151,933	413,619	2,628,142	983,656	5,690,006	2,257,020	5,028,958	3,767,398
Whiskey	gal.	460,875	8,844	362,307	16,285	514,560	......	457,217	34,325
Window Glass	box	177,521	4,909	640	......	......	......	......	......

AGRICULTURAL PRODUCTS AND PROVISIONS SHIPPED EASTWARD AND WESTWARD FROM OR TO PITTSBURGH OVER THE PENNSYLVANIA STATE SYSTEM, 1835-1850.

(Compiled from the ANNUAL REPORTS, 1835-1851)

		East 1835	West	East 1836	West*	East 1837	West	East 1838	West
Agricultural Produce	lb.	......	......	......	......	......	......	......	......
Bacon	lb.	5,249,639	......	3,667,180	......	5,640,936	11,120	8,211,175	......
Butter & Cheese	lb.	30,452	3,860	90,159	......	86,940	33,744	32,729	111,325
Clover & Grass Seeds	bu.	341	......	80,667	......	195	......	180	......
Corn & Other Grain	bu.	4,995	1,096	328,892	......	8,150	5,494	1,713	1,993
Cotton	lb.	16,626	......	209,566	......	584,720	55,090	1,045,350	......
Feathers	lb.	110,703	......	67,308	......	44,827	......	35,682	......
Hemp	lb.	4,443	197,200	107	......	34,059	579,902	908,232	392,132
Lard & Tallow	lb.	408,576	2,800	273,750	......	749,725	......	489,976	......
Potatoes	bu.	2,716	......	......	......	1,568	5,323	......	3,789
Provisions, not specified	lb.	43,182	4,517	29,747	......	2,335	......	12,235	......
Salted Beef	bbl.	1,347	......	183	......	287	......	......	......
Salted Pork	bbl.	345	......	1,343	......	2,072	......	1,007	991
Wheat	bu.	212	......	1,427,247	......	128,008	26	48,557	......
Wool	lb.	998,205	66,229	867,790	......	325,693	342,200	865,677	......

* The *Annual Report* for 1836 does not give figures for goods shipped westward from Philadelphia.

AGRICULTURAL PRODUCTS AND PROVISIONS SHIPPED EASTWARD AND WESTWARD FROM OR TO PITTSBURGH OVER THE PENNSYLVANIA STATE SYSTEM, 1835-1850—Continued

(Compiled from the ANNUAL REPORTS, 1835-1851)

		East 1839	West	East 1840	West	East 1841	West	East 1842	West
Agricultural Produce	lb.	......	......	......	......	......	......	......	......
Bacon	lb.	11,449,586	......	7,203,177	......	9,601,832	......	13,286,233	......
Butter & Cheese	lb.	27,426	45,773	393,336	28,433	598,318	......	956,454	......
Clover & Grass Seeds	bu.	1,092	......	371	......	......	......	......	......
Corn & Other Grain	bu.	18,226	3,377	3,562	6,064	3,042	......	66,417	......
Cotton	lb.	300	5,689	1,311,055	1,000	689,856	......	952,985	......
Feathers	lb.	43,468	......	144,120	......	207,913	......	482,247	......
Hemp	lb.	766,017	625,971	22,859	366,950	14,407	501,749	147,806	103,207
Lard & Tallow	lb.	334,645	......	634,761	......	825,369	......	1,362,685	......
Potatoes	bu.	29	2,099	......	4,528	......	......	......	......
Provisions, not specified	lb.	......	28,655	23,246	......	1,578,070*	......	1,651,789	......
Salted Beef	bbl.	......	......	125	8	......	......	......	......
Salted Pork	bbl.	857	......	1,235	2	2,266	......	2,658	......
Wheat	bu.	1,835	999	15,680	2,482	......	......	......	......
Wool	lb.	1,010,462	8,080	1,066,424	......	1,476,60	......	1,248,733	......

* In 1841 *Provisions, not specified* increase sharply because the individual totals are not always stated. Apparently items formerly listed under *Sundries* are also included here.

AGRICULTURAL PRODUCTS AND PROVISIONS SHIPPED EASTWARD AND WESTWARD FROM OR TO PITTSBURGH OVER THE PENNSYLVANIA STATE SYSTEM, 1835-1850—Continued

(Compiled from the Annual Reports, 1835-1851)

	East 1843	West	East 1844	West	East 1845	West	East 1846	West
Agricultural Produce ....lb.	....	....	849,374	70,653	77,198	....	194,624	....
Bacon ....lb.	23,004,922	....	19,105,805	....	15,155,344	....	21,661,236	....
Butter & Cheese ....lb.	1,433,266	....	1,645,472	....	1,126,750	....	1,475,826	....
Clover & Grass Seeds ....bu.	....	78	177,561	9,136	3,152	748	1,923	506
Corn & Other Grain ......bu.	22,690	9,170	....	15,170	....	32,753	3,867	36,487
Cotton ....lb.	1,080,337	....	1,125,746	....	965,041	....	1,000,971	....
Feathers ....lb.	396,473	....	584,279	....	773,908	....	410,199	....
Hemp ....lb.	1,289,236	319,892	881,961	388,669	865,444	244,372	1,287,886	154,734
Lard & Tallow ....lb.	2,673,436	....	2,665,039	....	2,659,286	....	3,220,599	....
Potatoes ....bu.	....	9,645	....	2,560	....	2,826	....	4,621
Provisions, not specified ...lb.	1,703,112	982,306	685,529	134,140	625,057	708,640	196,275	....
Salted Beef ....bbl.	317	....	75,099	....	} 4,575*	....	}	....
Salted Pork ....bbl.	3,124	....	26,531	....	}	....	}	....
Wheat ....bu.	441	5,181	490	3,303	....	1,267	21,236	2,620
Wool ....lb.	2,500,789	....	3,166,969	10,008	3,763,570	....	3,403,161	....

* In 1845 Salted Beef and Pork are combined.

AGRICULTURAL PRODUCTS AND PROVISIONS SHIPPED EASTWARD AND WESTWARD FROM OR TO PITTSBURGH OVER THE PENNSYLVANIA STATE SYSTEM, 1835-1850—Concluded.

(Compiled from the Annual Reports, 1835-1851)

	East 1847	West	East 1848	West	East 1849	West	East 1850	West
Agricultural Produce ....lb.	774,916	1,257,626	371,201	787,119	1,247,162	515,618	3,364,894	790,450
Bacon ....lb.	17,213,427	13,946	29,233,848	....	31,019,065	....	38,956,065	....
Butter & Cheese ....lb.	1,392,373	7,350	2,983,931	....	2,546,654	....	2,674,185	1,850
Clover & Grass Seeds ....bu.	10,404	152	5,913	....	4,725	....	874	....
Corn & Other Grain ....bu.	137,214	43,429	36,096	13,154	1,150	6,570	9,717	89,252
Cotton ....lb.	1,056,138	....	1,679,428	....	589,513	....	1,084,600	3,700
Feathers ....lb.	523,975	7,357	480,721	....	350,389	....	568,331	....
Hemp ....lb.	3,204,110	271,139	483,080	207,100	1,289,577	245,400	809,528	94,400
Lard & Tallow ....lb.	5,382,324	73,790	4,673,695	....	5,382,854	....	580,622	18,940
Potatoes ....bu.	18	1,574	....	250	....	....	275	1,147
Provisions, not specified ....lb.	....	....	....	....	....	....	....	....
Salted Beef ....bbl.	41,225	....	5,376	....	9,030	....	5,600	....
Salted Pork ....bbl.	....	....	....	....	....	....	....	10,420
Wheat ....bu.	61,268	530	13,486	....	6,300	....	12,346	....
Wool ....lb.	4,284,988	11,821	2,036,133	....	5,113,076	....	4,586,432	10,420

BIBLIOGRAPHY

BIBLIOGRAPHY

I. ORIGINAL SOURCES

A. MANUSCRIPT MATERIALS

1. *Private Papers*

a. Blythe, Ellen, Manuscripts. In Carnegie Library of Pittsburgh. Two letters describe Pittsburgh during the 1830's. Letters are detailed and give a clear picture of Pittsburgh's economic and social characteristics.

b. Craig Papers. In Carnegie Library of Pittsburgh. These papers consist of an extensive collection of letters and accounts dealing with Isaac Craig's business activities in Pittsburgh.

c. Denny Papers. In Historical Society of Western Pennsylvania. Collection is large and consists of correspondence and accounts.

d. Dick Papers. In Historical Society of Western Pennsylvania. This extensive collection of letters from John, James and David Dick, dealing with business and financial conditions in Pittsburgh and the vicinity, is especially pertinent to an economic study of Pittsburgh. The letters cover the period from 1825 to 1860.

e. O'Hara Papers. In Historical Society of Western Pennsylvania. These papers consist of correspondence, accounts, invoices, and other records relating to the provisioning of the Western posts from 1792-1803, as well as several account books relating to James O'Hara's own private business as a Pittsburgh merchant.

f. Reynolds Papers. In Historical Society of Western Pennsylvania. Collection consists of day books and ledgers of John Reynolds, Meadville merchant, 1816-1855; also ledgers and accounts of Thomas R. Kennedy.

g. Thaw Papers. In Historical Society of Western Pensylvania. The collection consists of letters and business papers, covering the period 1802-1840.

2. *Public Documents*

a. Pennsylvania Canal Accounts. Manuscripts found in Public Records Division, Pennsylvania Historical and Museum Commission in Harrisburg. Collection consists of four boxes of accounts from the various collectors along the Pennsylvania State System, 1831-1856.

b. Pennsylvania Governors' Papers. Manuscripts found in Public Records Division, Pennsylvania Historical and Museum Commission in Harrisburg. Collection consists of miscellaneous items concerning petitions and appointments to various public offices, as well as petitions on numerous other questions.

c. Pennsylvania Road and Turnpike Papers. Manuscripts in Public Records Division, Pennsylvania Historical and Museum Commission in Harrisburg. The collection of more than 100 volumes is conveniently catalogued, and consists of accounts, annual reports, petitions, and contracts pertaining to Pennsylvania roads.

B. PUBLISHED MATERIALS

   1. *Public and Private Documents*

      a. *American State Papers; Documents, Legislative and Executive,* 1789-1828, 5 vols., Washington, 1832.

      b. *Annals of Congress of the United States,* 1789-1824, 42 vols., Washington, 1834-1856; *The Congressional Globe: Containing Sketches of the Debates and Proceedings,* 1833-1873, 109 vols.

      c. Breck, Samuel, *Sketch of the Internal Improvements Already Made by Pennsylvania, with Observations upon her Physical and Fiscal Means for their Extension,* Philadelphia, 1818.

      d. Carey, Matthew and Bioren, John, *Laws of Commonwealth of Pennsylvania,* 6 vols., Philadelphia, 1803.

      e. Hazard, Samuel, *The Register of Pennsylvania Devoted to the Preservation of Facts and Documents and Every other Kind of Useful Information Regarding the State of Pennsylvania,* 16 vols., Philadelphia, 1829-1835.

      f. Monongahela Navigation Company, *Annual Reports and Accompanying Documents,* 1840-1851, Pittsburgh, 1871.

      g. Pamphlets, Canal, Carnegie Library of Pittsburgh, 4 vols. A collection of pamphlets relating to the Pennsylvania State System and internal improvements of Pennsylvania.

      h. Pennsylvania and Ohio Canal Company, *Annual Reports,* 1837-1851. (One volume collection in Ohio State Library, Columbus, Ohio. No publication date.)

      i. Pennsylvania Canal Commissioners, *Journals,* 1825-1851. The *Journal* of the Canal Commissioners was submitted annually to the Legislature of Pennsylvania, and was reprinted in both legislative journals.

      j. Pennsylvania Canal Commissioners, *Annual Reports,* 1825-1851. The *Annual Reports* are scattered in the various legislative journals. A complete set of records are in the possession of the Pennsylvania Law Library, Harrisburg.

      k. Pennsylvania *Executive Documents.* Published either in connection with the legislative journals or separately to 1843; from 1843 to 1886 the reports of the executive department were published in a series called *Executive Documents.*

      l. Pennsylvania *Journal of the House of Representatives,* 1800-1850, Harrisburg.

      m. Pennsylvania *Journal of the Senate,* 1800-1851, Harrisburg.

      n. *United States Census Reports,* 1790-1860, Philadelphia and Washington.

      o. United States *House Executive Documents,* 1800-1851, Washington.

      p. United States *House Journal,* 1800-1851. Washington.

      q. United States *Senate Journal,* 1800-1851. Washington.

   2. *Almanacs and Directories*

      a. Cramer, Zadok. *The Navigator Containing Directions for Navigating the Monongahela, Allegheny, Ohio and Mississippi River.* Sixth edition, Pittsburgh, 1808. Preceding editions 1801, 1802, 1804, and 1806, followed by 1811, 1814, 1817, 1818, 1821, 1824, with title pages almost unchanged from that of 1808.

b. Cramer, Zadok, *Pittsburgh Magazine Almanack,* 1802-1828; 1831, 1834. Pittsburgh, 1802-1834. Title varies slightly.

c. Cummings, Samuel, *The Western Pilot, Containing Charts of the Ohio and of the Mississippi Rivers . . . and Gazetter,* Cincinnati, Ohio, 1839.

d. Fahnestock, Samuel, *Pittsburgh Directory for the year 1850,* Pittsburgh, 1850.

e. Harris, Isaac, *Harris' Pittsburgh Business Directory for the year 1837,* Pittsburgh, 1837.

f. Harris, Isaac, *Harris' Pittsburgh and Allegheny Directory with the Environs, for the year 1839,* Pittsburgh, 1839.

g. Harris, Isaac, *Harris' General Business Directory of the Cities of Pittsburgh and Allegheny for the year 1841,* Pittsburgh, 1841.

h. Harris, Isaac, *Harris' General Business Directory of the Cities of Pittsburgh and Allegheny, for the year 1844,* Pittsburgh, 1844.

i. Harris, Isaac, *Harris' General Business Directory of the Cities of Pittsburgh and Allegheny, for the year 1847,* Pittsburgh, 1847.

j. Jones, Samuel, *Pittsburgh in 1826, Containing Sketches Topographical, together with a Directory of the City, and a View of its Various Manufactures, Population and Improvements,* Pittsburgh, 1826.

k. Lyford, William S., *The Western Address Directory Together with Historical, Topographical, and Statistical Sketches (for the year 1837) of those Cities and Towns in the Mississippi Valley, for the year 1836,* Baltimore, 1837.

l. Riddle, James M., *The Pittsburgh Directory for 1815, Containing the Names, Professions and Residence of the Heads of Families and Persons in Business in Borough of Pittsburgh With an Appendix containing a Variety of Useful Information,* Pittsburgh, 1815. Republished by Colonial Trust Company, 1905.

m. Taylor, John, *The Honest Man's Almanac for the year 1813,* Pittsburgh, 1813.

3. *Newspapers*

   a. *Cleveland Herald,* 1821-1840.

   b. *Ebensburg Sky,* (Pa.), 1831-1837.

   c. *Louisville Public Advertiser,* 1821-1833.

   d. *Missouri Gazette and Public Advertiser,* 1819-1821.

   e. *New Orleans Commercial Bulletin,* 1833-1850.

   f. *Niles' Weekly Register,* 73 Vols. Baltimore, 1811-1848.

   g. *Pittsburgh Chronicle,* 1842-1850.

   h. *Pittsburgh Commonwealth,* 1805-1818.

   i. *Pittsburgh Saturday Visitor,* 1836-1850. (Title varies.)

   j. *Pittsburgh Gazette,* 1796-1851. (Title varies.)

   k. *Iron City and Pittsburgh Weekly Chronicle,* 1841-1842.

   l. (Pittsburgh) *Mercury,* 1812-1845. (Title varies.)

   m. *Pittsburgh Post,* 1842-1851.

   n. (Pittsburgh) *Tree of Liberty,* 1800-1804.

   o. (Pittsburgh) *Times,* 1836-1837.

   p. *Wheeling Times and Advertiser,* 1840-1850. (Title varies.)

4. *Contemporary Accounts*

  a. *Austin Papers*, 2 vols., edited by Eugene C. Barker, in the American Historical Association, *Report*, 1919.

  b. Cumming, Fortescue, *Sketches of a Tour of the Western Country through the States of Ohio and Kentucky*, Reuben G. Thwaites, ed., *Early Western Travels*, (IV) 32 vols., Cleveland, 1904.

  c. Fordham, Elias P., *Personal Narrative of Travels in Virginia, Maryland, Pennsylvania, Ohio, Indiana, Kentucky, and of a Residence in the Illinois Territory, 1817-1818*, edited by Frederic A. Ogg, Cleveland, 1906.

II. SECONDARY SOURCES

  A. PUBLICATIONS OF LEARNED SOCIETIES, PERIODICALS AND MONOGRAPHS

    1. Baxter, Frances, "Rafting on the Allegheny and Ohio, 1844," in the *Pennsylvania Magazine of History and Biography*, LI, 1927.

    2. Bishop, Avard L., "Corrupt Practices Connected with the Building and Operation of the State Works of Pennsylvania," in the *Yale Review*, XV, February, 1907.

    3. Callender, Guy S., "The Early Transportation and Banking Enterprises of the State in Relation to the Growth of Corporations," in the *Quarterly Journal of Economics*, XVII, 1902-1903.

    4. Crall, F. F., "A Half Century of Rivalry Between Pittsburgh and Wheeling," in the *Western Pennsylvania Historical Magazine*, XIII, October, 1930.

    5. DeBow, J. D. B., *DeBows Review of the Southern and Western States*, 20 vols., New Orleans and Washington, 1846-1861.

    6. Downes, Randolph C., "Trade in Frontier Ohio," in the *Mississippi Valley Historical Review*, XVI, 1929-1930.

    7. Dunbar, Rowland, "The Mississippi Valley in American History," in the Mississippi Valley Historical Association, *Proceedings*, IX, 1915-1916.

    8. Fish, Carl Russell, "The Decision of the Ohio Valley," in the American Historical Association, *Report*, 1910.

    9. Galpin, William F., "The Grain Trade of New Orleans, 1804-1814," in the *Mississippi Valley Historical Review*, XIV, 1927-1928.

    10. McCarthy, Charles, "The Anti-Masonic Party, A Study in Political Anti-Masonry in the United States, 1827-1840," in the American Historical Association, *Report*, 1902.

    11. Pelzer, Louis, "Economic Factors in the Acquisition of Louisiana," in the Mississippi Valley Historical Association, *Proceedings*, VI, 1912-1913.

    12. Way, R. B., "The Commerce of the Lower Mississippi in the Period 1830-1860," in the Mississippi Valley Historical Association, *Proceedings*, X, 1916-1917.

  B. UNPUBLISHED THESES

    1. Douds, Howard C., Merchants and Merchandising in Pittsburgh, 1759-1800. Master's Thesis, University of Pittsburgh, 1936.

    2. Kline, Harriet E., Financial and Industrial Aspects of the Panic of 1837 in Pittsburgh. Master's Thesis, University of Pittsburgh, 1933.

C. GENERAL ACCOUNTS

1. Ambler, Charles H., *A History of Transportation in the Ohio Valley*, Glendale, California, 1932.

2. Andrews, J. Cutler, *Pittsburgh's Post Gazette*, Boston, 1936.

3. Baldwin, Leland D., *The Keelboat Age on Western Waters*, Pittsburgh, 1941.

4. Bishop, James L., *A History of American Manufacturing from 1808 to 1860*, 2 vols., Philadelphia, 1864.

5. Boucher, John N., *History of Westmoreland County*, 3 vols., New York, 1906.

6. Buck, Solon J., and Elizabeth H., *The Planting of Civilization in Western Pennsylvania*, Pittsburgh, 1939.

7. Channing, Edward, *A History of the United States*, 5 vols., New York, 1932.

8. Craig, Neville B., *The History of Pittsburgh with a Brief Notice of its Qualities of Communication and other Advantages for Commercial and Manufacturing Purposes*, Pittsburgh, 1851.

9. Day, Sherman, *Historical Collections of the State of Pennsylvania*, Philadelphia, 1843.

10. Dewey, Davis Rich, *Financial History of the United States*, New York, 1934.

11. Dunbar, Seymour, *A History of Travel in America*, 1 vol. edition, New York, 1937.

12. Durrenberger, Joseph A., *Turnpikes: A Study of the Toll Road Movement*, Valdosta, Georgia, 1931.

13. Fish, Carl Russell, *The Rise of the Common Man, 1830-1850*, Vol. VI of *A History of American Life Series*, 12 vols., edited by Arthur M. Schlesinger and Dixon R. Fox, New York, 1939.

14. Gephart, William F., *Transportation and Industrial Development in the Middle West*, New York, 1909.

15. Godcharles, Frederic A., *Daily Stories of Pennsylvania*, Milton, Pennsylvania, 1924.

16. Habermehl, John, *Life on the Western Rivers*, Pittsburgh, 1901.

17. Hall, James, *The West: Its Commerce and Navigation*, Cincinnati, 1848.

18. Harlow, Alvin F., *Old Towpaths, The Story of the American Canal Era*, New York, 1926.

19. Hulbert, A. B., *The Ohio River*, New York, 1905.

20. Hulbert, A. B., *Historic Highways of America*, 16 vols., various dates of publication.

21. Killikelly, Sarah H., *The History of Pittsburgh, Its Rise and Progress*, Pittsburgh, 1906.

22. Kohlmeier, A. L., *The Old Northwest as the Keystone of the Arch of American Federal Union*, Bloomington, Indiana, 1938.

23. Kussart, Mrs. S., *The Allegheny River*, Pittsburgh, 1938.

24. Livengood, James W., *The Philadelphia-Baltimore Trade Rivalry, 1780-1860*, Harrisburg, Pennsylvania Historical and Museum Commission, 1947.

25. Monette, J. W., *History of Discovery and Settlement of the Valley of the Mississippi by three Great European Powers . . . to 1846,* 2 vols., New York, 1847.

26. Newton, J. E. (ed.), *History of the Panhandle,* Wheeling, West Virginia, 1879.

27. Reizenstein, Milton, *Economic History of the Baltimore and Ohio Railroad,* Baltimore, 1897.

28. Scharf, J. Thomas and Westcott, Thompson, *A History of Philadelphia,* 1609-1884, 3 vols., Philadelphia, 1884.

29. Schotter, H. W., *The Growth and Development of the Pennsylvania Railroad,* Philadelphia, 1927.

30. Searight, Thomas B., *The Old Pike, A History of the National Road With Incidents, Accidents and Anecdotes Thereon,* Uniontown, Pa., 1894.

31. Storey, Henry W., *A History of Cambria County,* 2 vols., New York, 1907.

32. Thurston, George H., *Allegheny County's Hundred Years,* Pittsburgh, 1888.

33. Thurston, George H., *Pittsburgh and Allegheny in the Centennial Year,* Pittsburgh, 1876.

34. Thurston, George H., *Pittsburgh as It is or Facts and Figures Exhibiting the Past and Present of Pittsburgh, Its Advantages, Resources, Manufactures and Commerce,* Pittsburgh, 1857.

35. Thurston, George H., *Pittsburgh's Progress, Industries and Resources,* Pittsburgh, 1886.

36. Whitaker, Arthur P., *The Mississippi Question,* New York, 1934.

37. Whitaker, Arthur P., *The Spanish-American Frontier,* New York, 1936.

38. White, Edward, *One Hundred and Fifty Years of Unparalleled Thrift,* Pittsburgh, 1908.

39. Wilson, Erasmus (ed.), *Standard History of Pittsburgh,* Chicago, 1898.

40. Winter, Wm., D., *Marine Insurance: Its Principles and Practice,* New York, 1919.

INDEX

INDEX

A

Aetna Fire Insurance Company, agent, Nathaniel Holmes, 187.

Alexandria, steamboat in Mississippi trade, 36.

Allegheny City (Northside), center of textile industry in 1850, 192-193.

Allegheny County, manufacturing of, compared with Pittsburgh, 15; value of manufacturing in 1810, 15.

Allegheny County Mutual Insurance Company, 188.

Allegheny Mountains, aided Pittsburgh manufacturing, 9; description of ridges, 69, 69n; location, 2; trade barrier, 4.

Allegheny-Portage Railroad, cost of repairs, (1836), 109; part of Pennsylvania State System, 88.

Allegheny River, French Creek, a tributary, 53-54; head water of navigation, 144; importance to Pittsburgh, 53; in 1850, 194-195; include Conemaugh River in trade area, 53; include Juniata River in trade area, 53; introduction of steamboats, 55-56; Kiskiminetas, a tributary, 53; location, 1; types of boats, 54; used Erie Canal as outlet, 67; volume and type of trade, 54-59; wharf, 132-134.

Allegheny River town, Meadville (Pennsylvania), 58; Olean (New York), 144.

Allegheny River trade, area covered, 53; volume and value of French Creek trade, 55.

Allegheny Valley, important lumber area, 57.

American Fire Insurance Company, agent George Cochran, 187, 188.

Anderson, John and Son, Pittsburgh manufacturers, 192.

Anshutz, Rahm and Company, Pittsburgh merchants, 129.

Army expeditions, Pittsburgh as focal point for frontier, 8.

Auction sales, 135-136.

Austin, Moses, description of Mississippi River obstacles, 33n; devises general rules for Mississippi River navigation, 35, 35n.

Austin, Stephen, son of Moses Austin, 35.

B

Bakewell and Company, Pittsburgh glass manufacturers, 123.

Bakewell, Pears and Company, Pittsburgh glass manufacturers, 193.

Baltimore, aided by National Road, 85; banks suspend specie payment in 1837, 168; part of triangular trade with New Orleans and Pittsburgh, 30; trade rivalries with Wheeling, 146, 149; trade rival to Philadelphia, 85-86.

Baltimore and Ohio Railroad, 153-154.

Bank of Pennsylvania, opens branch at Pittsburgh (1804), 159-160.

Bank of Pittsburgh, loan to Pittsburgh and Greensburg Company, 76; organized in 1814, 161.

Bank of United States (First), failed to renew charter (1811), 160; (Second), opened 1817, 161.

Banks, Bank of Pennsylvania established Pittsburgh branch (1804), 159-160; Bank of Pittsburgh organized, 1814, 161; blamed for post-war depression, 163-164; during War of 1812, 160-161; established in Pittsburgh, 1800-1850, 171n; Exchange Bank opened (1836), 165; Farmers Deposit Company, (1844), 165; Farmers and Mechanics Bank organized 1814, 161; robbed, 164; George A. Cook, banking house opened (1830), 165; Pittsburgh Manufacturing Company opened (1812), 160; Mechanics Bank opened (1837), 168; Merchants and Manufacturers Bank opened (1833), 165; Nathaniel Holmes, private

238   PITTSBURGH'S COMMERCIAL DEVELOPMENT

Farmers Deposit Company, new name of Pittsburgh Saving Fund Company, 1844, 165.
Fayette County, source of iron, 3.
Firemen's Insurance Company, 188.
Flatboats, arrival at New Orleans, 1817-1819, 32n; description, 30; used in Monongahela River coal trade, 65.
Flour milling, early beginnings in Pittsburgh, 12.
Forbes, General John Murray, cut road to Pittsburgh, 69.
Forbes Road, 69-70.
Fordham, Elias P., describes forests in America, 57.
Forest, steamboat in Allegheny River trade, 56.
Fort Louden, 78-79.
Forward, Walter, speaker at Right of Way Bill Convention (1846), 154-155.
France, in Ohio Valley, 69; to receive Louisiana territory from Spain, 38; wartime trade restrictions, 16-17.
Franklin, Allegheny River town, 55; dependent on New Orleans, 53.
Freeman, Richard, Pittsburgh merchant, 129.
French Creek (also Allegheny River), tributary of Allegheny River, 1, 53-54; volume and type of trade, 55.
Fulton, Robert, steamboat navigation on Mississippi River, 31n.

Gallatin, Albert, 81.
General Pike, steamboat in Ohio trade injured by ice, 34.
Glass industry, comparison between 1800 and 1850, 193; value of, in 1803, 14; in 1810, 15; in 1815, 19; in 1817, 21; in 1819, 22; in 1826, 25; in 1836, 26; in 1837, 26; in 1839, 27; in 1850, 28, 193.
Glass manufacturers, need for coal, 3.
Gratz Brothers, frontier traders, 2.
Great Britain, captured Washington, 161; flooded American markets after War of 1812, 21, 163; in Ohio Valley, 69; wartime trade restrictions, 16-17.
"Great Fire," of 1845, 148-149; losses, 188-189.

Hamilton and Brown, Pittsburgh brewers and manufacturers, 132.
Harris, Isaac, compiler of *Directory of 1837*, 26, 116; compiler of *Directory for 1841*, 27; describes roads, 76; Pittsburgh printer, 132.
Harrisburg, road to be built to Pittsburgh (1806), 74.
Hartley, Robert, Pittsburgh leather manufacturer, 122, 123, 196.
Hero, The, steamboat sunk on Mississippi River, 33.
Holmes, Nathaniel, agent for Aetna Fire Insurance Company, 187; Pittsburgh banker, 164.
Hulings, Marcus, agent of Major Isaac Craig, opened up lumber trade in Allegheny Valley, 57.

Insurance company, Aetna Fire Insurance Company, 187; Allegheny County Mutual Insurance Company, 188; American Fire Insurance Company, 187; American Fire Insurance Company (1837), 188; Beaver County Insurance Company, 188; branch office of Insurance Company of North America opened in Pittsburgh (1808), 187; Citizens Insurance Company incorporated (1849), 189; demand for created by "Great Fire," 189; Firemans' Insurance Company, 188; hard hit by "Great Fire," 188-189; in 1826, 187-188; in 1837, 188; Insurance Company of North America, 187; need for in Pittsburgh, 186-187; Penn Insurance Company, 188; Philadelphia Fire and Inland

R

S